THE LANGUAGE CONSTRUCTION KIT

The Language Construction Kit

by Mark Rosenfelder

YONAGU BOOKS

Chicago • 2010

Paperback   ISBN 978-0-9844700-0-6
Hardcover   ISBN 978-0-9844700-1-3

ed. 1.2

Contents

Introduction

This book is intended for anyone who wants to create artificial languages— for a fantasy or an alien world, as a hobby, as an interlanguage. It presents linguistically sound methods for creating naturalistic languages, which can be reversed to create non-naturalistic languages. It suggests further reading for those who want to know more, and shortcuts for those who want to know less.

The above is a sample of a constructed language (CONLANG) of my own, Verdurian. If you're curious, it reads, **Ďitelán mu cum pén veaďen er mësan so Sannam**, meaning "Go forth in peace to love and serve the Lord." The letter **ď** sounds like the *th* in *then*; the vowels are similar to those of Spanish.

Before I could write this little inscription I had to:

- Decide on the sounds of the language
- Create the lexicon
- Create the grammar
- Design an alphabet
- Modify the alphabet for cursive handwriting
- Translate the text

We'll cover all of this in the book.

The order of the steps above is significant. Working backwards (e.g. creating a text and then devising a grammar to match) will lead to an inconsistent if not incoherent work. A bad example is Hergé's Syldavian; since he basically made it up in pieces, as he needed it, it's impossible to create a consistent phonology or morphology for it, based on the scraps of the language provided in the Tintin books.

You can also use this book as a backhanded introduction to LINGUISTICS. To make an artificial language, after all, you have to know a lot about real languages.

For the impatient

Some books, especially the ones sold in airports, have a lot of padding... the author had an idea for an essay and wrote it as a book.

Not this one. We have a lot of material to cover, and to any expert the presentation will look pretty damn breezy.

However, I've tried to put the most important information first, overall and within each chapter. For instance, the first chapter tells you all you need to know to make a naming language, suitable for filling out a map or making character names. You don't have to be an expert on all this stuff.

Well, unless your professor assigned it, in which case, yes, *everything* will be on the final.

Using this book

Overall structure

We'll start with some overviews. The next chapter is on how to make a very basic language for creating names. After that, we'll look at the process for creating a more detailed language.

The meat of the book is a series of chapters that expand on the major parts of a grammar: sounds, word building, syntax, semantics, pragmatics.

After that are some special topics:

- How to create a set of related languages
- Devising writing systems

I've included an annotated grammar of one of my conlangs, Kebreni. The grammar itself serves as a model, but I've also discussed some of my linguistic sources, why I made the choices I did, and what I'd do differently today.

Finally there are some resources: some basic wordlists, and a bibliography.

But how do I start?

This seems to be a poser for some people. I suppose it's the conlanging equivalent of a writer staring in desperation at a blank page.

Well, first, read the book. You won't be using all the information at once, but it's good to scout out the territory and know what's there so you can go back to it when you need it.

Create an outline for your grammar (see the naming language chapter for an example). Now you can go through the book again and pick alternatives that appeal to you. *There aren't any wrong choices.* You want a language with ejectives, tones, SOV order, and five cases? Sure, why not?

Think of it as inventing a cartoon character. You choose a particular type of eye, a size and shape of nose, a body shape. The creativity comes in the way the character fits together— it doesn't consist of creating *mind-boggling new organs.*

Don't read this sentence!

Oops, too late. Don't read *this* one, then.

Anyway, the point is, you don't have to read the book straight through. When you're reading new material, you can absorb it up to a point— then your brain glazes over and it's not really registering any more.

That's fine— just go back to that section later. You can also try alternating reading with creating: read a chapter, then try applying it to your conlang.

What's it for?

Think about what the language is for.

- Naming people and places. For this you need a brief outline and a wordlist.

- Translating small or large texts, or simply creating the language as an artistic creation— an ARTLANG. For this you'll need a full grammar; its length will depend on how complete the language is. Translating a text, by the way, is a great way to find what bits of the grammar are missing.

- An auxiliary language or AUXLANG. Here your choices should be determined by simplicity and accessibility.

- Exploration of a logical concept— e.g. you'd like a language with as few words as possible; or you want to organize the lexicon scientifically, or it's going to be all gestures. Obviously such experiments aren't constrained by natural languages, but it's still useful to know what's out there, and you should be aware of assumptions that are built into your native language.

Typographical conventions

I've put technical terms in SMALL CAPS. This tells you two things:

- I didn't make the term up, so you can safely use it in your grammar.

- You can get more information by Googling. (If you get a choice between (say) Linguist List and Wikipedia, look at the former. Wikipedia isn't bad at basic linguistic terms, but it can be wrong or misleading.)

Italics are used when I'm discussing a word or phrase. If it's not in English I'll provide a gloss in 'single quotes'.

Example sentences are provided with both a word-for-word GLOSS and a free translation. I recommend this for your grammars as well— it makes it much easier to see the structure of the language.

> **U men^j a i u n^j evo n^j et khl^j eba.**
>
> by 1s.GEN and by 3sm.GEN not bread-GEN
>
> *He and I don't have any bread.*

Hyphens are used when a word can be separated into pieces: **khl^y eb-** is "bread", **-a** is the singular genitive suffix. Periods are used when the meanings can't be separated: e.g. **men^y a** is a 1st person singular genitive pronoun and can't be divided up.

For more on glossing, see p. 216.

When we get to phonetics:

> **boldface** refers to a letter, or informally to a sound
>
> / / slashes indicate a phonemic representation
>
> [ ] brackets are used for phonetic representations

> **Sidebars**
> Sidebars give tips, warnings, or interesting facts, or provide pointers to additional reading.

Your brilliant conlanging career

Conlangers sometimes follow a predictable trajectory.

- First— perhaps before knowing a thing about other languages— they play with their native language— perhaps something as simple as respelling it or creating a new alphabet. Or they create a badass fantasy language that looks like Elvish or Dwarvish.

- Then, depending on personal tastes, they re-invent Esperanto or create a Romance language.

- After learning some linguistics they create a KITCHEN SINK language— one which contains every linguistic feature they've heard of.

It's a natural process and nothing to worry about. But it stands to reason that your efforts will improve over time. So instead of making the first language you do your main conculture's speech, maybe you should work on its ancestor, or a neighboring language.

I wish I'd done it that way myself! My best known and best developed language is Verdurian, but I think most of my later languages are much better done.

Web resources

There are a lot of great resources on the web. But URLs rot quickly, so instead of listing sites in this book, I'll list a single permanent URL that will be kept up-to-date with a list of links:

http://www.zompist.com/resources/

Acknowledgements

Thanks to everyone who read or recommended the web LCK, or provided corrections. I'm sorry I didn't keep names at the time, but Ivan Derzhanski stands out in memory, and John Lawler was an early booster.

Thanks to Daniel von Brighoff and Jeff Burke for reviewing the book, and to Jeffrey Henning and my wife Lida for pushing to get it done.

12 LANGUAGE CONSTRUCTION KIT

Thanks to everyone on the ZBB for turning this isolated hobby into a community.

Mark Rosenfelder

March 2010

A naming language

The size of this book may be intimidating— *I have to know all that?* But conlangs don't all have to be huge. For instance, you might just need some names on a map, or an inscription or two. For that, a NAMING LANGUAGE will do.

An example is Tolkien's Black Speech, of which we have little more than the famous fragment

> **Ash nazg durbatulûk, ash nazg gimbatul, ash nazg thrakatulûk agh burzum-ishi krimpatul.**
>
> *One Ring to rule them all, One Ring to find them, One Ring to bring them all and in the Darkness bind them.*

Short as it is, this text allows us to learn quite a bit about the grammar of the Black Speech. We can start by noting that the sounds seem similar to English, except for **gh** and whatever **û** represents. There are characteristics that, for English speakers, convey an alien, nasty flavor:

- Many CLOSED syllables (that is, ones that end in a consonant).

- Plenty of STOPS; compare LIQUID-heavy Elvish words like *Lothlorien.*

- Many voiced stops in particular. Final -*zg* looks very alien, though it's just a voiced -*sk* and occurs naturally in English (as in *he's gone*).

How about the meaning? We know the word *nazgûl*, so we know that *nazg* means 'ring'. Given that, we can create a GLOSS (a word by word translation):

ash nazg	one ring
durbatulûk	rule them all
ash nazg	one ring
gimbatul	find them
ash nazg	one ring
thrakatulûk	bring them all
agh	and
burzum-ishi	in the darkness
krimpatul	bind them

Let's look closer at the verbs, which I've highlighted. The two verbs which have "them all" in their glosses share a common element *atulûk*. The two that just have "them" share the element *atul*. So we know at least two bits of verbal morphology:

-atul-	them
-ûk	all

Now, it's quite possible that *-atul-* is actually two elements— say, *-at + -ul*. Since the examples are all infinitives, perhaps the Black Speech, like English, explicitly marks infinitives. Let's guess that it does, so we have:

-at-	infinitive
-ul-	them
-ûk	all

How about *burzum-ishi*? Later on we have the name *Lugbúrz* for Sauron's Dark Tower, so *burz* means 'dark'. *-um* might be a NOMINALIZER (like *-ness*) or a marker of definiteness. So *-ishi* must be 'in', which we must call a POSTPOSITION rather than a preposition since it follows the noun.

A mini-grammar

Putting it all together, we have a mini-grammar like this:

Sounds

Consonants: b t d k g z sh th gh m n r l ...

Vowels: i a u û ...

Morphology

-at-	infinitive
-ul-	them
-ûk	all
-um	abstract nominalizer
-ûl	person nominalizer

Syntax

numerals before nouns
adjectives after nouns (at least in compounds)
postpositions
subjects before verbs

Lexicon	
agh	and
ash	one
burz	dark
durb-	rule
gimb-	find
ishi	in
krimp-	bind
lug	tower
nazg	ring
thrak-	bring

If you're writing a naming language, I recommend creating a mini-grammar like this, so that even if there isn't much material, it's all consistent. For instance, if Tolkien needed an object 'me', he would want to remember that 'them' was formed using a suffix.

If Hergé had kept notes like this, he might have kept from creating six different forms of the definite article in Syldavian!

Hints for naming languages

- Note the sounds you use— at the least, those different from English. Keep this list small so it doesn't get cumbersome or contradictory.

- Don't pile on diacritical marks, apostrophes, or odd spellings just to make the words look different— you'll regret it later.

- Start with geographical terms like *city, hill, mountain, forest, lake, river, coast.*

- Add some adjectives that combine easily with these: *big, small, new, high, blue, long.* That immediately gives you a number of names: New City, Long Lake, Blue Mountain...

- Different languages don't all work the same! Vary the order of adjectives and nouns; use compounds instead of separate words; use different sound systems. Features or people can be named with sentences ("The forest sings") instead of noun phrases ("strong arm").

- If you plan to make the bad guys speak a language with lots of k's and kh's and consonant clusters, you're not the first. Here are a few words from real languages to suggest ways to make words sound foreign: *Anauá, Neznanovo, Hyōgo, Torbat-e*

Heydarīyeh, Oaro, Ferkéssédougou, Fianarantsoa, Thavung, Yun-kunytjatjara, quliuutailat.

- Don't sprinkle the map with a hundred meaningless names. You'll only annoy yourself, perhaps years later, when you want to turn the naming language into a real language. Look at a map of a nation whose language is entirely unfamiliar— perhaps Turkey or Japan. The names aren't just random; they contain repeated elements— very likely the geographical terms and common adjectives mentioned above.

The overall process

The bulk of this book leads you through all the decisions you'll have to make creating a language, and considers the various ways languages deal with these.

Now, you may be thinking, "Do I *hafta*? It's *loooong* and it's on *dead trees* and stuff." So, let's look at it from a very high level.

Sounds

Even for a simple language, write down all the sounds it uses. Without this, you'll end up with a huge and contradictory set.

Here's a set of sounds (a PHONETIC INVENTORY) to get you started: the Standard Fantasy Language Inventory.

Consonants	labial	dental	velar	glottal	Vowels front	back
stops	p	t	k		i	u
	b	d	g		e	o
fricatives	f	s sh	kh	h		a
	v	z zh	gh			
nasals	m	n	ng			
liquids		l, r				
semivowels	w	y				

> **Um, p t k w t f?**
>
> The format and labels of this table are explained in the next chapter. This sort of table is appropriate for all languages; English alphabetical order is not!

Train yourself to check this table when creating words. Want a word *chuth*? Nope, can't do it: *ch* and *th* aren't in the chart. (*But I really want it!* Fine, add them to the chart.)

Don't confuse *sounds* with *letters*. English *sh, ch, ng* are all single sounds despite being written with two letters (they are DIGRAPHS); while *x* is two sounds written with a single letter.

If you want a language for a novel or a game intended for English speakers, it's best to spell the consonants as in English: *sh* instead of *š* or *ʃ* or *sz* or *ch*.

The trouble with c

The sample inventory lacks **c**. This is intentional: the average reader will read c with English values, generally *s* before *i/e* and *k* elsewhere. If that's what you want, fine, but why not just use *s* and *k*? And if it's not, you're just inviting trouble. Tolkien intended *c* to be always *k*, with the result that most readers mispronounce names like *Celeborn*.

Often it's effective to think about *removing* features from English. For instance, what about making a language without a *p* or an *l*?

If you read nothing else in the long middle of the book, read the chapter on sounds. It's not hard, it's the basis for everything else in linguistics, and you will avoid a lot of silly-looking mistakes if you know something about phonetics.

Lexicon

Keep a lexicon, as in the Naming Language chapter. Keep it alphabetical in your language, not in English; this will prevent you from reusing words (e.g. using *lug* for 'bring' when you already used it for 'tower').

If you write on a computer, you can easily search for the English word; if not, maintain a separate English list.

Use a column format, like this. You'll thank me later. (The middle column allows for easy searching for grammatical categories, gives a place later to add special information like declension type, and saves space in the gloss column— you don't have to write *bear (v)*. Plus, tables are easy to convert to HTML.)

lug   n   tower

How do you make up all the words? There are several methods.

- Create them one at a time, as you need them (for maps, sample sentences, or texts). This is the best method, since it makes you think about what you're doing, gives the language a hand-crafted quality, and helps keep you from inventing too many roots.

- Use a word generating tool, such as **gen** on my website. This is fine for when inspiration lags, but you'll probably end up with a formless mess, where you have simple roots for complex concepts (maybe *mopa* for 'religion') with no evident relation to anything else (since you picked *naba* for 'god' and perhaps even *gupu* for 'religious').

- Borrow words from a natlang. Maybe not French. Pick something like Kikongo or Aymara or Malayalam and if anyone notices they'll probably be flattered.

- Make a proto-language first, then change the words using the Sound Change Applier. This is advanced stuff and we'll get to it later (p. 155), but it's actually the easiest, quickest way to create a realistic vocabulary.

You should get in the habit of *doubling up definitions*. That is, instead of making a word for 'travel', make one for 'travel, voyage, trip'. Similarly, you probably don't need separate words for

> home, house
> rod, staff
> hole, pit
> stream, brook
> spurt, gush
> happy, content
> vast, huge, immense
> angry, mad, wrathful
> country, nation, land
> way, method
> soldier, warrior

This will save you work later on when you need one of the alternative words. It also makes your language seem less like a clone of English— its words have their own range of meanings rather than just echoing ours.

On the other hand, be aware of English words that have several very different meanings— you probably shouldn't duplicate these in your language. For example:

> right (direction / correct)
> fat (grease / chubby)
> earth (soil / planet)
> patient (sick person / untiring)
> people (persons / ethnic group)
> miss (long for / fail to hit)
> glass (material / container)

fly (insect / move in air)
fall (autumn / drop)
bear (animal / carry)

What words do you need? It depends on what you want the language for. For names and maps, just invent the roots you need. For a reasonably complete language sketch, think about verbs of motion, body parts, kinship terms, simple adjectives, and everyday objects.

At the end of the book there are vocabulary lists with different purposes (p. 241).

Inflections

English has just a few INFLECTIONS— plural -s, past tense -ed, participle -ing, and so on. You may be tempted to reproduce these exactly, but there are many alternatives.

As a place to start, many languages have inflections for all PERSONS (*I/you/he*) in singular and plural, e.g. Quechua:

rimani	I walk
rimanki	you (singular) walk
riman	he/she/it walks
rimanchik	we walk
rimankichik	you (plural) walk
rimanku	they walk

An advantage of this system is that you can usually omit the pronouns.

Many languages use inflections where we would use small grammatical words (PARTICLES), or entire expressions. For instance:

- modalities (I can, I should)
- aspects of the action: is it completed or still going on, is it repeated
- evidentiality: do I know this for a fact; is it just probable; is it quite unlikely
- definiteness (like our definite articles)
- direction and location (like our prepositions)

The main section of the book will give you many more ideas.

As in other areas, consider *removing* features English has. Do you really need to mark the plural, or even tense?

Derivations

You can multiply the utility of your basic roots, and make your language more consistent, by creating a system of DERIVATIONS, which might simply be prefixes or suffixes. Some of the most useful:

- person who does
- place
- collection
- tool
- characteristic adjective
- causative
- diminutive

Here's a set of words run through these derivations:

	Roots				
	war	book	tree	cow	star
person	soldier	librarian	forester	cowboy	astronomer
place	battlefield	library	forest	barn	sky
collection	campaign	bookshelf	woods	herd	cluster
tool	weapon	pen	axe	prod	telescope
adjective	warlike	bookish	wooden	bovine	stellar
causative	make war	write	plant	stupefy	deify
diminutive	fight	pamphlet	sapling	calf	firefly

Five roots turned into 40 words. Naturally you don't have to use all the possible variations; I filled out the whole table just to show how it could be done.

You should find ways of combining arbitrary roots as well, whether through compounding or phrases: consider English *battleground, skyscraper, blackbird, mother country, tree house, dish of the day.*

Syntax

Syntax includes most of the stuff that most English speakers hardly even realize is part of the language. At the very least, you want to cover the following:

- What's the sentence order: subject / verb / object, as in English? Or something else?

- What's the order within noun phrases? Where do adjectives, articles, and numbers come in relation to the noun?

- Do you have prepositions, postpositions?

- Do you mark cases?

- How are numbers formed and used?

- How do you form questions?

- How do you make negations and negative questions?

- How do you make relative clauses (*The man who stole my name*)?

- What happens when the subject or object of a verb is itself a sentence? (*It's possible he's a liar; He claims he's a chicken*).

Goodies

For extra credit, work out some of the following.

- **Greetings and common expressions.** For some reason, people in books can learn another language perfectly *except* for titles, 'yes', 'no', and 'hello', which they insist on saying in their native tongue forevermore.

- The **calendar**: days of the week, years of the month. These can add some flavor to a narrative— though don't expect readers to actually remember your names. Don't assume that a week is seven days and that there are 12 months.

- The overall **style** used in your language: blunt, polite, pedantic. Do people curse you by saying *You stink* or *May the dust of your ancestors settle in the privy of a diarrheic*?

- Speech patterns that **carry over into English**. If a language doesn't have articles, or the *s* sound, these features could be represented in your translations: *Shtranger is at door, mashter.* (Not for the main characters, please.)

Alphabet

Alphabets are fun to make, and you can use them to write secret notes to yourself. Just a few hints for now:

- Think in terms of *sounds*, not English letters.

- You don't need separate upper and lower case forms. On the other hand, numbers and simple punctuation are useful.

- Don't rush and use the first squiggle you think of for each sound; you'll end up with a dull, repetitive alphabet. Doodle a bunch of ideas and pick only the best ones.

For extra credit, think about how your people write— carving in stone, incising clay, brushing on papyrus, writing with brush or pen, gripping a stylus with their tentacles— and create letterforms that reflect that. Carving curved lines is difficult, for instance; and a stylus is more easily used to punch holes or make an impression than to draw.

Feedback

When I was a lad, it was foolish to expect anyone to be interested in your conlang, except perhaps the future readers of your epic trilogy. And it's still a hobby principally for the self-motivated.

But there are outlets today if you want feedback. You can publish your grammatical sketch on the web, or on one of the websites devoted to discussing or showcasing conlangs.

See the web resources page for places to show your work:

> http://www.zompist.com/resources/

Copyright

Some people are terribly worried about people stealing their languages. But frankly, unless your conlang accompanies a blockbuster TV show or movie, your problem is going to be getting people to look at it, not having people so excited that they want to plagiarize it.

Can you copyright a language? At this point, no one knows— it's never been contested in court.

But it's quite clear that you can copyright your *work*— your grammars, lexicons, and sample texts. If you're American, you get copyright protection even on unpublished work. If you're really worried, you can register your work (even in manuscript form) with the Library of Congress.

This isn't to say people won't repost your stuff— there are a billion people connected to the Internet, and some are jerks. Copyright may not help you (the jerk may not even be in your country); polite requests and escalation to their ISP may work better.

Models

Natural and unnatural languages

I personally like naturalistic languages, so my invented languages are full of irregularities, quirky lexical derivations, and interesting idioms.

It's easier to create a "logical" language, and desirable if you want to create an auxiliary interlanguage, à la Esperanto. The danger here is a) creating a system so pristine, so abstract, that it's also impossible to learn; or b) not noticing when you reproduce some illogicality present in the models you're using. (Esperanto actually contains an embarrassing number of irregularities.)

Non-Western (or at least non-English) models

Looking at some non-Indo-European languages, such as Quechua, Chinese, Turkish, Arabic, or Swahili, can be eye-opening.

Learn other languages, if you can. Or just skim a grammar for nice ideas to steal.

- Bernard Comrie's *The World's Major Languages* contains meaty descriptions of fifty languages.

- Anatole Lyovin's *An Introduction to the Languages of the World* surveys all the world's language families, and gives detailed sketches of some important languages Comrie skips.

If you don't know another language well, you're pretty much doomed to produce ciphers of English. Checking out grammars (or this book) can help you avoid duplicating English grammar, and give you some neat ideas to try out; but the real difficulty is in the lexicon. If all you know is English, you'll tend to duplicate the structure and idioms of the English vocabulary.

How do I write lessons?

The easiest format for creating a language is a REFERENCE GRAMMAR, such as the grammar of Kebreni in this book. I'd write that first anyway, so you don't confuse yourself. When you're using the language as opposed to learning it, it's useful to have (say) all the information about pronouns in one place.

You can follow the format of any language textbook you like. Or look at the Verdurian course on my site.

Lessons consist of a reading, new vocabulary, grammatical notes, and exercises, all advancing in difficulty through the book.

List all the topics you want to teach, in digestible chunks (say, half a page each), then sort by difficulty and utility. For instance, here are the topics for the first two lessons of my Verdurian course:

Basic sentence order
Articles
Yes-no questions
To be (the six basic forms)
Possessive pronouns
Subject pronouns
Gender
Verbs (how to form the 3s from the citation form)
Double negatives

Stuff you can easily live without, like comparatives and causatives, goes near the end. (Or just leave it in the reference grammar.)

Difficulty depends on your language, of course— e.g. English adjectives are easy and can be taught right away; Russian or Latin ones have forbidding declensions and should be left till after nouns are mastered.

The outline can help determine your readings— e.g. you need a reading that introduces basic questions and past tense, or one that focuses on using numbers.

Keep new vocabulary to a minimum in each chapter; this can be the hardest thing about writing lessons. Keep a list of the words you've used so far. As you create the readings, re-use words from the list if possible, and if not, add them to the list (and to the vocabulary section for that lesson).

You can save a lot of time by making open-ended exercises— e.g. "Continue the conversation between the wizard and the barbarian."

Am I done yet?

At some point, after writing four pages of your grammar or forty, you may wonder when a language is done.

One answer you may not want to hear: Never. You can always find something else to write about... there are thousands of books about English, and there are still things we don't know about it.

Or maybe this sounds better: As soon as it meets your needs. You don't need a hundred-page reference grammar to fill out a map. Writing some dialog for a movie might take a careful phonology, a fairly full morphology, and a hasty outline of the commonest sentence types.

I find that a language is fairly presentable after I've created a bunch of sample sentences for the syntax section and about three readings— the process of creating these naturally points out anything I haven't covered yet. For one of my latest languages, Lé, that amounts to about 150 sentences, with a lexicon of about 920 words. It's complete enough that I know I can write texts in the language without having to change the grammar itself much.

Verdurian has a lexicon of over 6000 words. That's enough that I can write quite a bit without having to add to the lexicon... though it's not that hard to find gaps, either.

Sounds

Non-linguists will often start with the alphabet and add a few apostrophes and diacritical marks. The results are likely to be something that looks too much like English, has many more sounds than necessary, and which even the author doesn't know how to pronounce.

You'll get better results the more you know about PHONETICS (the study of the possible sounds of language) and PHONOLOGY (how sounds are actually used in language).

If you read just one book on linguistics besides this one, make it J.C. Catford's *A Practical Introduction to Phonetics*. Catford goes through the possible sounds systematically, with practical descriptions of how to produce each one even without having heard them.

Linguists use PHONES to refer to a particular sound used in a language.

Phonetic notation

Language textbooks usually describe sounds by comparison with English, adding recipes for producing unusual sounds. Linguists instead use the IPA (International Phonetic Alphabet), a set of symbols with precise meanings.

I'll ease into using the IPA, since it isn't that helpful till you know something about phonetics. For now, IPA symbols will be in brackets, and I'll use customary English representations in boldface. E.g. **sh** [ʃ] refers to the English **sh** sound as in *shirt* and tells you that its IPA symbol is ʃ.

If an IPA symbol isn't given, it's the same as the English representation— e.g. the symbol for **f** is [f].

There's an IPA chart at the back of the book (p. 270)

Consonants

You know about vowels and consonants— though the distinction between them isn't as airtight as you heard in school. Consonants can be further organized, however. The most important division is a two-dimensional distinction between PLACE OF ARTICULATION and degree of CLOSURE.

Place of articulation

Consonants are formed by obstructing the flow of air from the lungs. The first thing to check is where the obstruction occurs; by convention we start at the lips and move inward.

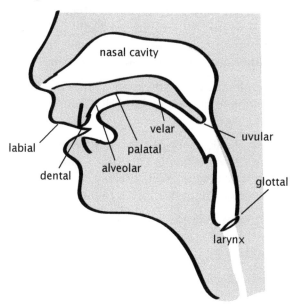

- LABIAL: lips alone (**w**)

- LABIODENTAL: lips and teeth together (**f, v**)

- DENTAL: tongue against teeth (**th**: unvoiced [θ], voiced [ð]; French or Spanish **t, d**)

- ALVEOLAR: tongue behind the teeth (**s, z**, English **t, d**, Spanish **r**)

- PALATO-ALVEOLAR: tongue further back from the teeth (**sh** [ʃ], American **r** [ɹ])

- PALATAL: tongue touching the top of the palate (Spanish **ñ** [ɲ], Italian **gn**, Sanskrit **c**)

- VELAR: back of the tongue against the back of the mouth (**k, g, ng** [ŋ])

- UVULAR: tongue compressing way back in the mouth (Arabic **q**, French **r**). To pronounce an uvular **q**, pronounce a series of **k**'s while sliding your tongue back as far as it will go. You'll notice a difference in pitch: **q** is about an octave lower than **k**. The k in *milk* is part of the way there (compare *Mick*).

- GLOTTAL: constricting the throat (**h**, glottal stop [?] as in John Lennon saying *bottle*).

The Roman alphabet doesn't have enough symbols, so languages are forced to use letters ambiguously, or use digraphs or diacritics. English and French **t** aren't the same sound, for instance: French **t** is formed by touching the tongue to the teeth, English **t** by touching the alveolar ridge behind the teeth.

Degree of closure

Consonants also vary depending on *how much* they obstruct the airflow.

- STOPS (also called PLOSIVES) stop it entirely: **p t k b d g**. In the middle of a word, as in *happy*, this is so fast that we're hardly conscious of the closure. The stop can be lengthened, however, and then we can see there's actually a brief silence while the air-flow is stopped. Compare *back kit, Beckett.*

- FRICATIVES just impede the airflow, creating a noticeable hiss-ing sound: **f s sh** [ʃ] **kh** [x]. A fricative can be prolonged indefi-nitely.

- AFFRICATES consist of a stop releasing into a fricative at the same place of articulation, such as **t + s** in *tsetse*. English **ch** is actually an affricate, consisting of **t + sh** [tʃ]; likewise **j** is **d + zh** [dʒ].

- APPROXIMANTS impede the airflow only slightly; there's no hissing sound, only a slight change in sound quality: **r l w y**.

  Confusingly, the IPA for **y** is [j]. Don't mistake this for English **j**.

- If the airflow isn't obstructed at all, what you have is a VOWEL.

More distinctions

Voicing

Consonants can be VOICED or UNVOICED; voicing just means letting the vocal cords vibrate.

Unvoiced and voiced consonants usually come in pairs: **p/b, t/d, k/g, f/v, sh/zh**, and so on. Sometimes there are gaps:

- German has unvoiced **kh** [x] (which it spells **ch**) but not voiced **gh** [ɣ] (which however exists in Dutch).

- Spanish has unvoiced **s** but not voiced **z**.

- Standard Arabic has voiced **b** but not unvoiced **p**.

- Often approximants only appear in voiced form. Nonetheless it's possible to have an unvoiced **r l w y**. For some English speakers, *wh* is pronounced as an unvoiced **w**[ʍ].

Vowels are normally voiced; we'll see some exceptions later.

Voicing isn't entirely binary; languages can differ in VOICING ONSET TIME (VOT), which is when the voicing starts. English has relatively late VOT— we start voicing initial **b, d, g, j** pretty late; French, by contrast, has early VOT. English also tends to stop voicing pretty early if the consonant ends a word. We really distinguish "voiced" consonants at the beginning and end of the word by other cues.

Nasalization

Instead of simply stopping the airflow, we can re-route it through the nose, producing NASAL consonants: **m n ng** [ŋ].

The mouth does the exact thing for **b** as for **m**; the difference is that the nasal passage is open for **m**. Thus we call **m** a NASAL STOP, or just a NASAL, with a labial place of articulation.

Similarly, **n** is a nasal dental or dental-alveolar, and **ng** [ŋ] is a nasal velar. If a language has other places of articulation, it can have other nasals, e.g. labiodental [ɱ], palatal [ɲ].

Aspiration

Stops may be released lightly, or with a noticeable puff of air— ASPIRATION. In English, we aspirate unvoiced stops at the beginning of a word (*pot, tall, cow*), but not after an **s** (*spot, stall, scow*). French and Spanish doesn't have this initial aspiration (and if you retain it while speaking these languages you'll have a gringo accent).

In Chinese, Hindi, or (Cusco) Quechua, there are separate series of aspirated and unaspirated stops. In Chinese and Quechua, in fact, there isn't a series of voiced stops at all. *Beijing*, for instance, doesn't start with a **b** at all, but an unaspirated **p**.

The IPA symbol is [ʰ]; so the Chinese labial stops are [p pʰ] .

Palatalization

A PALATALIZED consonant is pronounced by raising the tongue toward the top of the mouth. This happens to be about the position for **y**, and a palatalized consonant may sound to an English speaker as if there's a **y** (IPA [j]) after or before it.

Russian and Gaelic have palatalized and unpalatalized versions of most of their consonants. For instance, да, да [da da] 'yes, yes' sounds very different from дядя [dʲadʲə] 'uncle'.

Palatalization is an example of CO-ARTICULATION: the consonant is pronounced at (or nearly at) its normal place of articulation, but with the tongue raised. So palatalized [nʲ] isn't quite the same as palatal [ɲ].

Labialization

A LABIALIZED consonant is pronounced with the lips rounded. For instance, Latin *aqua* 'water' was pronounced [akʷa] with labialized k. This isn't the same as the cluster [kw]; with true labialized [kʷ], the lip-rounding is *simultaneous* with the [k].

Any of the stops can be labialized, and fricatives too.

Glottal games

Most sounds are produced by air moving from the lungs. It's also possible to create a small amount of airflow by moving the larynx up or down, without any pulmonic airflow at all.

Try it! Touch your Adam's apple and sing an [a], varying from high to low pitch; you'll feel the larynx moving. Now do it silently. Finally, keep the vocal cords closed as for [ʔ], put the tongue in [k] position, and raise the larynx suddenly— that should produce an EJECTIVE [k'], a sort of throaty puff.

Now keep your lips closed as for [b], and move the larynx *down* while voicing; this should produce a strangled-sounding [ɓ], an IMPLOSIVE. There's also implosives [ɗ] and [ɠ].

The consonant grid

Where non-linguists tend to list sounds in alphabetical order, linguists prefer to use a PHONOLOGICAL GRID, with place of articulation across the top, and degree of closure down the sides.

The grid for American English looks like this.

	labial	labio-dental	alveolar	alveolar-palatal	velar	glottal
stops	p		t		k	
	b		d		g	
fricatives		f	s	sh		h
		v	z	zh		
affricates				ch		
				j		
approximants	w		r, l	y		
nasals	m		n		ng	

Voicing is a third dimension in English; voiced sounds can simply be placed next to the unvoiced equivalent.

This is where the **p t k** order comes from: the stops are listed in order of place of articulation.

Rhotics

In programming, there's an aphorism that 10% of the functionality takes 90% of the effort. In phonetics we might say the same about **r** and **l**, which are quite messy.

There are a number of RHOTIC (**r**) sounds:

- American **r** [ɹ] is an approximant, but there are two ways of forming it (which sound about the same):

  ° A RETROFLEX **r** [ɻ] is pronounced by curling the tongue up behind the alveolar ridge. Some languages, such as Hindi, have a series of retroflex consonants, such as the stops [ʈ] and [ɖ].

  ° A BUNCHED **r** is pronounced by bunching up the tongue thickly under the palate; the tip is drawn back into the body of the tongue.

- In much of England **r** is a post-alveolar approximant— like the retroflex **r** but the tongue pointed at the alveolar ridge, not curled back. (However, younger speakers seem to be adopting a sound more like a w!)

- Another type of **r** is a TAP [ɾ], where the tongue tip is brushed briefly against the alveolar ridge. This can sound like a **d**; thus "veddy" for "very" in attempts to capture certain accents. Spanish single, non-initial **r** (as in *caro*) is a tap; it's also common in Scottish English.

- **R** can be TRILLED [r], which is like a repeated tap caused by vibrating the tongue against the alveolar ridge. Initial and double **r** in Spanish are trilled (as in *rueda, carro*).

- French **r** is a uvular approximant or trill [ʀ].

Don't confuse any of these realizations with a *dropped* **r**— that is, one that's not there! Many English dialects are NON-RHOTIC, meaning that syllable-final **r** is dropped.

Laterals

LATERALS (**l** sounds) are so called because they're made with a closure, like a stop, but leaving an opening at the sides of the tongue for airflow.

- English has two distinct **l** sounds:

    ° CLEAR **l** is formed with the closure on the alveolar ridge; it occurs at the beginning of a syllable, as in *Luke*.

    ° DARK **l** [ɫ] is formed by retracting the tongue (VELARIZATION); it occurs at the end of a syllable, as in *cool*. Velarization can be applied to other consonants as well.

    Many languages have a clear **l** in all positions; using a dark **l** in (say) Spanish will mark you as an *anglófono*.

- Russian (among other languages) has a *dental* **l**, with the tongue touching the teeth. If you want a Slavic accent, make your **l**'s dental.

- Then there's palatal **l** [ʎ], as in Italian *voglio*. Spanish **ll** used to be pronounced this way, and still is in some dialects.

- If the edges of the tongue are closer to the sides of the mouth, so that there's a noticeable hissing sound, you have a LATERAL FRICATIVE [ɮ]. Welsh **ll** is an *unvoiced* lateral fricative [ɬ]. (You may pause to congratulate yourself that you can now work out a triple-barreled term like that. If you can't, re-read the consonants section!)

Phones, phonemes, and allophones

I've talked about (say) different realizations of English **l** or **p**. However, we need to be more precise about what this means.

Each language has a set of PHONEMES— classes of sounds (phones) that speakers treat as "the same sound". By convention,

- **phonemes** appear between **slashes**: /l/, /p/...

- **phones** appear between **brackets**: [l], [p]...

This allows us to be brief and precise. For instance, we say that English /p/ is realized as [pʰ] initially and as [p] elsewhere. (The absence of the ʰ indicates a lack of aspiration.) The two phones [pʰ] and [p] are called ALLOPHONES of /p/.

You can think of phonemes as how sounds are represented in the speaker's mental grammar. Speakers are often quite unaware of allophonic variation. We don't think of the *p* in *pot* and *spot* as different, though phonetically they are.

Phonemes vs. letters

Often phonemes correspond to letters, but don't confuse them; letters are an aspect of writing systems, which are a separate topic. The same language may have multiple writing systems— e.g. Yiddish can be written in Hebrew or Roman letters; Turkish was once written in Arabic script and now uses Roman; Mandarin can be written using Chinese characters or in a dizzying variety of romanizations.

Letters don't correspond one-for-one with phonemes— notoriously so, in English. Digraphs like **ch** represent a single phoneme /č/. A letter can represent different phonemes; e.g. **s** can represent /s/, /z/, or /š/. And a single phoneme may be spelled in many ways: e.g. English /f/ can be spelled **f** or **ph**.

Phonemes may be written using IPA, but often this isn't very convenient. For a conlang, you can think of the phonemes as your romanization scheme— for most purposes, your writing system. If you like š better than ʃ, by all means use it for the phoneme.

But I'm †Σℏ ₵øℕℓæŇ₲iℕ4₵øℜ!

Maybe you've been making conlangs since you were eight and you use a lot of personal symbols. Well, knock it off.

Once your conlang leaves your desk, you need to make it accessible to other people. Even if you carefully explain that % means [ʃ], they'll forget or won't care.

Plus, all those cool symbols you found buried in the Unicode manual have some actual meaning, and the people who know that meaning will just be confused when you misapply them.

Phonemes vs. allophones

Here are some more examples of phones vs. allophones:

- English /t/ is [tʰ] initially, [t] after an [s], often an unreleased [t˺] finally, and often a glottal stop [ʔ] medially (as in *button*).

- English /l/ is clear [l] initially, dark [ł] finally.

- English /m/ is usually labial, but it's labiodental [ɱ] before [f].

- In some English dialects, dropped final /r/ reappears before a vowel: *I fear a disaster* = [aj fir ə dɪzɑstə]. In this case we may say that there's still an underlying phoneme /r/, but it's normally realized as [ə], and only as [r] before a vowel. But for some speakers, an [r] is added between vowels whether or not written English has an **r**: e.g. *I saw a cat* = [aj sɔr ə kæt]. For them, this intrusive r isn't a phoneme at all.

- Spanish /s/ is usually [s], but it's voiced [z] before a voiced consonant: *los dedos* = [loz deðos].

Allophones vs. dialectal realizations

Don't confuse allophones with dialectal variation. Allophones exist within a *single speaker's* dialect.

For instance, the different ways different English varieties pronounce /r/ are not allophonic. Each individual has a particular REALIZATION they always use— e.g. a Scottish speaker always has /r/ as flapped [ɾ].

Different dialects can have different phonemes. For instance, European Spanish has a /θ/ phoneme; in Latin American Spanish it's merged with /s/. Some English dialects have a separate unvoiced /w̥/ for *wh*; others just MERGE this with /w/.

Phonemic analysis

Phones are very precise and not controversial: if you see [pʰ] you know we're talking about an unvoiced aspirated labial stop. (Though a few symbols aren't as precise as they could be; e.g. [t] can be used for either a dental or an alveolar stop.)

Phonemes, however, represent an analysis of the language, and there are often multiple ways to do this, and it's not always possible to say that one way is the best.

For instance, is /č/ a phoneme of English? Native speakers do think of it as a "sound"; they're often surprised to learn that phonetically it's made of two sounds [t] + [ʃ]. Calling /č/ a phoneme also makes some observations about English phonology neater. But we could also analyze it as a cluster /tʃ/.

How do you know if a given sound is a phoneme or an allophone? The classical test is to find MINIMAL PAIRS— e.g. *bat* and *pat* show that /b/ and /p/ are separate phonemes in English. We can't find minimal pairs for [pʰ] in *pat* and [p] in *spat*— they never distinguish words; we say they are in COMPLEMENTARY DISTRIBUTION.

Sometimes a phonological puzzle has no accepted solution. In Mandarin, the palatals **j q** occur only before high front vowels; they contrast with three separate series: the dental sibilants **z c**, the retroflexes **zh ch**, and the velars **g k**, none of which appear before those vowels. We'd like to say that the palatals are allophones of one of the other series, but it's not clear which one!

Cross-language comparisons

Strictly speaking, only phones should be compared across languages. For instance, you can say that both English and Mandarin have [p] and [pʰ] phones.

But it's misleading and confusing to say that they both have /p/ *phonemes.* You can find references to /p/ in grammars of both languages, but they don't mean the same thing. English /p/ has [p] and [pʰ] allophones and contrasts with /b/; Mandarin /p/ is always [pʰ] and contrasts with /b/, which is normally [p], but may be realized as [b] in unaccented syllables.

Informally, linguists do talk about (say) how many languages have an /a/. Just don't take this too seriously. Without reading the individual grammars, you don't know what it means that the language has an /a/— what actual realizations it has or doesn't have.

Some consonants are more common than others. For instance, virtually all languages have the simple stops [p t k]. Lass's *Phonology* gives examples; see also David Crystal's *The Cambridge Encyclopedia of Language,* p. 165. Online, search for UPSID (the *UCLA Phonological Segment Inventory Database*) or WALS (the World Atlas of Language Structures).

Inventing consonants

The amateur way of creating consonants it to mix letters— I encountered one conlang with a sound "between an **n** and an **m**".

You can pick from the many sounds English doesn't have— e.g. add palatalized ñ and a glottal stop ʔ. But it's more naturalistic and more interesting to add entire series— or remove them. Cusco Quechua, for instance, has three series of stops— aspirated, non-aspirated, and glottal-ized— but doesn't distinguish voiced and unvoiced stops.

Or you can add places of articulation. For instance, while English has three series of stops, Hindi has five (labial, dental, retroflex, alveolo-palatal, and velar), and Arabic has six (bilabial, dental, 'emphatic' (don't ask), velar, uvular, glottal).

Vowels

Vowels vary in several dimensions. The most important are height, frontness, and roundedness.

Height

HEIGHT refers to the height of the tongue within the mouth; there's also a tendency to open the mouth wider as the tongue lowers, so lower vowels are also called OPEN.

The usual scale is HIGH [i, u], MID [e, o], LOW [a].

Many languages, including English, have four steps instead. Instead of mid there are two heights:

- MID-HIGH or CLOSED: English /e, o/ as in *say, so,* French é and the [o] in *eau;* the Italian **e, o** in *cera, voce.*

- MID-LOW or OPEN: English /ɛ/ as in *set;* French è and the **o** in *donner;* Italian **e, o** in *sella, cosa.*

  For English speakers who distinguish *Don / Dawn* and *cot / caught,* the open **o** or /ɔ/ is the second of these pairs. But if you pronounce these words the same, that's not an open **o** but an [a]! You can produce /ɔ/ by starting with /ɛ/ and retracting the tongue; see *Frontness* below.

The word *closed* is a mnemonic for closed /o/. The word *open* has open **e** (so don't think about the **o**, which is also closed!).

Frontness

FRONT vowels are pronounced with the tongue pushed forward, to the front of the mouth. [i e ɛ] as in *me, may, meh* are all front vowels.

BACK vowels are pronounced with the tongue retracted— e.g. [u o ɔ] in *do, doe, dawn.*

In between are CENTRAL vowels, such as the muddy schwa [ə] found in the unstressed syllables of *China, about, photograph.*

English /a/ as in *pot* may be central, but for some speakers it's a back vowel /ɑ/. The **a** in *cat* is /æ/, a low front vowel.

The vowel grid

You can arrange the vowels in a grid according to these two dimensions. The bottom of the grid is usually drawn shorter because there isn't as much room for the tongue to maneuver as the mouth opens more.

To get a feel for these distinctions, pronounce the phones in the diagram, moving from top to bottom or side to side, and noting where your tongue is and how close it is to the roof of the mouth.

Tenseness

Once you understand the vowel grid, you can appreciate the distinction of TENSE vs. LAX. Graphically, tense vowels lie toward the edges of the diagram; lax vowels are closer to the center. The names refer to the fact that the tongue is held more tensely forward or backward in order to produce these sounds.

The standard vowels used for phonetics, the CARDINAL VOWELS, are as tense as possible. English speakers, however, tend to pronounce /u/ and /ɛ/ more centrally than the cardinal vowels.

Many languages, including English, have tense/lax versions of almost all their vowels. Here's the full diagram for my dialect of American English, using sample words:

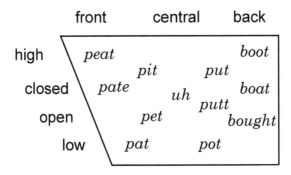

And using IPA:

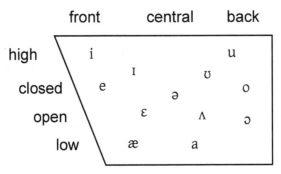

Roundedness

A ROUNDED vowel is pronounced with the lips rounded, like English /u o/, as opposed to UNROUNDED vowels like /i e/.

There's a strong tendency for front vowels to be unrounded, and back vowels to be rounded, as in English, Spanish, or Italian.

- French **u**, **œ** and German **ü**, **ö** are FRONT ROUNDED vowels. To pronounce **ü**, your lips should be in the position for **u**, and your tongue for **i**. Or to put it another way, say [i] and purse your lips. The IPA for ü is [y]; don't confuse this with English **y**.

- Russian **ы** and Japanese **u** [ɯ] are BACK UNROUNDED vowels. To pronounce [ɯ], say [u] and unpurse your lips.

Here's an expanded version of the basic vowel grid showing the IPA symbols for unrounded then rounded vowels in each position:

	front	central	back
high	i • y	ɨ • ʉ	ɯ • u
	ɪ • ʏ		
closed	e • ø	ə • ɵ	ɣ • o
open	ɛ • œ		ʌ • ɔ
low	æ • Œ		ɑ • ɒ

Other distinctions

Vowels can vary along other dimensions as well:

- LENGTH: vowels may contrast by length, as in Latin, Greek, Sanskrit, Japanese, and Old English. Estonian has three degrees of length.

  Length just means that the vowel is pronounced for a longer time. E.g. Latin *pōtus* 'drunken' [po:tus] contrasts with *potis* 'able' [potis]. As a complication, short vowels may be laxed compared to their long counterparts.

  Don't confuse this with the English "long vowels"— these do derive from Old English long vowels, but they're mostly diphthongs now.

- NASALIZATION: like consonants, vowels can be nasalized. French, for instance, has four nasalized vowels [œ ɔ ɛ ɑ] as in *un bon vin blanc*.

- VOICING: Vowels are normally voiced, but may be unvoiced in particular circumstances; e.g. Japanese often devoices vowels between two unvoiced consonants; e.g. the *u* [u̥] in *kusa* 'grass'.

  An unvoiced vowel may have a fricative (hissing) quality. Phonetically, English **h** can be taken as the unvoiced form of the following vowel.

SEMIVOWELS like **y**, **w** [j w] can be thought of as ultra-short vowels. Fronted [y] has a corresponding approximant [ɥ], found in French— e.g. *huile* [ɥil].

Rhotics, laterals, and nasals can be prolonged, and thus can take the place of vowels— they're SYLLABIC. English *murk, vessel, lesson* are [mr̩k ves̩l lesn̩]. Dictionaries like to show a vowel [mʌrk lesən], but there aren't really two separate phones there.

Diphthongs

A DIPHTHONG is a sequence of two different vowels in the same syllable, as in English *coy, cow, guy* /koj kaw gaj/. Phonetically, the vowels are not really distinct; the position of the vocal organs glides from one position to the other.

English has a tendency to diphthongize its closed vowels: e.g. *day* is pronounced [dej], *go* is [gow]. Don't carry this habit over to languages with purer vowels— e.g. French *thé, tôt* are [te, to] not [tej, tow].

The diphthongs mentioned above end with a semivowel; they can also begin with one, as in *cute* [kjut] or Chinese *tiān* [tjɛn] 'heaven'; or you can have a TRIPHTHONG beginning and ending with a semivowel: *xiǎo* 'little' [ɕjɑw].

A single vowel is sometimes called a MONOPHTHONG, usually in the context of sound change. In Southern American English, for instance, /aj/ has monophthongized to /a/.

Vowel systems

As with the consonants, if you're inventing a vowel system, don't just add an exotic vowel or two. Invent a vowel system by adding or removing entire classes of vowels.

Vowel systems vary greatly in complexity. Some of the simplest are those of Quechua (three vowels, **i u a**) and Spanish (five: **i e a o u**). Simple vowel systems tend to spread out; a Quechua **i**, for instance, can sound like English *pit, peat,* or *pet.* Spanish **e** and **o** have open and closed allophones.

English is fairly rich in vowels, with a dozen or so. French has 16.

What makes an good phonetic inventory?

People sometimes post phonetic inventories on my board and anxiously await comments. This mystifies me... it's a bit like a painter showing you which colors he intends to use. It's only a first, small step.

Still, if you're anxious, here are a few guidelines.

- Don't throw in every sound discussed above. New conlangers often throw everything they've learned into one language— a KITCHEN SINK conlang.

- It's a bit tacky to simply use all and only the sounds of English. Or, as in the Standard Fantasy Language, English plus **kh**.

- Think in terms of *features*, not sounds. E.g. add a series of retroflex stops, or nasalized vowels, not just one or two new sounds.

- On the other hand, if your language is aimed at non-conlangers— e.g. it's the background for a novel— your readers are going to ignore exotic sounds anyway. In that case it can be more effective to *remove* English sounds than to add new ones.

Stress

Don't forget to give a stress rule. English has unpredictable stress, and if you don't think about it your invented language will tend to work that way too.

French (lightly) stresses the last syllable. Polish and Quechua always stress the second-to-last syllable. Latin has a more complex rule: stress the second-to-last syllable, unless both final syllables are short and aren't separated by two consonants.

If the rule is absolutely regular, you don't need to indicate stress orthographically. If it's irregular, however, consider explicitly indicating it, as in Spanish: *corazón, porqué*.

In English, vowels are REDUCED to more indistinct or centralized forms when unstressed. This is one big reason (though not the only one) that English spelling is so difficult.

Tone

Tone proper

Mandarin syllables have four TONES, or intonation contours: high level; rising; falling-rising, and high falling. These tones are parts of the word, and can be used to distinguish words of different meanings: *mā* 'mother', *má* 'hemp', *mǎ* 'horse', *mà* 'curse'. Cantonese and Vietnamese have six tones.

Tones are often described on a five-point scale, 5 being the highest. The Mandarin tones are 55, 35, 214, and 51. They may be understood better with diagrams of relative pitch:

mā   má   mǎ   mà

The diacritics are mnemonics for the diagrams.

Tones are complicated by TONE SANDHI, where neighboring tones influence each other. For example, Mandarin's third tone changes to second before another third tone: *wǒ hěn hǎo* 'I'm fine' is pronounced *wó hén hǎo*.

Some answers to questions people often have about tone:

- Tones are not absolute, but relative to one's normal pitch— indeed, relative to the intonation of the sentence as a whole.

- Songwriters may or may not try to match the tones of the lyrics to the melody. In Mandarin songs tone tends to be ignored; in Cantonese not.

Pitch-accent systems

If that seems a bit elaborate, you might consider a PITCH-ACCENT system, where intonation contours belong to words, not syllables. Japanese and ancient Greek are pitch-accent languages.

In (standard) Japanese, syllables can be either high or low pitch; each word has a particular 'melody' or sequence of high and low syllables— e.g. *ikebana* 'flower arrangement' has the melody LHLL; *sashimi* 'sliced raw fish' has LHH; *kokoro* 'heart' has LHL. It sounds as if a tone has to be remembered for each syllable; but this turns out not to be the case. All you must learn for each word is the location of the 'accent', the main drop in pitch. Then you apply these three rules:

- Assign high pitch to all MORAS (= syllables, except that a long vowel is two moras, and a final -n or a double consonant takes up a mora too).

- Change the pitch to low for all moras following the accent.

- Assign low pitch to the first mora if the second is high.

Thus for *ike'bana* we have HHHH, then HHLL, then LHLL.

Channels

The Amazonian language Pirahã has an extremely simple phonological inventory, with tones. This allows it to be communicated by multiple CHANNELS: normal speech, humming, whistling.

Whispering can be considered a channel too; it can readily be understood though all voicing information is lost.

Phonological constraints

Every language has a series of constraints on what possible words can occur in the language. For instance, as an English speaker you know somehow that *blick* and *drass* are possible words, though they don't happen to exist, but *vlim* and *mtar* couldn't possibly be native English words.

Designing the PHONOLOGICAL CONSTRAINTS (also called PHONO-TACTICS) in your language will go a long way to giving it its own distinctive flavor.

Start with a distinctive syllable pattern. For instance,

- Japanese basically allows only **(C)(y)V(V)(n)**: *Ran-ma, A-ka-ne, Ta-te-wa-ki Ku-noo, Ru-mi-ko Ta-ka-ha-shi, Go-ji-ra, Too-kyoo, kon-kuu-ru, su-shi,* etc.

- Mandarin Chinese allows **(C)(i, u)V(w, y, n, ng)**: *wǒ, shì, Měi-guó, rén, wén-yán, chī-fàn, màn-huà, Wáng, pǔ-tōng-huà,* etc.

- Quechua allows **(C)V(C)**: *Wall-pa-ku-na sa-ra-ta mi-kuch-kan-ku, ach-ka a-llin ha-tun mo-soq pu-ka wa-si-kuna,* etc.

- English goes as far as **(s) + (C) + (r, l, w, y) + (V) + V + (C) + (C) + (C)**: *sprite, thanks-giv-ing.*

> **C and V?**
>
> C stands for any consonant, V for any vowel. Parentheses mean that an element is optional. So **(C)V(C)** means that a syllable must contain a vowel, but can optionally have an initial and/or final consonant.

Try to generalize your constraints. For instance, **m + t** is illegal at the beginning of a word in English. We could generalize this to [nasal] + [stop]. The rule against **v + l** generalizes at least to [voiced fricative] + [approximant].

Some of you will immediately think of *Vladimir.* But notice that that's a borrowing— new English words are still very unlikely to have **vl**. But it's true that some constraints are harder than others— even in borrowings like *psychology* we don't try to pronounce [ps]— though the French do for *psychologie.*

Working backwards

If you already have a lexicon, you can deduce the phonotactics by examining it and seeing what sort of syllables you've allowed.

For instance, if you have a word *bapada,* all the syllables are CV. If you have *strumpsk,* you're allowing CCCVCCCC. But try to be more specific: probably you don't actually allow clusters of any three arbitrary consonants. If you have words like *stroi, skrum, prek, blat,* that's more like (s)C(r,l)VC.

Divide clusters however they sound best to you— e.g. *bastroi* could be *bas-troi* (CVC CCVV) or *ba-stroi* (CV CCCVV) or even *bast-roi* (CVCC CVV). Be consistent, though.

Then look at all the syllable types you're allowing and decide if you really want to allow them all. Maybe you decide final CCCC is too much and have to change *strumpsk.*

Assimilation

Another process to be aware of is ASSIMILATION. Adjoining consonants tend to migrate to the same place of articulation. That's why Latin *in-* + *-port* = *import, ad* + *simil-* = *assimil-.* Consonants can assimilate in voice to; that's why our plural *-s* sounds like **z** after a voiced stop, as in *dogs* or *moms.*

It's also why Larry Niven's *klomter,* from *The Integral Trees,* rings false. **m** + **t** (though not impossible) is difficult, since each sound occurs at a different place of articulation; both sounds are likely either to shift to the dental position (*klonder*) or the labial (*klomper*). Another possible outcome is the insertion of a phonetically intermediate sound: *klompter.*

Alien mouths

If you're inventing a language for aliens, you'll probably want to give them *really different* sounds (if they have speech at all, of course). The Marvel Comics solution is to throw in a bunch of apostrophes: "This is Empress Nx'id"ar' of the planet Bla'no'no!" Larry Niven just violates English phonological constraints: *tnuctipun.* We can do better.

Think about the shape of the mouth of your aliens. Is it really long? That suggests adding a few more places of articulation. Perhaps the airstream itself works differently: perhaps they have no nose, and therefore can't produce nasals; or they can't stop breathing as they talk, so that all their vowels are nasal; or the airstream is at a higher velocity, producing higher-pitched sounds and perhaps more emphatic consonants. Or perhaps their anatomy allows odd clicks, snaps, and thuds that have become phonemes in their languages.

Several writers have come up with creatures with two vocal tracts, allowing them to pronounce two sounds at once, or accompany themselves in two-part harmony.

Or, how about sounds or syllables that vary in *tonal color*? Meanings might be distinguished by whether the voice sounds like a trombone, a violin, a trumpet, or a guitar.

Suggesting additional sounds is difficult and perhaps tiresome to the reader; an alien ambience can also be created by *removing* entire phonetic dimensions. An alien might be unable to produced voiced sounds (so he sounts a pit like a Cherman), or, lacking lips, might be stymied by labials (you nust do this to de a thentrilocooist, as ooell).

Orthography

Once you have the sounds of your language down, you'll want to create an ORTHOGRAPHY— that is, a standard way of representing those sounds in the Roman alphabet.

You have something very close to this already— your phonemic realization. There's nothing wrong with just using this as your orthography. You have some choices, however.

Don't try to be too creative here. For instance, you could represent /a e i o u/ as **ö é ee aw ù**, with the accents reversed at the end of the word. An outlandish orthography is probably an attempt to jazz up a phonetic system that didn't turn out to be interestingly different from English. Work on the sounds, then find a way to spell them in a straightforward fashion.

If you're inventing a language for a fantasy world, take account of how English-speaking readers will mangle your beautiful words. Tolkien is the model here: he spelled Quenya as if it were Latin, didn't introduce any really vile spellings, and kindly indicated final **e**'s that must be pronounced. Still, he couldn't resist demanding that **c** and **g** always be hard (I couldn't either, for Verdurian), which probably means that a lot of his names (e.g. *Cirdan*) are commonly mispronounced.

Marc Okrand, inventing Klingon, had the clever idea of using upper and lower case letters with different phonetic values. This has the advantage of doubling the letters available without using diacritics, but it's not very aesthetic and it sure is a tax on memory.

As an example of different approaches, here are some alternative transliterations for the same Verdurian sentence.

Mira rasfolžeca řo fäse meᵈ imočul.

Mira rasfolzheca rho faase medh imochul.

Miɾa ɾasfolȝɛka ʀo faːsɛ mɛð imotʃul.

A loving mother does not abandon a strayed son.

The first is the one I actually use, inspired by Czech orthography— č for ch, š for sh, etc. The second uses digraphs, uglier but more suitable for naïve English speakers and for ASCII applications, such as the early web. (In the Unicode era you can generally find any character you want.) The third uses IPA; never a bad choice, but sometime awkward (e.g. if you use unusual vowels *and* need to mark tone or nasalization).

Avoid **ee** and **oo** for [i u]; they're highly marked as English spellings. If people can handle *sushi* they can handle *mira.*

If you're inventing an **interlanguage**, of course, you shouldn't worry about English conventions; create the most straightforward romanization you can. You're only asking for trouble, however, if you invent new diacritic marks, as the inventor of Esperanto did.

Multiple transliterations

A sense of variation among the nations of your world can be achieved by using **different transliteration styles** for each. In my fantasy world, for instance, Verdurian *Ďarcaln* and Barakhinei *Dhârkalen* are not pronounced that differently, but the differing orthographies give then a different feeling. Surely you'd rather visit civilized Ďarcaln than dark and brooding Dhârkalen? (Tricked you. It's the same place.)

However, these systems should be motivated— ideally each orthography is a good representation of the native writing system (or, for unwritten languages, its phonology). Verdurian and Barakhinei each have their own native alphabets, so the differing orthographies suggest this.

Developing multiple languages, even if they're just naming languages, can give a map a pleasing sense of complexity. For instance, here are some of the names from the continent of Arcél on Almea:

Witsiʔpopok	*Smë*
Žonyān	*Gleŋ*
Bélésàɔ	*Ȟšanda*
Uytai	*Rimasača*
Siad βo	*Praȟmai*

These ten names represent eight different language families, of widely different phonologies and phonotactics. None of the diacritics or unusual characters is decorative; all are straightforward representations of the particular languages.

Diacritics

Some advice: never use a diacritical mark without giving it a specific meaning, preferably one which it retains in all uses. I made this mistake in Verdurian: I used ö and ü as in German, but ë somewhat as in Russian (indicating palatalization of the previous consonant), and ä as a mere doubling of a. I was smarter by the time I got to Cuêzi: the circumflex consistently indicates a low-pitch accent.

Avoid using **apostrophes** just to make words look foreign or alien. Since apostrophes are used in contradictory ways (they represent the glottal stop in Arabic or Hawai'ian, glottalization in Quechua, palatalization in romanized Russian, aspiration or a syllable boundary in Chinese, and omitted sounds in English, French, and Italian), they end up suggesting nothing at all to the reader.

Writing systems

The next chapter discusses grammar, but once you have a phonology, you can create an ALPHABET or other writing system for your language. If you want to do so now, turn to the section on *Writing Systems* (p. 176).

Acoustic phonetics

So far we've been concentrating on ARTICULATORY PHONETICS— how sounds are produced. There's also ACOUSTIC PHONETICS— how they are perceived by the ear and brain. To explain this would take a fairly long digression into the physics of sound waves, and wouldn't really improve your conlangs. But a couple of facts may be of interest.

Naively, we may feel that we speak a sound at a particular frequency. Really the sound wave is composed of a series of harmonics at various frequencies, with various peaks. The lowest peak is the FUNDAMENTAL FREQUENCY, which we perceive as the pitch of the voice. The higher peaks are called FORMANTS.

- As you raise the pitch of your voice, the fundamental frequency changes, but the formants do not.

- The location of the formants changes for each vowel.

Here's a plot of the first two formants (F_1 and F_2) for a particular speaker, in this case Canadian professor Kevin Russell:

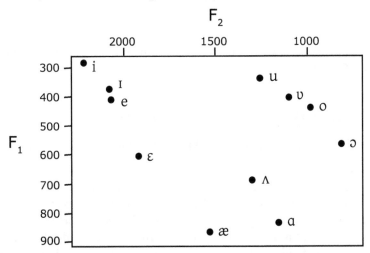

By this time, this picture should remind you of something— namely, the charts of vowels earlier in the chapter. So now you know what's really going on: openness corresponds largely to variation in F_1, and frontness to F_2.

Russell's web page (see the Web Resources page) contains a good short introduction to acoustic phonetics.

Word building

This section concentrates on techniques for building the vocabulary, or the LEXICON as linguists call it.

How many words do you need?

Where the conlang bug bites, the **Speedtalk** meme is sure to follow. Let Robert Heinlein explain it:

> Long before, Ogden and Richards had shown that eight hundred and fifty words were sufficient vocabulary to express anything that could be expressed by "normal" human vocabularies, with the aid of a handful of special words— a hundred odd— for each special field, such as horse racing or ballistics. About the same time phoneticians had analyzed all human tongues into about a hundred-odd sounds, represented by the letters of a general phonetic alphabet.
>
> ... One phonetic symbol was equivalent to an entire word in a "normal" language, one Speedtalk word was equal to an entire sentence.
>
> –"Gulf", in *Assignment in Eternity*, 1953

This is a tempting idea, not least because it promises to save us a good deal of work. Why invent thousands of words if a hundred will do?

The unfortunate truth is that **Ogden and Richards cheated**. They were able to reduce the vocabulary of Basic English so much by taking advantage of IDIOMS like *make good* for *succeed*. That may save a word, but it's still a lexical entry that must be learned as a unit, with no help from its component pieces. Plus, the whole process was highly irregular. (*Make bad* doesn't mean *fail*.)

The Speedtalk idea may seem to receive support from such observations as that 80% of English text makes use of only the most frequent 3000 words, and 50% makes use of only 100 words. However (as linguist Henry Kučera points out), there's an *inverse relationship between frequency and information content*: the most frequent words are function words (prepositions, particles, conjunctions, pronouns), which don't contribute much to meaning (and indeed can be left out entirely, as in newspaper headlines), while the least frequent words are important content words. It doesn't do you much good to understand 80% of the words in a sentence if the remaining 20% are the most important for understanding its meaning.

The other problem is that **redundancy isn't a bug, it's a feature**. Claude Shannon showed that the information content of English text was about one bit per letter— not too high considering that for random text it's about five bits a letter. Sounds inefficient, huh? On the other hand, we don't actually hear every sound (or, if we're accomplished readers, read every letter) in a word. We use the built-in redundancy of language to understand what's said anyway.

To put it another way: y cn ndrstnd Nglsh txt vn wtht th vwls, or shouted into a nor'easter, or over a staticky phone line. Similarly distorted Speedtalk would be impossible to understand, since entire morphemes would be missing or mistaken. Very probably the degree of redundancy of human languages is pretty precisely calibrated to the minimum level of information needed to cope with typical levels of distortion.

However, go ahead and play with the Speedtalk idea. It's good for some hours of fun, working out as minimal a set of primitives as you can; and the habit of paraphrase it gives you is very useful in creating languages. Just don't take it too seriously; if you do, your punishment is to learn 850 words of any actual foreign language and be set down in a city of monolingual speakers of that language.

Alien or *a priori* languages

If you're making up a language for a different world, you want words that don't sound like any existing language. Just make up words that use the sounds and the phonotactics of your language.

This can fairly quickly get tiresome. I don't advise you to sit down and come up with a hundred words at once; you're likely to run out of inspiration, or find that all the words are starting to sound the same. You may also be creating new roots where you could more easily derive the word from existing roots.

It's not hard to write computer programs that will randomly generate words for your language (even respecting its syllable structure— see **gen** on my website). If you use them, remember that sounds (and syllable types) are not equiprobably distributed in natural languages. English uses many more t's than f's, more f's than z's.

Resist the temptation to give a meaning to every possible syllable. Real languages don't work like that (unless the number of possibilities is quite low). Even if you're working on a highly structured interlanguage, you'll want some maneuvering room for future expansion. And the speakers of your language shouldn't have to throw out an old word whenever they want to construct a coinage or an abbreviation.

You will want a mixture of word lengths for variety; but don't invent too many long words. It's better to derive long words by combining shorter words, or adding suffixes. Or, imitating the way English is full of polysyllabic borrowings from Latin and Greek, or Japanese is full of Chinese loanwords, create two languages, and build words in one out of components from the other.

A few half-recognizable borrowings

You can vary how alien your language looks to English speakers. For instance, I designed Flaidish to look and sound not too different from English:

> **Lana voss zepo cepple, zynen gess?**
>
> *The girl isn't a virgin, is she?*

Cuêzi is intended to be mellifluous; its phonology is reminiscent of Greek and Latin, with mostly CV syllables and plenty of **l** and **r**:

> **Pomi namasiōmo radē tībal ōisizirītu.**
>
> *We defeated the men who had stolen the horse.*

I intended Verdurian to look mildly familiar, as if it could be a distant relative of the European languages. For example:

> **So cuon er so ailuro eu drukî. Cuon ride še slušir misotém ailurei. So ailuro e arašó rizuec.**
>
> *The dog and the cat are friends. The dog laughs at the cat's jokes. The cat is quite amusing.*

To achieve this impression, I borrowed from a number of earthly languages— e.g. **ailuro** 'cat' and **cuon** 'dog' are adapted from Greek; **sul** 'only' from French; **rizir** 'amuse' from Spanish; **druk** 'friend' and **slušir** 'hear' from Russian. The friendly orthography and the simple (C)(C)V(C) syllable structure also help make the language inviting.

By contrast, another language, Xurnese, was intended to look more alien:

Ir nevu jadzíes mnošuac. Toš to ray do šasaup rile šizen. To am šus bunji dis kes denjic. Syu cu šus izrues šač.

My niece is dating a sculptor. She can see no flaws in him. He hopes one day to govern a province. Myself, I don't envy that province.

Some un-English clusters (**mn**) and plenty of fricatives contribute to this, as well as the lack of evident cognates (though **dis** 'day' is related to Latin *dies*).

Elkarîl, spoken by non-humans, looks even more forbidding, largely due to its consonant clusters and non-English sounds. The doubled consonants are implosives.

On qichidd qurd qîl-kunmegg-nguj.

We classify gold among the five noble elements.

If you're creating an auxlang, you probably want maximum recognizability. You can't do much better than Interlingua:

Esseva in le mundo scientific— specialmente le branca medical— que interlingua vermente se monstrava utile post su apparition in 1951.

It was in the scientific world— especially the area of medicine— that Interlingua truly showed its utility after its appearance in 1951.

Borrowing existing lexicons

Interlanguages are often based on existing languages; for instance, Esperanto is chiefly based on French, Italian, German, and English. Here the problem of creating words largely reduces to one of acquiring enough good dictionaries.

A few language creators have tried to approach the task systematically— e.g. Interlingua is based on nine languages, and usually adopts the word found in the most languages.

Lojban uses a wider variety of languages, including some non-Western ones, and uses a statistical algorithm to produce an intermediate form. The intention is to provide some mnemonic assistance to a very wide variety of speakers. It's an intriguing idea, although the execution is so subtle that the language is often mistaken for *a priori*.

Sound symbolism

Some linguists claim to have found some common meaning patterns among human languages. For instance, front vowels (**i**, **e**) are said to suggest smallness, softness, or high pitch; low and back vowels (**a**, **u**, **o**) to suggest largeness, loudness, or low pitch. Compare *itty-bitty, whisper, tinkle, twitter, beep, screech, chirp*, with *humongous, shout, gong, clatter, crash, bam, growl, rumble*; or Spanish *mujercita* 'little woman' with *mujerona* 'big woman'. Cecil Adams took advantage of this pattern when he commented, on the subject of penis enlargement surgery, that "if nature has equipped you with a ding rather than a dong, you'll just have to live with it."

Exceptions aren't hard to find, of course— notably *small* and *big*.

Inventing alien languages, authors also simply make use of what we might call phonetic stereotypes. Tolkien's Black Speech, for instance, makes heavy use of guttural sounds and is full of consonant clusters, while his Elvish tongues are more vocalic, and have plenty of pleasant-sounding l's and r's.

Derivational morphology

This was discussed under *The overall process*; but it's worth repeating. A way to build families of words— a DERIVATIONAL MORPHOLOGY— is a basic conlanging tool, one that allows a single root to multiply into half a dozen words or more.

There are several ways to build words:

- SUFFIXES or PREFIXES (collectively called AFFIXES) can be added to the base form of the word (the ROOT).

- INFIXES are inserted within a root. My conlang Kebreni, for instance, has the infix *-su-* for "made of X": *siva* 'sand' → *sisuva* 'sandy'; *kam* 'oak' → *kasum* 'oaken'.

- VOWEL CHANGE is extensively used in the Semitic languages for both inflectional and derivational morphology. For instance, Arabic KTB 'write' has such forms as *yaktubu* 'he writes', *kitba* 'writing', *kitāb* 'book', *maktaba* 'library', *kātib* 'writer'.

- REDUPLICATION, where a root is repeated, is often used to indicate plurality, repetition, or emphasis— e.g. Malay *balik* 'go back' → *bolak-balik* 'go back and forth', *cabik* 'tear' → *cabik-cabik* 'tear to pieces'.

- COMPOUNDS simply join two roots together. There are several patterns:

  ° Concatenation, as in English *blackboard, typewriter, disk drive*, or Mandarin *diànhuà* 'electric-speech' = 'telephone'.

  ° A special compounding form; we're familiar with this from Greek, where *psukhē* 'mind' has a combining form *psukho-*, seen in *psychology*. (The inventor of *psychedelic* got this wrong.)

  ° Verb phrase, as in French *gratte-ciel* 'skyscraper', or English *forget-me-not*.

  ° An entire sentence— e.g. the name *Michael*, Hebrew for 'Who is like God?', or Mohawk *tekalistó:lalaks* 'typewriter', lit. 'it presses steel', or the Cheyenne name *Hestaneoo?e* 'stands in the wind'.

Derived words often show slightly different roots: *Florence/Florentine, divide/division, Eros/erotic, ten/-teen*. The culprit is sound change; we'll go over that in the Language Families chapter (p. 149).

As we've seen here, words have an internal structure. They can be divided into MORPHEMES, pieces which have a single meaning. Some words have just one morpheme (*some, have, just, one* in this sentence), others have two or more: *word/s, inter/nation/al/ly, build/ing*.

A FREE MORPHEME can stand alone as a word; a BOUND MORPHEME only occurs combined with other morphemes— e.g. English *-ing* or *-ed*, or the underlined syllables in *<u>ruth</u>less, un<u>kempt</u>, con<u>vert</u>, ra<u>sp</u>berry*.

On not reinventing English

- If the literal meaning of an expression doesn't make sense (e.g. "make good", "go all out", "have it in for someone", "look lived-in"), you're dealing with an IDIOM. Translate using expressions that make sense literally ("succeed", "work at full capacity", "have a grudge against someone", "seem inhabited"), or create your own idioms ("laugh at hell", "play bee", "circle your eye at someone", "be breathed and worn").

- Look through the foreign-to-English section of a bilingual dictionary. Look at the range of English meanings particular foreign words have: think about what kind of root concept could cover all of them.

For instance, Latin *fēlix* is defined as 'fruitful, lucky, happy, fortunate, successful'. That suggests that the Latin term covers material good fortune as much as good feelings.

- Look at the foreign words used to translate a single English word: try to see what distinctions the foreign language is making where English uses that one word.

  E.g. for 'captain', my Latin dictionary suggests *centurio* for infantry, *praefectus* for cavalry, and *nāviculārius* or *magister* for ships.

  For 'beautiful' it has *pulcher; (of form) formōsus.* That laconic hint suggests that *formōsus* prototypically refers to one aspect of beauty, shapeliness.

  Mandarin has six words for our 'brother-in-law':

  > *jiěfu* husband of older sister
  > *mèifu* husband of younger sister
  > *nèixiōng* elder brother of wife
  > *nèidì* younger brother of wife
  > *dàbó* elder brother of husband
  > *xiǎoshū* younger brother of husband

- Look up the etymology of the English word. See if you can come up with an alternative process. E.g. *etymology* derives from Greek roots *etumon* 'true sense (of a word)' + *-logia* 'study'. Hmm, how about 'word-origin' or 'grandfather-meaning'?

- Consider a whole class of related English words— verbs of motion, for instance. Design the related class of words in your language, dividing up the conceptual space in your own way.

- For a fantasy language, think about the culture that your language serves. What concepts are most important to it? They will likely have many synonyms, or even be reflected directly in the grammar. What's its history or mythology? Those will probably generate a number of derived words, similar to our *tantalizing* from Tantalus, or *quixotic* from Don Quixote.

- Browse through the *Semantics* chapter (p. 92) for plenty of things to think about.

- Also see my book on word-building, *The Conlanger's Lexipedia.*

Grammar

Once you've bundled together some words and perhaps an alphabet, you may think you're done. If you do, it's likely that you've just created an elaborate cipher for English. You still have the grammar to do, bucko.

Morphology and syntax

To linguists a GRAMMAR is the description of the entire language, including phonology and semantics. To non-linguists it largely means MORPHOLOGY, the formation of words, and perhaps SYNTAX, the formation of sentences.

A written grammar will often cover morphology first, then syntax. I'm going to proceed by features instead, such as cases, tenses, questions, and relative clauses. That's because the same feature may be handled by either morphological or syntactic means (or both).

How to use this chapter

Consider each feature a question about your language: How do you form plurals? What do the verbs do? How do you ask questions?

Each section will offer examples of how various languages handle that feature. You can adopt one of the solutions, or look in other grammars for more ideas, or try to come up with something on your own. But put *something* in your grammar to answer the question.

Grammaticalization

For any given feature, it's an option to not handle it at all. Maybe your language just doesn't deal with plurality or evidentiality (p. 70). If you're creating a fantasy conlang, you may wish to include some very non-English-like features. If you're creating an auxlang, you may prefer to only have features similar to those of your source languages.

All the features discussed here can be *expressed* in any language, but perhaps only by adding explicit modifiers (e.g. if plural isn't marked, you can state the number of things). That is, languages differ in what they GRAMMATICALIZE. English, for instance, grammaticalizes person and number in its verbal system, while Japanese does not. On the other hand Japanese verbs have positive and negative forms, as well as levels of deference.

Grammaticalization can also occur over time. E.g. many prepositions in Mandarin derive from (and often can still function as) verbs, such as *yòng* 'using' ← 'use', *gěi* 'for' ← 'give', *gēn* 'with' ← 'follow'. The English past tense *-ed* derives from the verb *did*.

Fusional, agglutinative, isolating?

INFLECTIONS are affixes used to conjugate verbs and decline nouns. Examples from English are the *-s* added to verbs for the 3rd person present form, the *-s* added to pluralize nouns, and the *-ed* of the past tense. Languages such as Russian or Latin have complex, not to say baroque, inflectional systems.

In AGGLUTINATIVE languages, each affix has a single meaning. E.g. in Quechua *wasikunapi* 'in the houses', the plural suffix *-kuna* is separate from the case suffix *-pi*. In *mikurani* 'I ate', the past tense *-ra-* is separate from the personal ending *-ni*.

By contrast, in FUSIONAL languages a single inflection may encode multiple meanings. E.g. in the Russian form *domóv* 'of the houses', the *-óv* ending indicates both plurality and the genitive case; it doesn't bear any evident relationship to other plural endings (e.g. nominative *-á*) or the singular genitive ending (*-a*). In Spanish *comí* 'I ate', the *-í* ending represents the 1st person singular, past tense, indicative mood— quite a job for one vowel, even accented.

Usually the same root is used throughout a paradigm; but sometimes a SUPPLETIVE form is used. For instance, Latin *ferō* 'bear' has the perfect stem *tul-*. An example from English is *went*, the past tense of *go*.

In an ISOLATING language, there are no suffixes at all; meanings are modified by inserting additional words. In Mandarin, for instance, *wǒ chī fàn* could mean 'I eat' or 'I was eating', depending on the context; the verb is not inflected at all. For precision, adverbs or particles can be brought in: *wǒ chī fàn zuótiān* 'I was eating yesterday', *wǒ chī fàn le* 'I've eaten' (i.e. 'I ate and finished').

In practice natural languages are mixed. Some inflections in fusional languages have a single meaning; Quechua does have a few fusions; and Mandarin does have a few suffixes and grammatical particles.

Conlang creators seem to gravitate toward agglutinative or isolating languages; but there's something to be said for fusional inflections. They tend to be compact, for instance. You can't beat -í for succinctness.

POLYSYNTHETIC languages incorporate nouns or other roots within the verb. For instance, Nishnaabemwin *naajmiijme* 'fetch food' incorporates *miijim* 'food'; in Ainu *Kane rakko o-tumi-osma* 'The war started because of the golden sea otter' the verb incorporates *tumi* 'war'. The Cheyenne name *Nahkôxhoveoʔeooʔestse* is a complete polysynthetic sentence, 'A bear stands in the shade'.

The incorporated form may differ from the noun normally used as a standalone word; e.g. Nishnaabemwin *naadaabkwe* 'go get one's money' includes an element *-aabikw-* for 'money' which differs from the standalone *zhoon'yaa*.

Got nouns, verbs, and adjectives?

Why not get rid of one or two of them?

It's not hard to get rid of **adjectives**. One easy way is to treat them as verbs: instead of saying "The wall is red", you say "The wall reds"; likewise, instead of "the red wall" you say "the redding wall". Quite a few languages do in fact treat adjectives as a type of verb.

With such tricks you can even get rid of the verb **be**, which according to some theorists is responsible for most of the sloppy thinking in the world today. (Heinlein was careful to ban 'to be' from Speedtalk.) About the only response this notion deserves is: would that clear thinking was that easy.

You can extend the idea to get rid of **nouns**. For instance, in Lakhota, ethnic names are verbs, not nouns. There's a verb 'to be a Lakhota' the present forms mean 'I am a Lakhota, you are a Lakhota, etc.'

You can have some fun with this. "The rock is under the tree" could be expressed as something like "There is stonying below the growing, greening, flourishing", or perhaps "It stones whileunder it grows greeningly." If we really encountered a language like this, however, I'd have to wonder whether we weren't just fooling ourselves. If there's a word that refers to stones, why translate it as 'to stone' rather than simply 'stone'?

Jorge Luis Borges, in "Tlön, Uqbar, Tertius Orbis", posits a language without nouns; but this was because its speakers were Berkeleyan idealists who didn't believe in object permanence. However, linguists really do not like using semantic classes— or metaphysics— to define syntactic categories. (It's not the right level of analysis; and it tends to obscure how languages really work by making them all look like Latin.)

Jack Vance (in *The Languages of Pao*) posited a language without **verbs**. For instance, "There are two matters I wish to discuss with you" comes out something like "Statement-of-importance– in-a-state-of-readiness– two; ear– of [place name] – in-a-state-of-readiness; mouth– of this person here– in-a-state-of-volition." Vance may be in a state of pulling our legs.

What noun inflections are there?

NOMINAL MORPHOLOGY covers the inflections on nouns. (Again, it's up to you whether to use inflections at all— maybe you prefer particles, or something more complex.)

Case

CASE is a way of marking nouns by function. For instance, Latin *mundus* 'world' has these forms in the singular:

mundus	subject or NOMINATIVE: the world (is, does, ...)
mundum	object or ACCUSATIVE: (something affects) the world
munde	VOCATIVE: O world!
mundi	possessive or GENITIVE: the world's
mundo	indirect object or DATIVE: (given, sold, etc.) to the world
mundo	ABLATIVE: (something is done) by the world

Putting a noun through its paces is called DECLINING. Latin has five distinct patterns of case endings, which are called DECLENSIONS.

Latin is fusional— the plural endings have nothing to do with the singular endings.

Our possessives (like *world's*) started as genitive case forms. Most of our pronouns have nominatives (*I, we, he...*) and accusatives (*me, us, him...*).

Conlangers generally either love case (because it makes a language compact and frees up word order) or hate it (because English doesn't do much with it).

Finnish has an impressive fifteen cases, shown below for the singular of *kirja* 'book':

kirja	NOMINATIVE	book (subject)
kirjan	ACCUSATIVE	book (object)

kirjan	GENITIVE	book's
kirjana	ESSIVE	as a book
kirjaa	PARTITIVE	certain objects (it's complicated)
kirjaksi	TRANSLATIVE	turned into a book
kirjassa	INESSIVE	in the book
kirjasta	ELATIVE	from (inside) the book
kirjaan	ILLATIVE	into the book
kirjalla	ADESSIVE	at the book
kirjalta	ABLATIVE	from (outside) the book
kirjalle	ALLATIVE	toward the book
kirjoin	INSTRUCTIVE	by means of the book
kirjoineen	COMITATIVE	along with the book
kirjatta	ABESSIVE	without a book

You won't go wrong inventing a case that corresponds to a preposition in English. But cases can also mark a syntactic role that has no special marking in English— e.g. the COMPARATIVE for something compared.

Case particles

Case can be indicated with particles instead of affixes. For instance, Japanese *o* marks the accusative, while *no* is a genitive.

It can be argued that English *'s* is really a particle, because it attaches to a NP (noun phrase), not to a noun: in *the king of England's daughter*, the daughter belongs to *the king of England*, not to *England* (the noun marked by the possessive).

Ergativity

Many languages have a different arrangement of cases. Consider these roles:

   A: *subject* of TRANSITIVE sentences: *I broke the window*
   B: *object* of TRANSITIVE sentences: *I broke **the window***
   C: *subject* of INTRANSITIVE sentences: ***The window** broke*

English treats subjects (A and C) together as the NOMINATIVE, B as the ACCUSATIVE. But we could group B and C together instead as the ABSOLUTIVE case, leaving A in the ERGATIVE case.

Basque is an example:

Gizona heldu zen.
The man arrived.

Neskak gizona ikusi zuen.
The girl saw the man.

Gizona 'man' is absolutive in both sentences, though he's what we'd consider a subject when he's arriving; *neska* 'girl' gets ergative *-k* in the second example because she's a transitive subject.

Some languages, such as Dyirbal, use the nominative/ accusative system for 1st and 2nd person pronouns (I, we, you), and the ergative/absolutive system for nouns and for 3rd person pronouns. In Pashto, present tense is nominative/accusative while past tense is ergative/absolutive.

Novel case systems

Ergativity may seem exotic, but it uses the same semantic roles as Indo-European languages. The basic questions are:

> *What happened? (V)*
> *Who did it? (S)*
> *What was affected? (O)*

In my conlang Elkarîl, spoken by non-humans, I wanted something different. Each sentence has three case roles and two verbs, answering these questions:

> *What happened at a physical level?*
> *What did it happen to?*
> *What was the immediate cause?*
> *What was this for?*
> *Who desired it?*

These can be seen, in order, in this sample sentence:

Qop ngôt âThulbelidd bôchiq tînsh nrêl.

hit (head GEN-Moonlight) apple mischief child

The child, acting out of mischief, made an apple fall on Moonlight's head.

There are complications, but in general these five items must be supplied in any Elkarîl sentence, just as (in general) our sentences must include subject, verb, and object.

Head marking

If a language doesn't have case it may rely on word order to indicate the relationship between a verb's arguments; but there is another alternative: HEAD-MARKING on the verb. For instance, in the Swahili *Kitabu umekileta?* 'Did you bring the book?', the verb *leta* has prefixes indicating the subject (*u-* 'you') and the object (*-ki-*, a third person prefix agreeing in gender with *kitabu*). (*-me* marks the perfect tense.) The gender-specific object marker on the verb allows free word order even without case marking on the nouns.

Gender

Most Indo-European languages have GENDER, typically MASCULINE/ FEMININE/NEUTER; many have lost the neuter. Algonquian languages have ANIMATE/INANIMATE genders instead.

English speakers, used to gender only in their pronouns, are baffled and amused at the arbitrary nature of gender, perhaps shown most strikingly by the French terms *le vagin* ('the vagina', masculine) and *la verge* ('the cock', feminine). On the other hand, kinship terms usually match natural gender: *l'oncle* ('the uncle', masculine), *la tante* ('the aunt', feminine).

If adjectives are inflected, they show GENDER AGREEMENT with their nouns: *le bon oncle* 'the good uncle', *la bonne tante* 'the good aunt'.

Gender need not be masculine/feminine, though if not the more general term NOUN CLASS may be used. Swahili, for instance, has eight noun classes, none of them masculine/feminine: one is for animals, one for human beings, one for abstract nouns, one forms diminutives, etc.

Conlangers used to avoid gender, back when they were mostly creating auxlangs. But it's a nice addition to a naturalistic language.

What is gender for?

People ask, what is gender **for**? Gender is remarkably persistent: it's persisted in the Indo-European, Semitic, and Bantu language families for at least five thousand years. It must be doing *something* useful.

A few possibilities:

- It helps tie adjectives and nouns together, reducing the functional load on word order and adding useful clues for parsing.

- It gives language (in John Lawler's terms) another dimension to seep into. In French, for instance, there are many words that vary only in gender: *port/porte, fil/file, grain/graine, point/pointe, sort/sorte*, etc. Changing gender must have once been an easy way to create a subtle variation on a word.

- It allows indefinite references to give someone's sex, which makes gossip easier, at least.

- It offers some of the advantages of obviative pronouns (p. 73): one may have two or more third person pronouns at work at the same time, referring to different things.

- It can support free word order without case marking, as in the Swahili example on p. 62.

Is gender sexist?

Many people have worried that gender is somehow inherently sexist. It's certainly a little disturbing that in masculine/ feminine systems, a group of mixed sex is usually referred to by masculine nouns or pronouns. (In some languages you use the neuter instead, while in Zayse you use the feminine.)

This probably bugs English speakers precisely because gender is so vestigial in English. French speakers are used to arbitrary rules— e.g. *la personne* (f.) is used for either sex.

It's also difficult to maintain that gender reflects sexism when such languages as Turkish and Chinese lack it; these cultures were not historically noted for sexual equality. And other forms of discrimination (e.g. those based on race, class, or religion) have no linguistic expression at all.

As this example shows, it's not clear how well natural languages reflect cultures. On the other hand, it's fun to have your conlangs reflect your con-society (see p. 140). Should the orcs have personal pronouns that reflect edibility? Why not?

Other possibilities for nouns

Other things can be signaled on the noun. An incomplete list:

- PLURALITY, as in English.

- Some languages have special DUAL forms for pairs of items, or PAUCAL forms for a small number.

- HONORIFICS, e.g. Japanese *o-*. These may show respect for the referent (e.g. *ocha* 'tea', *otōsan* 'father') or for the hearer (e.g. when talking to a superior you may use honorific forms in general).

- POSSESSION: in Quechua, there are suffixes (corresponding to the personal pronouns) indicating who owns something: *wasi* 'house' → *wasiy* 'my house', *wasiyki* 'your house', *wasin* 'his/her house'.

- Other forms indicating attitude: DIMINUTIVES for affection or small size, AUGMENTATIVES for honor or large size, DESPECTIVES showing disdain.

- Verbal features can be applied to nouns too. For instance, the past tense suffix might be attached to a noun to refer to things that used to exist or no longer have the quality described by that noun— something like our *ex-* as in *ex-wife*.

There's no reason you can't invent your own categories, especially for alien cultures. Type of movement? Value? Interestingness? Degree of threat?

Derivation or inflection?

Some of you may wonder whether a given affix is an inflection, or part of derivational morphology. That's a good question and there isn't a clear-cut dividing line. But we usually reserve 'inflection' for mandatory markings— perhaps based on Latin, where e.g. both singular and plural are marked on the noun. There's also a tendency for derivational affixes to be applied first, closer to the root. And often derivational processes have limited productivity.

Mass and count nouns

Nouns can be divided into MASS and COUNT nouns. Count nouns can be counted: *one cow, two houses, three French hens.* Mass nouns are treated as, well, a mass that can't be counted: *water, grain, wallpaper, cattle.*

The distinction can be quirky: *pea* is a count noun while *corn* isn't; *beans* can be counted and *rice* not. The determination can vary by language.

To be precise, you can count things named by mass nouns, but you need a MEASURE WORD to define the quantity counted:

> one grain of rice
> two sacks of rice
> three carloads of corn
> forty head of cattle
> six sheets of paper
> ten reams of paper

Mandarin treats almost all nouns as mass nouns; there is a large set of measure words which are conventionally used for a class of objects. For instance, *sān ge rén* 'three persons', *zhèi zhǎn dēng* 'this lamp', *nèi tiáo niú* 'that cow', where the middle words are measure words.

What verb inflections are there?

VERBAL MORPHOLOGY covers the inflections on verbs. For traditional reasons, we speak of CONJUGATING verbs, and a particular pattern of verb forms is a CONJUGATION.

Person and number

You may be familiar with endings that show person and number from the Romance languages, though they are found in many other languages as well. Here are the present tense forms for 'give' in several languages:

	French	Hungarian	Quechua	Swahili
1s	donne	adok	quni	nipa
2s	donnes	adsz	qunki	upa
3s	donne	ad	qun	apa
1p	donnons	adunk	qunchik	tupa
2p	donnez	adtok	qunkichik	mpa
3p	donnent	adnak	qunku	wapa

The "I / you / he" distinction is PERSON; and as with nouns, the singular/plural distinction is NUMBER. **1s** is a convenient abbreviation for "1st person singular"; older grammars might write something like **I. sing.**

The particular list often corresponds to the distinctions made in the personal pronouns; see below. (Quechua actually has two 1p verb forms: *qunchik* is inclusive 'we', *quniku* is exclusive 'we'.)

Note that the Swahili inflections are prefixes, not suffixes!

These basic inflections tend to be worn down, but they may derive from an earlier system which separated the person and number affixes. They're *almost* separable in Quechua: *-chik* is a pluralizer which includes the hearer, *-ku* is used for everything else.

An advantage of personal endings is that subject pronouns can be omitted— in Spanish, for instance, you say *doy* 'I give' rather than *yo doy*.

Bipersonal inflection

In Quechua and Swahili, the object can be incorporated into the verb as well. Klingon has this feature as well; probably people who studied it thought it was very alien!

The Swahili system is simple enough: *-ni-, -ku-, -m-, -tu-, -wa-, -wa-* are inserted before the root; e.g. *nikuona* 'I see you', *tumona* 'we see him'.

- There's a separate REFLEXIVE infix *-ji-* used when the subject and object are the same: *nijiona* 'I see myself'.

- For inanimates, the noun class suffix is used instead of third person *-m-* or *-wa-*; e.g. *nikiona* 'I see it (the book)', *-ki-* being the infix for *kitabu* 'book'.

Tense and aspect

Non-linguists use TENSE to refer to any PARADIGM or set of grammatical forms; but for linguists it refers to time. It's easily confused with ASPECT, which refers to the relationship of the event with the timeline.

Tense

Think of TENSE as a location on the timeline:

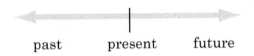

past   present   future

English has a morphological past tense (*I walked*), but no morphological future. Other languages have one; e.g. Latin *erimus* 'we will be'.

> **Fun time**
>
> Are there just three possible dots? No reason you can't have more: remote past, far future, just happened, about to happen, and so on. There's an Austronesian language which has four past tenses— last night, yesterday, near past, and remote past— and three future tenses— immediate, near, and remote.

Aspect

We can view the PROGRESSIVE aspect as zooming in on the event till we can see its full extent. The past progressive (*I was eating*) tells what you were doing for a span of time; the present progressive (*I am eating*) says what activity you're engaged in.

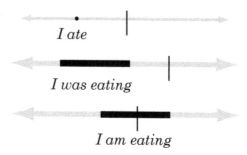

I ate

I was eating

I am eating

You can focus on the beginning of an event with an INCEPTIVE (*I started eating*) and on the end with a COMPLETIVE (*I finished eating, I just ate*).

The PERFECTIVE sees an event as a whole, as with Mandarin:

Yànméi shuì-le sān ge zhōngtóu.

Yanmei slept for three hours.

Here *le* marks the sleeping as an unanalyzed whole. An IMPERFECTIVE, by constrast, sees it as a process or a span in time.

Prototypically we see an event as a process when it's not over, so an imperfective generally (but not always) implies completion. Indeed, that's the etymological meaning: Latin *perfectus* means 'complete'. The English progressive could be described as an imperfective that emphasizes non-completion.

Languages differ in which viewpoint is UNMARKED: English and French have a special form for the imperfective; Chinese and Russian have one for the perfective.

Some languages, notably Mandarin, don't have a past tense, just a perfective— *wǒ chī fàn le* has the perfective particle *le*, which here emphasizes that the action is done. (It needn't be done in the past— we can easily say *míngtiān wǒ chī fàn le* 'I'll eat tomorrow'.)

PERFECT aspect refers to past or future events with present relevance or present consequences. You can think of it as the speaker telling you "And therefore...", leaving you to fill in the blanks. Examples:

- English *John has arrived* implies that John is still here, unlike *John arrived*.

- If someone rudely assumes you don't know generative linguistics, you can correct their assumption with *I've read Chomsky*.

- Mandarin *Xiǎo Huáng jiù yào lái le* 'Little Huang is about to arrive', with perfect *le*, is anticipatory; it implies "Get ready!"[1]

Older grammars often use "perfect" to refer to perfectives or completives.

HABITUAL aspect describes a cyclical or recurring activity.

An example is Lithuanian *Atsikel davau anksti* 'I used to get up early'. English *would* can be a habitual marker: *We would travel to Europe every year.*

Interactions

The definitions above are the prototypes; natural languages get a little messy.

- In English, we have a morphological past tense (the *-ed* form) and form the perfect with *have* (*I've read, I'd read*). But...

  ° *I've been to Japan* is an EXPERIENTIAL perfect— it asserts that the action happened at least once.

  ° *I've lived here ten years* is a "past perfect", but semantically it's a present progressive— the action is still going on.

  ° We use the "past perfect" as a remote past tense, to contrast with the narrative focus: *When I arrived, she had already left.*

  ° Our "present tense" doesn't always refer to the present: *Tomorrow we leave for France.*

- In spoken French, the ordinary way to refer to past events is using the morphological "present perfect": *je l'ai vu* 'I saw it'. This contrasts with a morphological imperfective: *je le voyais* 'I was seeing it'.

- In Mandarin, using perfect *le* can be used simply to end the speaker's turn.

---

[1] Yes, confusingly, Mandarin uses *le* as both perfective and perfect. The perfective follows the verb; the perfect always ends the sentence.

Irrealis forms

Languages often have specially marked forms for events that aren't quite real for some reason: they're hypothetical, or conditional, or merely desired. These may be grouped as IRREALIS forms.

In Indo-European languages the usual term is SUBJUNCTIVE MOOD, as opposed to INDICATIVE. The French subjunctive, for instance, is used for desired, doubtful, or hypothetical events, among other things. A neat distinction can be made between

- indicative *Je cherche un homme qui a vu la victime* "I'm looking for a man who saw the victim", which implies that the man exists, and

- subjunctive *Je cherche un homme qui ait vu la victime*, which implies that the man might not exist.

English tends to express this sort of thing using MODAL verbs: *may, might, could, should,* etc. English modals have some strange behavior that you shouldn't assume is universal: they don't have infinitives; past tense *might, could...* are also used as separate modals with a slightly different meaning.

The future is inherently doubtful, and IMPERATIVES naturally express desired but not certain events, so an irrealis form might be adapted for these uses.

Other possibilities for verbs

A brief review of some other distinctions that might be marked on the verb:

- A NEGATIVE mood

- EVIDENTIALITY: whether the speaker knows about the action from personal experience, or from hearsay, or merely considers it probable. The languages of the Vaupés river basin distinguish five levels of evidentiality: visual perception; non-visual perception; deduction from obvious clues; hearsay; and mere assumption.

- Whether the verb simply describes a state (STATIC) or reports a change in state (DYNAMIC). In English these are often separate verbs; compare Arabic *rukūbun* which may mean static 'ride' or dynamic 'mount'. In some languages these are distinguished morphologically.

- Degree of DEFERENCE between speaker and listener; e.g. Japanese has neutral and polite forms for each verb.

- Basque verbs can inflect to encode information about the **listener**. For instance, *ekarri digute* is a neutral way of saying 'They brought it to us'; *ekarri zigunate* means the same, but also indicates that the listener is a woman addressed with the informal personal pronoun.

I'm here for an argument

Verbs can be categorized by how many objects they have; or in more modern terms, their VALENCE, or number of ARGUMENTS.

- Some verbs have no arguments at all. In English we require a dummy subject for these: *It's raining.*

- Verbs with single arguments are INTRANSITIVE: *The cat howled. The rain fell. Jesus wept.*

- Verbs with two arguments are TRANSITIVE: *The cat ate the mouse. The rain disturbed us. I like zombies.*

- An important subcategory of these are REFLEXIVES, where the subject and object are the same: *I washed myself. Goths hate themselves.*

  Romance languages often use reflexives where the subject is simply unknown or impersonal: *Se habla español* "Spanish is spoken (here)", literally "Spanish speaks itself".

- Verbs with three arguments are DITRANSITIVE. In Latin, for instance, verbs like 'give' take a DIRECT OBJECT (which appears in the accusative) and an INDIRECT OBJECT (in the dative): *Puella librum agricolae dat* 'The girl gives a book to the farmer'. In English the indirect object may be expressed as a prepositional phrase, or the two objects may simply be concatenated ('The girl gives the farmer a book'). Verbs of appointment or naming take two accusatives in Latin: *Mē augurem nōmināvērunt* 'they named me augur'.

- Verbs with four arguments are TRITRANSITIVE. These include CAUSATIVES (*John made me give the book to Sarah*) or actions with a beneficiary (*We gave the woman money for her daughter*).

  Many languages have a morphological causative; e.g. Quechua *wañuy* 'die', *wañuchiy* 'cause to die', i.e. 'kill'.

There isn't a clear dividing line between a verb argument and additional information (e.g. an adverbial or a prepositional phrase). Some rough-and-ready tests:

- If they're required, they're arguments. E.g. we can omit the destination of a movement (*I went*), but it's odd to omit the beneficiary of an act of giving (*I gave the book*).

- Arguments can be passivized: *The book was given to me.* We can't say *Norway was gone to by me.*

Many English verbs can be used either transitively or intransitively: *I broke the window; the window broke.*

A language will have methods for adding or removing arguments. E.g. you can eliminate the subject with the PASSIVE (*The book was read*). Often an argument normally indicated with a preposition can be promoted to a main argument via an APPLICATIVE affix on the verb. Expressions like *He walked a mile* could be called syntactic applicatives: the normally intransitive *walk* has been given an additional argument.

Languages differ in how particular actions are classified, or what the subjects and objects are. Examples:

- In French *renoncer* 'renounce, give up' is intransitive— what you give up takes a prepositional phrase, where in English it's a simple object.

- Spanish *gustar* has the opposite argument structure to English 'like': *I like books = Me gustan los libros*, literally "Books please me."

- Mandarin often inserts a default object where we'd use a naked verb: *kàn shū* 'look at books = read', *chōu yān* 'draw smoke = smoke'; *chī fàn* 'eat a meal = eat'.

What are the personal pronouns?

PERSONAL PRONOUNS are often arranged into a simple grid like this one for Mandarin:

	s	p
1	wǒ	wǒmen
2	nǐ	nǐmen
3	tā	tāmen

That's singular and plural NUMBER along the top, and the three PERSONS down the side. English messes up the neat grid by dividing the 3s pronouns by sex and combining 2s and 2p:

	s	p
1	I	we
2	you	you
3	he, she, it	they

Many distinctions can be made, or omitted, in the pronouns:

- GENDER (not necessarily just in the third person)

- *no* gender (many languages don't distinguish *he* and *she*— e.g. Turkish has a single 3s pronoun *o*)

- NUMBER (as with nouns, there may be DUAL or PAUCAL forms)

- *no* number (cf. English *you*)

- ANIMACY (cf. *he/she* vs. *it*)

- whether *we* includes *you* (INCLUSIVE we) or not (EXCLUSIVE we)

- FORMALITY or politeness— e.g. many European languages have informal and polite forms in the 2nd person; these may be called T/V FORMS after French *tu, vous*

- there may be two sets of third persons (PROXIMATE and OBVIATIVE)— imagine having two forms of 'he' to distinguish two different persons. Potawatomi has a third set, the further obviative

- there may be INDEFINITE pronouns, such as French *on*: *L'on y danse* 'People dance there'

I invented an alien race once that used different pronouns on land and underwater (they were amphibians), and had the inclusive/exclusive and proximate/obviative distinctions. They also had a pronoun for group minds, and pronouns for each of their three sexes. The complete list was impressive.

Other forms

As a rough guide, pronouns should have the same number and case distinctions as nouns, and the same personal and number distinctions as verbs. E.g. it'd be a little odd to have a dual or an accusative case for nouns but not pronouns.

But some variation is fine— e.g. English pronouns have a case distinction (subject/object) that its nouns don't. And of course verbs don't have to be marked by number and person at all.

The Romance languages have CLITIC forms of the pronouns, which stop just short of being verb inflections: e.g. French *Je le vois*, 'I see him'; Spanish *Dígame*, 'Tell me'.

Do subject pronouns appear?

If the person is marked on the verb as in Spanish, or people are just good at inferring who did something as in Japanese, subject pronouns can be omitted; the language is said to be PRO-DROP. (But Russian and Portuguese have both required subject pronouns *and* personal verb inflections.)

Are pronouns necessary?

A hoary old technique for making fantasy characters seem alien is to eliminate 'I' and 'you', perhaps in favor of descriptions: *This one advises against the maneuver.* In traditional European culture, one avoided personal pronouns in favor of titles: *Your excellency is well informed about wine.*

Before you throw out the pronouns, consider how you'd translate *I said to myself one day, you know, your career isn't giving you the life you deserve.* Are you happy to live with *This one said to this one's self one day, this one knows, this one's career isn't giving this one the life this one deserves?*

What are the other pronouns?

Esperanto has a table of CORRELATIVES which is a neat way of organizing the non-personal pronouns. For English, it looks like this:

	query	this	that	some	none	every
adjective	which	this	that	some	no	every
person	who	this (one)	that (one)	someone	no one	everyone
thing	what	this (one)	that (one)	something	nothing	everything
place	where	here	there	somewhere	nowhere	everywhere
time	when	now	then	sometime	never	always
way	how		thus	somehow		
reason	why					

More traditionally, the first column comprises INTERROGATIVE PRONOUNS, the second two are DEMONSTRATIVES, and the remainder are INDEFINITE PRONOUNS. Adjectives like *some, no, every* are also called QUANTIFIERS.

It's easy and diverting to regularize the table, although natural languages generally leave holes, which must be filled in with phrases (*in that way, for no reason*). You can also extend the table with other quantifiers (*many, most...*), or with other types of question (*how many? with what emotion?*).

In some languages, such as Russian, the interrogative pronouns ("*Who* did it?") and the RELATIVE pronouns ("Is this the man *who* did it?") are different.

Generally, if nouns decline, these pronouns decline the same way. Sometimes they're worse— English, for instance, retained separate 'from' and 'to' forms for pronouns of place (*here* / *hence* = 'from here' / *hither* = 'to here') long after such distinctions were lost for ordinary nouns.

Make your language count

Are the numbers based on tens, or something else? Many human number systems are based on fives or twenties instead, and there are a few oddities, such as base 4 (e.g. Bam) or base 6 (Kanum). My pronoun-happy aliens had a duodecimal (base 12) system. Intelligent machines would surely prefer hexadecimal (base 16)...

How do you form higher numbers? 'Forty-three', for instance, may be formed in several ways:

> forty three
> four three
> forty with three
> three and forty
> four tens and three
> eight fives and three
> fifty less seven — note the *subtractive* process
> twice twenty and three

Naming numbers involves addition ('fourteen' = 4 + 10) and multiplication ('forty' = 4 * 10). Both may be indicated simply by concatenation, but make sure your rules don't conflict (e.g. concatenated 'four-ten' can't mean both 14 and 40).

Where nouns decline, numbers may also. Or they may not. In Latin, you stop declining the numbers at four.

In Indo-European languages we are used to unanalyzable roots for the numbers; but in other families number names are transparent derivations, often related to the process of counting on fingers and toes:

- Choctaw 5 *tahlapi* 'the first (hand) finished'

- Klamath 8 *ndan-ksahpta* 'three I have bent over'

- Unalit 11 *atkahakhtok* 'it goes down (to the feet)'

- Shasta 20 *tsec* 'man' (considered as having 20 countable appendages)

Derivations

A number of useful words can be derived from numbers:

- ORDINALS— first, second, ...

- FRACTIONS— half, third, ...

- frequency— once, twice, ...

- multiples— double, triple, ...

For extra credit, think about basic arithmetic. How do you say -1, 5/7, 1.23, 2 + 2 = 4 out loud?

What about adjectives?

Adjectives can be something like nouns, something like verbs, or like neither.

- If they're like nouns (and they inflect), they generally AGREE with their head noun in gender, case, and number— for instance Russian *krasivoy devuškam* 'to the pretty girls', both words being feminine plural datives.

- If they're like verbs, they conjugate like verbs— e.g. Japanese *omoshirokatta desu* 'it was interesting'.

Do you allow ADJECTIVE COMPLEMENTS such as *good to eat, eager to go, afraid of dogs, new to the city*?

Comparatives

How are comparative expressions (*holier than thou, less holy than thou, as holy as thou*) formed? How about superlatives (*the most holy*)?

- You can have fixed expressions, like English *less holy than thou*, French *moins saint que toi*.

    There may be a special verb rather than 'be', as in Mandarin *tā bǐ nǐ gāo* 'he is taller than you', literally 'he/she compare you tall'.

- You can have special inflections, such as English *holier*, Latin *sanctior*.

- It may operate on a subclause; e.g. Nishnaabemwin:

    Washme ndoo-gnooz pii dash mBill

    more I.am.tall than then 3s.prox.Bill

    I am taller than Bill

Derivations

It's useful to have some regular derivations for or from adjectives:

opposite (un-)
lack (-less)
surfeit (-ful)
possibility (-able)
liking (-phile)
disliking (-phobe)
inhabitant (-er, -ian, -an, -ese)
weakening of meaning (-ish)
strengthening of meaning (to the max)
adverb (-ly)

The articles

In English and even more so in French, nouns feel naked by themselves, preferring to be accompanied by ARTICLES— *a, the*. A (French *un, une*, Spanish *una, uno*) is an INDEFINITE article; *the* (French *le, la*, Spanish *el, la*, Arabic *al-*) is a DEFINITE article. The Romance articles have plural forms as well.

Many languages, such as Latin, Russian, Quechua, and Mandarin, get by quite happily without articles.

It may help to understand what the distinction really means. Ordinarily it's pragmatic: *the* can be paraphrased 'You know which one I'm talking about'. Consider:

> *I saw a man at the rodeo. The man had on a horrid plaid suit.*

A man in the first sentence signals that this character is being introduced in this conversation; *the* in the second sentence signals that he's old news— in fact he's the same guy we started talking about.

The before *rodeo* is a little trickier because we haven't mentioned rodeos before. But again, *the* indicates that the speaker expects that the hearer can figure out which rodeo— if not, he'd have said *a rodeo*.

Word order serves the same function in Russian. There you'd say, in effect,

> *I saw man in rodeo. Man wore horrid plaid suit.*

When he's introduced, the man lives near the end of the sentence; when he's old news, he appears at the front.

(Actually, they don't have many rodeos in Russia.)

Sentence order

Linguists like to talk about the order of subject, object, and verb, which of course can occur in just six combinations:

> SVO (as in English or Swahili)
> SOV (Latin, Quechua, Turkish)
> VSO (Welsh)
> OVS (Hixkaryana)
> OSV (Apurinã)
> VOS (Malagasy)

The last three are for some reason rare, although they do exist.

Combinations and complications are common. For instance:

- Simple German sentences are SVO; but subclauses are SOV, and if there's an auxiliary the participle moves to the end of the sentence:

Mein Vater *ist* vor einigen Tagen nach London *gefahren.*

My father has several days ago to London travelled.

- French is basically SVO (*Je cherche les femmes* 'I'm looking for the women'), but if the objects are pronouns it's SOV: *Je les cherche* 'I'm looking for them'.

Languages with case marking can easily move entire constituents around. We can do this in English (*the man nobody knows*, OSV; *Not a word said I*, OVS), but this comes across as highly stylistically marked, and perhaps imitates the freer word order of Latin.

Noun phrase order

Consider articles, numbers, quantifiers, adverbs, adjectives, possessives, subordinate clauses— e.g.

> *The ten very happy robots who passed the bar exam*

You can generally divide phrases into HEADS and MODIFIERS. Some languages are very consistent about placing all modifiers before, or all after the head. English isn't very consistent but tends to be HEAD-FINAL. Japanese is head-final too, but it's more consistent— the subordinate clause, like everything else, comes before the noun:

> **Shihōshiken ni gōkakushite totemo ureshii jūtai no robotto**
>
> bar.exam DAT pass-do-GERUND very happy-POS.PRES ten-body of robot

There's some tendency for NP and sentence order to match. The verb is considered the head. For instance, in Welsh, the verb begins the sentence, and nouns precede adjectives.

The head of a prepositional phrase is a preposition, so a strictly head-final language, like Japanese, has postpositions.

You have yes-no questions, right?

How do you ask questions? English has a rather baroque procedure (inverting subject and verb). Other languages simply make use of a rise in intonation, or add a particle at the beginning of the sentence (e.g. Polish *czy*), or the end (Mandarin *ma*), or to the verb (Quechua *-chu*).

Many languages offer ways of suggesting the answer to the question. For instance, the Latin particle *num* expects the answer 'no' (*Num ursī cerevisiam imperant?* 'Bears don't order beer, do they?)', while *nōnne* expects 'yes' (*Nōnne ursus animal implūme bipēs?* 'Bears are featherless bipeds, aren't they?').

Where questions are formed by appending a particle (e.g. -ne in Latin, or -chu in Quechua), the particle can be added directly to the word being questioned. We can only achieve the same effect in English by emphasis ('Is the *bear* drinking beer? Is the bear drinking *beer?*') or by rearrangement ('Is it beer that the bear is drinking?').

One way of asking a question in Mandarin is to offer the listener a choice: *Nǐ shì bu shì Běijīng rén?* 'You're from Beijing?', literally 'You be, not be Beijing person?'

Some folks get by without having words for 'yes' or 'no'. The usual workaround is repeat the verb from the question: "Do you know the way to San José?" can be answered "I know" or "I don't know", as in Portuguese:

> —**Você conhece o caminho que vai a São José?**
>
> —**Conheço.** *'I know'*

How about other questions?

We talked about the interrogative pronouns above (p. 75).

English usually moves the question word to the beginning of the sentence (i.e. it's FRONTED), but other languages don't, asking in effect "You said *what?*" or "She's going out with *whose* boyfriend?"

Again, some languages have different pronouns for relative clauses ("The man who fishes") and questions ("Who is this man?").

Negation

There are many options:

- Add a particle before the verb (as in Russian *ya ne znayu* 'I don't know' or Spanish *no sé*)

- ...or after the verb (as we used to do: *thou rememberest not?*)

- ...or both (French *je ne sais pas*)

- use a special mood of the verb (Japanese *nageru* 'throw', *nagenai* 'not throw')

- add a particle at the beginning or end of the sentence (e.g. Quechua *mana*, which however also requires a supporting suffix on the verb)

- use a special inflected auxiliary (e.g. Finnish *e-*)— it's as if 'not' was an inflected verb: I not, you not, he nots...

These can be mixed, as in English: auxiliaries are directly negated with -*n't*, while other verbs require DO-SUPPORT (insert 'do' and negate that).

Conjunctions and such

CONJUNCTIONS allow constituents to be paired, with some relationship between them— e.g. English *and, or, but, then*. (*But* has the same meaning as *and* but expresses contrast or surprise.)

Latin has a neat trick: to express *X and Y,* you can say *X Y-que,* using a clitic. The expression SPQR, *Senātus Populusque Rōmānus,* is an example of this construction: *the Senate and the Roman People.*

Latin also distinguishes INCLUSIVE and EXCLUSIVE OR: *vel X vel Y* means that you can have X or Y or both; *aut X aut Y* means you get one or the other but not both.

In many languages different conjunctions are used for different types of speech. E.g. in Athabaskan, NPs are conjoined with *ʔił* and clauses with *ts'eʔ.*

Quechua (before the Spanish conquest) got by without conjunctions at all. For adding things together, you can usually get by with juxtaposition. Or you can use the case ending *-wan* meaning *with*: in effect you say 'X and Y' by saying 'X with Y'. In questions, 'or' could be expressed by adding the interrogative suffix *-chu* to both elements; in statements you could use *manachayqa* 'otherwise', literally 'if not that...'

It's useful to have a set of logical and temporal connectors:

X because of Y

X, therefore Y

X, in order to Y

if X then Y

X while / before / after Y

X until / since Y

If clauses can be complex, as the condition may or may not be counterfactual; compare *If I were in charge* with *If this is Toledo we're almost home.*

Relative clauses

Subclauses are perhaps the most sophisticated aspect of syntax, allowing entire sentences to serve as constituents or modifiers. A few basic types:

- SENTENTIAL ARGUMENTS: a verb takes an entire sentence as its subject or object.
  - ° Verbs of saying or thinking may have a sentential object: *I think that you've been drinking.*
  - ° Sentences can appear as the subject. In English this requires adding a dummy subject (*It's possible that Grandma's drunk*), but your language could have something like *That Grandma's drunk possibles.*

- A preposition can take a sentence as its object: *after you were born, like a lion attacking a mouse, without you complaining* (compare *after Monday, like a virgin, without feathers*).

- A sentence can modify a noun, forming a RELATIVE CLAUSE: *the man who hated subways.*

That and *who* in the above examples are examples of SUBORDINATORS, particles which mark a subclause.

Quechua has an interesting way of forming clauses using participles. For instance:

[Chakra-y yapu-q runa-ta] qaya-mu-saq

[field-my plow-PARTICIPLE man-ACC] call-ALLATIVE-1s.FUT

I'll call [the man that plowed my field].

In English the subclause looks like an ordinary sentence, but in Quechua it's a participle: *the my-field-plowing man.*

Quechua is also an example of how to get by without relative clauses: rather than link up clauses, you can simply concatenate them, using a connective:

Chay phista serkamunñachá, chayta yachan.

He knows that this festival is approaching.
Lit., This festival is approaching. He knows that.

My conlang Old Skourene has no subclauses, only a wide array of conjunctions (underlined below).

Saŋkum psiukkasan <u>nsul</u>-mindntu <u>aŋ</u>-inbuştu boiḍunru <u>nen</u>-bşti ḍodrim.

successful-3sns expedition-his therefore-back-go-neg-3s but-attempt-int-travel-3s westward as-dur-go-neg-3p us-people

(Lit.) His expedition was successful / therefore he did not return / but tried to travel westward / as people do not go

His expedition was so successful that he did not return, but decided to travel farther west than anyone had gone.

Compare Pirahã, which also lacks relative clauses:

Ko Paitá, tapoá xigaboopaáti. Xoogiai hi goo tapoá xoáboi. Xaisigíai.

Hey, Paitá, bring back some nails. Dan bought those very nails. They are the same.

(I.e., Bring back the nails that Dan bought.)

Adverbials

Constituents can be added that specify when, where, or how the action took place. Some of the options:

- A single word: *here, yesterday.*
- A particle, as in English's separable verbs: *look at, watch out, fall out.* Some of these are idiomatic, but some have a predictable meaning; e.g. *up* often signifies completion: *burn up, use up, eat up.*
- A noun in the locative case: Latin *Rōmae* 'in Rome'; Quechua *urqukunapi* 'in the mountains'.
- A noun phrase: *all night, the Greek way.*
- A prepositional phrase: *in the alleyway, by subterfuge.*
- A postpositional phrase: Japanese *Kyōto ni* 'in Kyoto'.
- A subordinate clause: *when the cows come home, where the cats could find it, how Mom used to make it.*

Mandarin has a RESULTATIVE construction in which an additional verb suggests the result of the first:

Wǒ bǎ chábēi dǎ pò le.

I OBJ teacup hit break PERF

I broke the teacup (lit. I hit-broke it)

Transformations

It can be useful to think of your grammar as applying various TRANSFORMATIONS to simple sentences. You can think of these as operations that rearrange the structure of a sentence.

A simple example is auxiliary inversion, which English uses to form questions:

S Aux VP → Aux S VP

I can have a cheeseburger → Can I have a cheeseburger?

Note that this movement applies to entire constituents, not words:

[This cute little cat] can have a cheeseburger →

Can [this cute little cat] have a cheeseburger?

In 1957, in *Syntactic Structures*, Noam Chomsky introduced TRANSFORMATIONAL GRAMMAR (TG), also known as GENERATIVE GRAMMAR, which focused linguists' attention on syntax, with heavy use of transformations. There was hope for some time that TG would provide a model for how the mind processes language, and facilitate AI. Unfortunately no consensus was reached, and the field is rather a mess, with many theories that are more arcane than useful.

Rather than present any particular formalism, I'll provide an informal list of transformations.

The Axunašin and Xurnese grammars on my website provide examples of how to describe transformations in a conlang.

Do I need this?

There are some things you should look at here, to keep your "syntax" section from being a page long. But this is pretty advanced stuff. So you could come back to it when you're creating your *second* language.

Syntactic trees

Syntacticians devoted a good deal of time to creating TREE STRUCTURES and arguing over exactly how to group and name constituents.

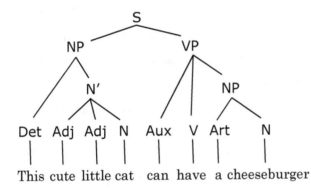

Frankly such diagrams aren't of much use in conlanging, but they do point out a universal to keep in mind: syntactic transformations apply to entire nodes of the tree— CONSTITUENTS.

The abbreviations NP (for NOUN PHRASE) and VP (for VERB PHRASE) are also worth picking up.

Asterisks mean don't do that!

TG uses asterisks as a quick shorthand to mark sentences that don't occur. For instance:

> *I can has cheezburgr.

Standard English doesn't allow two verbs to combine quite like this.

(Or does it? I purposely chose an example that should raise questions... the very joke of lolcat-speak is that it's ungrammatical. But people use it in other contexts— jocularly, but jocular language is still language. An asterisk always implies some context— usually "the standard dialect as I (or my informants) speak it". Any discussion of syntax is liable to produce surprising variations in what people find acceptable.)

Auxiliaries

To explain English auxiliary verbs, *Syntactic Structures* posited an AUX (auxiliary) node that broke down as follows

S → NP Aux VP

Aux → TENSE (MODAL) (have -en) (be -ing)

where the items in parentheses are optional. (-*en* comes from irregular past participle forms like *taken*.) Transformations apply the tense, -*en*, and -*ing* elements to the following node. For instance:

I Aux sing

→ I (PAST (can) (have -en) (be ing)) sing

→ I PAST (can) (have -en) (be ing) sing

→ I (PAST can) (have) (-en be) (ing sing)

→ I could have been singing

The analysis works neatly when some of the optional elements are omitted:

I PAST (have -en) (be ing) sing

→ I (PAST have) (-en be) (ing sing)

→ I had been singing

I PAST (can) (be ing) sing

→ I (PAST can) (be) (ing sing)

→ I could be singing

I PAST (can) (have -en) sing

→ I (PAST can) (have) (-en sing)

→ I could have sung

I PAST sing

→ I (PAST sing)

→ I sang

With a fairly simple rule, the wide variety of English verb forms is accounted for, with a neatness that captured many people's imaginations and led to decades of work in TG. (I should warn you that probably no one, including Chomsky, currently accepts the rule as working quite this way.)

Relative clauses

A relative clause like

The man that John hit yesterday prefers beer to wine.

can be seen as deriving by transformation from one sentence that's embedded in another:

> *The man [John hit him yesterday] prefers beer to wine.*

Chomsky called the underlying form of a sentence, before all transformations, the DEEP STRUCTURE. Once all the transformations apply you get the SURFACE STRUCTURE— the sentence as spoken.

RELATIVIZATION proceeds in two stages. First, the pronoun in the subclause is replaced with a relative pronoun (or with *that*):

> *The man [John hit him yesterday] prefers beer to wine.*

> → *The man [John hit that yesterday] prefers beer to wine.*

Then the relative pronoun is moved to the front of the phrase:

> → *The man [that John hit yesterday] prefers beer to wine.*

One advantage of breaking down constructions like this is that it suggests alternatives. For instance, you might leave out that second transformation— perhaps in your language you just say *The man John hit who yesterday...*

Cases in relativized clauses

Thinking about deep structures can also clarify the proper cases to use, if your language has cases. Compare

> *The cat [my sister brought it home] is dead.*

> *The cat [it ate fifty mice] is dead.*

The cat is the subject of the main clause, but it's the object of the first subclause.

> *The cat [which my sister brought home] is dead.*

> *The cat [which ate fifty mice] is dead.*

In English the subordinator is the same (*which*); we can tell its syntactic role by noticing whether the subclause has a subject or not.

In French, we need a different subordinator for each— *que* (accusative) for the first example, *qui* (nominative) for the second:

> *Le chat que ma sœur a apporté chez nous est mort.*

> *Le chat qui a mangé cinquante souris est mort.*

Limits on relativization

Your language may also put limits on what exactly can be relativized. The following examples are legal in English, for instance, but not in certain other languages.

> *the girl [you think [I love her]]*
>
>> → *the girl you think I love*
>
> *the neighbor [I traumatized his pastor]*
>
>> → *the neighbor whose pastor I traumatized*
>
> *the cat [I said [my sister brought it home]]*
>
>> →   *the cat that I said my sister brought home*

On the other hand, not everything is possible in English:

> *This is the man [my girlfriend's father is a friend of John and him]*
>
>> → * *This is the man that my girlfriend's father is a friend of John and.*

or (thanks to Leo Connolly for this example)

> *There's the barn [more people have gotten drunk down in back of it than any other barn in the county]*
>
>> →   *There's the barn that more people have gotten drunk down in back of than any other barn in the county.*

Some languages can handle such sentences simply by leaving the pronoun in the subclause. S.J. Perelman liked to do this in English:

> *"That's the man which my wife is sleeping with him!"*

Topicalization

Sentences can often be divided into TOPIC (what the sentence is talking about) and COMMENT (what's added to the discussion); see also the discussion under Pragmatics (p. 130).

English has several transformations that relate to TOPICALIZATION.

Fronting

Topics tend to come at the beginning of the sentence— it's best to state what we're talking about first. If the object is the topic, it can simply be moved to the front:

> *I know that girl.*

→ *That girl, I know her.*

Passivization

The PASSIVE can be considered a way of fronting the topic, or a way to alter the verb's argument structure, promoting an object to subject position.

I gave the sniper rifle to Zoey.

→ *The sniper rifle was given to Zoey.*

→ *Zoey was given the sniper rifle.*

As we just saw, 'to' clauses— indirect objects— can be passivized. But not, apparently, other prepositional phrases, not matter how important. So it looks like not all arguments are the same (p. 72).

The rascal headed for Cornwall Gardens.

→ **Cornwall Gardens was headed.*

In ergative languages (p. 61), you have an ANTIPASSIVE instead, which promotes an absolutive rather than an accusative or dative object.

Clefting

It's possible to highlight the new information by fronting, too. English has a process called CLEFTING that emphasizes the comment:

The city paid for the lights.

→ *It's the city that paid for the lights.*

→ *It's the lights that the city paid for.*

More comments on topics

Two other approaches to topics are worth mentioning. One is to mark it with its own clitic, like Quechua -**qa**; since any constituent can be marked as the topic, no movement transformation is needed.

Or a topic may be stated that has no case role in the sentence, as in Flaidish:

<u>Luckit teeren</u> Verduria zys kematt nellit.

human city-PL Verduria be.PROG muchly nice

Among human cities, Verduria is pretty nice.

Causatives

The English causative can be seen as a transformation which moves the subject of the subclause into the object position in the main clause:

> *I made [the child stopped crying]*
>
> → *I made the child stop crying.*

Even if you have a lexical causative, you may need to adjust cases. E.g. in this Quechua example, nominative *pay* 'he' turns into dative *payman* 'to him':

> **Pay wasiyta qawan** *He sees my house*
>
> → **Qawachisaq wasiyta payman** *I'll make him see my house*

Anaphora

Pronouns have been seen as replacing or standing in for nouns. There can be pro-adjectives or pro-verbs as well; the general term is ANAPHORA.

A pro-verb can replace an entire VP; an example in English is *do (so)*:

> *John slept with that girl and Bill slept with that girl too.*
>
> → *John slept with that girl and Bill did (so) too.*

French *le* can serve as a pro-adjective:

> **Zoë est belle et je le suis aussi.**
>
> *Zoë is beautiful and I am too.*

Arguably the English gloss has a pro-adjective too— a null morpheme that appears (doesn't appear?) just after *I am*.

In some accounts, pronouns appear via a similar transformation:

> *John told John, "John is John's own best friend."*
>
> → *John told himself, "You're your own best friend."*

Or do they? We might buy that for John, but what if the NP is *that fat old farmer I knew from my schooldays*? In a theory of production, it might make more sense to consider the deep structure as consisting of nothing but place markers with similar identity marked:

> *X told Y, "Y is X's only friend... for now."*

As part of production, we decide how to express the X's and Y's. Perhaps the default is pronouns, but some are expanded into full NPs.

Dick told George, "You are my only friend... for now."

Nominalization

A sentence can be turned into a noun phrase by replacing the verb with a NOMINALIZATION, and its arguments into set case roles:

> *[The army destroyed the city] shocked me.*
>
> → *The army's destruction of the city shocked me.*

Question and negative formation

Questions and negatives can be seen as proceeding by transformation:

> *The naming of cats is a difficult matter.*
>
> → *Is the naming of cats a difficult matter?*
>
> → *The naming of cats is not a difficult matter.*

Semantics

SEMANTICS is the study of meaning. Since I published the online LCK, the conlangs I've seen have grown much more sophisticated in phonology and morphology; but they rarely pay much attention to semantics. Let's see if we can change that.

Though any conlang can benefit from the material here, it should be of particular interest if you're making a language for aliens, or for unusual humans. There are many opportunities to underline the culture of the language's speakers. (See also p. 140.)

As a model, I've included an extensive semantics section to my Xurnese grammar online.

The meaning of meaning

We all know what *meaning* is, but no one can really explain it. It's somehow related to REFERENCE, but not the same. For instance, *Pam* refers to a certain very cute girl I knew in Evanston; but the relationship between Pam and the word 'girl' is less clear. *Girl* doesn't even refer to the set of all girls, though this does feel a little closer.

We can declare that 'girls' are a natural class and pretend we're done, but the concept of a 'natural class' doesn't really hold up. For one thing, classes are vague... when exactly does a *girl* become a *woman*? This is really a complex cultural construct which varies by class, region, and historical epoch. The choice may even reflect the speaker's emotional attachment more than any objective fact about the referent.

Meaning in pictures

I'm going to use a visual metaphor for meaning, like this.

The space represents things in any world (i.e. it includes imaginary or possible worlds). The dots are references to girls— i.e., actual uses of the word *girl*.

The boundary can be thought of as the meaning— it delimits girls from non-girls in some rational way. What way is that? We'll get back to this question after exploring some of the complications of meaning.

The structure of the lexicon

A key insight of Ferdinand de Saussure was that the whole problem of single-word meanings could be sidestepped by looking instead at language as a STRUCTURE. Meanings don't exist in isolation; they're circumscribed by their relationships with other words.

- Meanings may exist in BINARY OPPOSITION: *alive/dead, male/female, on/off.*

- Meanings may divide up a linear CONTINUUM: *good/bad, tall/short, beautiful/ugly.*

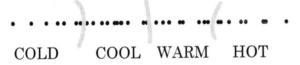

COLD   COOL   WARM   HOT

As shown, there may be multiple labels along the continuum. Different languages may divide up the same continuum differently; e.g. French doesn't have all-purpose words in between *chaud* and *froid*.

If you picture *ice/water/steam* as a continuum, Japanese divides this space in four: *kōri, mizu, yu, jōki.*

- Meanings may divide up a non-linear SEMANTIC SPACE— e.g. color, social classes, directions, parts of the body, time, geographical features.

Naturally, languages can divide up the same space in different ways. For instance, English divides *arm* and *hand* while Quechua has the same word for both, *maki.*

° A word may carve out a space for itself in opposition to other words— e.g. a *stool* is a kind of *chair*, but without a back.

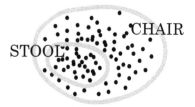

° Spanish distinguishes a *pez*, a living fish, from *pescado*, one that's been caught.

Hierarchies

Meanings can be organized into HIERARCHIES. For instance, a *lizard* is a *reptile*, which is a type of *animal*, which is a type of *life*.

In our visual metaphor, this might be covered by adding superterritories:

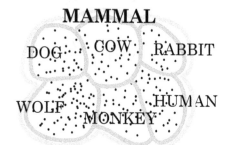

but it's more convenient, especially when there are multiple levels, to change metaphors and draw a tree structure.

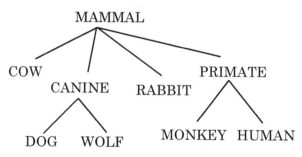

This chart happens to look like part of a scientific taxonomy, but it belongs to language, not science, and a language need not classify things as science does.

Sometimes the same word may label two adjoining levels of a hierarchy. E.g. English uses *man* for both males and humans where Latin has two words, *vir* and *homo*.

Languages differ in how they categorize. Naturally, this is most evident in the domain of pure culture. Consider how your conculture approaches things like social class, age, sexuality, family relationships, types of writing, virtue and vice, forms of government. Don't just translate English terms!

But even natural things may be categorized in different ways... e.g. is a whale classified with mammals or fish? Is the neck part of the chest or the head?

CATEGORIES are basic to scientific thought, and thus a staple of intelligence tests— e.g., you're presented with a knife, a potato, a cassava, and a basket, and told to group things together. The 'right' answer— the one that will pass the test— is to group together the food items, the potato and cassava.

But in a prescientific community, people group things by function. Kpelle tribesmen, given the same items, group the knife and the potato, because you use a knife to cut potatoes.

Different dividing lines

A language often has a recurrent set of dividing lines. For instance, English names family members and animals by age and gender:

> *man / woman / child*
>
> *bull / cow / calf*
>
> *stallion / mare / foal*
>
> *boar / sow / piglet*
>
> *dog / bitch / puppy*

Another dimension found in our lexicon, perhaps not so salient in our highly urbanized culture, is between castrated and uncastrated males: *ox, gelding, barrow, capon* are castrated bulls, horses, pigs, and chickens respectively.

In Mandarin, kinship terms encode relative age: e.g. *jiĕjie* is 'older sister', *mèimei* is 'younger sister'. (If you want to refer to any or all of your sisters, you can use the neat portmanteau *jiĕmèi*.)

Consider how verbs of motion are divided:

- English verbs of motion make a basic distinction between movement toward and away from the speaker: *come* vs. *go*.

- Russian makes a basic distinction between travel on foot (*idti*) or by vehicle (*ekhat'*), and secondarily between one-way movement and two-way or habitual movement (*khodit'* / *ezdit'*).

- Hua, spoken in the mountains of New Guinea, distinguishes coming and going, but also between movement upward and downward.

To help think about such issues, it helps to create a whole semantic field at once. E.g. don't just invent a word for 'brother' when you happen to need it; work out the whole kinship system. Or take a profession (farming, law, magic, robotics) and think about the words and distinctions it needs.

Consider using distinctions that aren't as important in English: animacy, shape, relative height, social class, relative value.

What gets a name?

Languages differ in what seems worth naming. You can get whole books— for instance, Howard Rheingold's *They Have a Word For It* or Adam Jacot de Boinod's *The Meaning of Tingo*— which list concepts or distinctions English doesn't have a word for. A sampling:

- Japanese *bakkushan*, a woman who looks beautiful from the back but not the front

- Inuit *areodjarekput*, to exchange wives for a few days

- Portuguese *dar um jeito*, find a clever way around an obstacle

- Quechua *mancharisqa*, a children's disorder caused by a fall or an argument

- French *meuble*, an item of furniture

- Tsonga *pyhakavaka*, the noise a naked person makes falling ass-first into the mud

- Latin *bōs*, a cow or bull— this is a curious lexical gap in English; we have a unisex plural (*cattle*) but no way to refer to just one of these animals!

Now, don't take this like unsophisticated journalists who think that if a word doesn't exist, the thing can't be talked about. Maybe it can be expressed with a longer expression or an obscure term.

Or maybe we can just borrow it. Terms such as *Weltanschauung, esprit de l'escalier, nomenklatura, mensch* might have once lived on such lists, but were useful enough to be borrowed into English.

Intention and utterance

In English 'meaning' is used also for *intention*, which is an unfortunate linguistic coincidence. We must distinguish the speaker's intention from a word's or sentence's significance.

An obvious example is IRONY: a speaker says *You're brilliant* to mean the opposite.

Reference mismatch and new senses

Somewhat more ambiguously, speakers might *use* a word differently from its meaning, till the meaning changes. In terms of our metaphor, we could say the meaning is remapped to fit its usual referents.

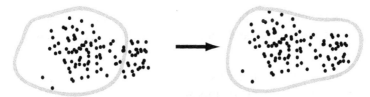

For instance, *girl* means an unmarried female; but it's often applied to mature women— even elderly ones, as in *The Golden Girls*. In the future it wouldn't be surprising if its lexical meaning shifted to just be 'female'.

More on speakers speaking

PHATIC communication is used to reinforce social bonds rather than convey information. For instance, English *How do you do?* is not a request for a medical diagnosis or even a request at all; it's a greeting.

We may also distinguish an UTTERANCE from a SENTENCE. An utterance is a single speaker saying something, at a particular moment in time, in a particular context. This gets so messy that linguists and logicians prefer to deal with sentences, abstract statements without context. The optimist hopes that by getting the abstract sentence right, we'll be in a better position to plunge into the grimy specifics of utterances. The pessimist may feel that focusing on 'sentences' is so artificial as to be counter-productive. If we want to learn how humans use language, we won't get far by throwing out most of our subject matter.

I'll focus on the interaction of language with the world in the chapter on Pragmatics.

Some oddities of meaning

Semantics is something like a rain forest: a huge area of obvious scientific interest, but not well mapped; paths have been hacked into it, but don't seem to meet up to allow us to form a coherent overview.

It's evident that words are much more complicated beasts than they look like in the dictionary. We deal seemingly effortlessly with a large mass of information about each word:

- Verbs have argument counts, and restrictions on what sort of thing each argument can be. (See p. 71.)

- Noun have classes. In English, the important distinction is not sex but count vs. mass noun: we know that *oats* and *peas* are count nouns but *cotton* and *wheat* are not. Other languages have this distinction but don't always agree on the contents of each class.

  There are often idiosyncratic ways of referring to associated words: e.g. birds and sheep come in *flocks*, cows come in *herds*, fish in *schools*.

- Adjectives are not absolute, but contextual. A *big* beetle is smaller than a *small* moose. Applied to a class X, *big* really means *big as X goes*. Or consider the meaning of *good* in *good friends* (= loyal or decent), *good food* (= delicious or unspoiled), *good grades* (= high), a *good shot* (= accurate), a *good worker* (= productive), *good weather* (= warm and not raining).

- Many adjectives can be used as an implied causative: e.g. a *warm coat* is one that makes you warm. On the other hand this doesn't work for all adjectives: a shoe that makes you taller can't be called a **tall shoe*.

- Some adjectives are gradable (e.g. *tall*), while some are binary (*female*). (And somehow this distinction is not erased when we make the binary adjectives gradable after all: *more female*).

- Some words can be used only with a few other words; e.g. *rancid* can only by used for a few things (oil, butter); we seem to be able to *scramble* only eggs and words. *Beautiful* can be applied freely to men but *pretty* can't.

Often the more we look at a word, the more we'll find. George Lakoff (in *Women, Fire, and Dangerous Things*) wrote a 46-page analysis of the single word *over*. We'll get into this more when we consider real-world knowledge (p. 137).

The complexity of meaning frustrates simplistic attempts to reduce meaning to reference or to componential analysis. Some words neatly decompose (e.g. *bull* = male + adult + bovine); other are more difficult (what are the components of *sculpt* or *pill*?).

Another naive formulation is that all the members of a class have "something in common", even if we are not sure what it is; Ludwig Wittgenstein pointed out that this is not the case for many words, such as *game*, whose instances have FAMILY RESEMBLANCES but do not all share a set of features.

Isn't the dictionary definition enough?

No, for several reasons. Children don't learn words from definitions, nor do speakers of non-written languages. It's hard to define common words like *go*, *dog*, or *low* without using more advanced concepts (e.g. *position, carnivore, height*), or without defining words in terms of each other (*low* = 'not high', *high* = 'not low').

Plus, it provides no basis for understanding semantic change: if 'girl' means 'young female', how can it be extended to older women?

Technical terms *are* defined by formulas— e.g. the *radius* is the distance from the center of a circle to the outside. You haven't learned these words if you don't know the formula, and it either applies or it doesn't. But don't assume that all words work this way.

Language and logic

Many linguists have tried to reduce language to logic; but perhaps the attractive simplicity of logic is due to it being underdeveloped. Logic has quite a few rules devoted to conjunction and quantification; rather than these being the only special operators needed, it may be that logicians have only gotten around to fully analyzing five words: *and, or, every, some,* and *no.*

Grammarians generally go farther; the morphology and syntax sections of a grammar are essentially the language's operators, with the predicates and arguments left to the lexicon. But the lexicon is not merely a list; we know quite a bit about each word. (Foreign-language lexicons are brief because they omit many complications, and because by providing glosses they leverage our own real-world knowledge. Even so, following the dictionary too slavishly will get you in trouble.)

The school of GENERATIVE SEMANTICS in the 1970s produced SEMANTIC STRUCTURES based on predicate calculus; e.g. they would relate *Joan killed the rapist* to

CAUSE(Joan, DIE(rapist))

Some went on to treat nouns as predicates, leading to something like

EXISTS x, y SUCH THAT
    NAMED(x, "Joan") &
    RAPES(y) &
    CAUSE(x, DIE(y))

Perhaps the same meaning underlies other sentences: e.g. *The rapist was killed by Joan* has the same semantic structure, but undergoes an additional passive transformation; *Did Joan kill the rapist?* has the same structure plus an element Q which queries truth value.

Many an ambitious grad student felt that, with just a few more semesters of work, the appropriate transformations could be modeled in LISP.

It's worth playing with, just to see how far it can be taken. But as a model of either meaning or how the brain processes language, it's at best very incomplete.

- Meanings aren't entirely preserved under transformations, notably when quantifiers are involved: *The target was not hit by many arrows* doesn't mean the same as *Many arrows didn't hit the target.* (The second sentence is compatible with many arrows hitting the target; the first isn't.) William Poundstone in *Labyrinths of Reason* wrote a fascinating essay focusing on why *All ravens are black* and *All non-ravens are non-black*, though logically equivalent, are epistemologically different.

- Words like *kill* don't behave syntactically precisely like their presumed components, such as *cause to die*; in particular each component can have separate adverbials:

  On Tuesday Joan caused the rapist to die on Thursday.

  *On Tuesday Joan killed the rapist on Thursday.

- The initial attraction of such representations is their simplicity (e.g. the same deep structure underlies many surface structures). But the more you analyze, the more complex the predicate calculus gets. E.g. a *painter* isn't just an x for whom PAINTS(x) is true— Leonardo is a painter even if he's not painting right now. A painter *habitually* paints. On the other hand, someone can be a *rapist* without habitually raping.

- Componential analysis isn't very satisfactory anyway; there's no explanation for the primitives, and many proposed primitives don't seem that primitive anyway.

- As Michael Tomasello points out, children learn linguistic generalizations late; what they learn first are scores of individual constructions. Often they learn questions before statements, which means they can't be conceiving of questions as statements plus an added element. Even ideas like "direct object" seem to come pretty late.

- The procedure assumes that surface syntactic details are not very important— they are mere stylistic variation. But that's a dubious assumption at best. Conveying factual information isn't the only thing language does, and often it's not even the most important thing.

Semantic change

Words change meaning over time; the process is not predictable, but does follow a number of common patterns.

If the old meaning is still in use, the word simply has multiple SENSES, or to put it in Greek, it shows POLYSEMY. Often senses diverge so much that their original connection is no longer clear.

Here are some examples from various languages, using Leonard Bloomfield's classification:

Narrowing

Old English *dēor* 'wild animal' → *deer*

OE *mete* 'food' → *meat*

OE *fugel* 'bird' → *fowl*

OE *steorfan* 'die' → *starve*

drink ('beverage' → 'alcoholic beverage')

Japanese *kimono* ← 'wearing thing'

Widening

Old English *hund* 'dog' → *hound*

OE *brid* 'nestling' → *bird*

Old Chinese **krôŋ* 'Yangtze' → Mandarin *jiāng* 'large river'

Latin *passer* 'sparrow' → Spanish *pájaro* 'bird'

'Christian' in medieval times often simply meant 'human being'

Metonymy (nearness in space or time)

Latin *bucca* 'cheek' → French *bouche* 'mouth'

OE *cēace* 'jaw(bone)' → *cheek*

the pulpit (place for preaching → the clergy)

Washington (city and capital → the USA, or the federal government)

Latin *cathedra* 'chair' → Spanish *cadera* 'hips'

Synecdoche (whole/part)

OE *tūn* 'enclosure' → *town*

Middle English *stofe* 'heated room' → *stove*

muscle → 'enforcer'

style (Middle English 'stylus' → 'way of writing')

Italian *banco* (bench → merchant's counter → (financial) bank)

Hyperbole (stronger to weaker)

terribly (with terror → very)

lame (crippled → insipid, dumb)

German *laufen* 'run' → 'walk' in some dialects

German *sehr* 'sorely' → 'very'

Litotes (weaker to stronger)

OE *culle* 'hit' → *kill*

French *baiser* 'kiss' → 'have sex'

Degeneration

> Old English *cnafa* 'boy' → *knave*
>
> OE *ceorl* 'commoner' → 'rustic' → *churl*
>
> Middle English *villein* 'rustic' → *villain*
>
> ME *sely* 'blessed' → 'innocent' → *silly*
>
> ME *huswif* 'matron' → *hussy*
>
> *disease* (discomfort → illness)

Elevation

> Old English *cniht* 'boy' → *knight*
>
> OE *praettig* 'cunning' → *pretty*
>
> ME *fonned* 'foolish, infatuated' → *fond*
>
> Old French *mareschalc* 'horse handler' → *maréchal* 'high military official'
>
> Latin *casa* 'hut' → Spanish, Italian 'house'

Then there's EUPHEMISM, the replacement of offensive words. This is by no means a new phenomenon; Indo-Europeans replaced the names of some wild animals— e.g. the bear was called 'the brown one' in Germanic, 'the honey-eater' in Slavic.

Personal pronouns are subject to a constant shift in Japanese, as any references to oneself come to seem disrespectful— e.g. *boku* 'I' once meant 'servant', but today it's almost offensive.

Terms for disliked things can be subject to a similar repeated replacement process— e.g. *moron* and *retarded* were originally invented as euphemisms, and now serve as insults.

Pay attention to the etymology section of the dictionary; not only is it a treasure trove of ideas, but it demonstrates that the average word's history is likely to be circuitous. If you have a proto-language, a sure sign of amateurishness is that all the cognates have the same gloss.

C.S. Lewis's *Studies in Words* masterfully traces the histories of ten words— *nature, sad, wit, free, sense, simple, conscience, world, life, dare say*— both in English and in the languages that influenced it.

Metaphor systems

One of the primary means of extending language is METAPHOR. In school we're taught about nonce metaphors (*John is a pig; my love is like a red, red rose).* More interesting to the grammarian are metaphors which have become lexicalized:

> *kid* (young goat → child)
> *chick* (young bird → girl)
> *ruminate* (chew the cud → think something over)
> *schmaltzy* (full of fat → cloying)
> *cell* (room → unit of biological tissue)
> *cool* (not too cold → unruffled → hip, neat)
> *sketch* (rough drawing → précis)

Many more metaphors are hidden in the etymology section of your dictionary:

> *evolve* = unroll
> *spirit* = breath
> *simple* = folded once
> *chief* = head
> *radical* = at or by the roots
> *depend* = hang from
> *introduce* = lead into
> *govern* = steer (a boat)
> *translate* = carry across
> *invest* = clothe (→ establish → lay out money)

One continuum may be likened to another; this provides terms for the extremes and sometimes points in between:

HEAVY IS IMPORTANT	*heavy* (matters, prose)	*light* (subjects, banter)
SHARP IS SMART	*sharp*	*dull*
SOFT IS MERCIFUL	*soft-hearted*	*hard-hearted*

Hard also shows that a metaphor need not involve the whole continuum: we also have *hard-headed* = stubborn, but no opposite involving 'soft' for the non-stubborn.

Even more productive are METAPHOR SYSTEMS, which can generate many expressions and be extended by speakers. Here are some examples collected by George Lakoff and Mark Johnson in *Metaphors We Live By*:

ARGUMENT IS WAR

> *Your claims are indefensible.*
> *He attacked every weak point in my argument.*
> *His criticisms were right on target.*
> *He shot down all my arguments.*

LANGUAGE IS CARRYING

It's hard to get that idea across to him.
It's difficult to put my ideas into words.
Your words seem hollow.
Try to pack more thought into fewer words.

The conduit metaphor

Lakoff and Johnson call this the CONDUIT METAPHOR, and point out that it's so basic that we may not even recognize it as a metaphor. It can be seriously misleading as a picture of language, especially in the implication that "meaning", whatever that is, is perfectly reconstituted in the listener's mind.

HAPPY IS UP / SAD IS DOWN

> *I'm feeling up.*
> *My spirits rose.*
> *I'm depressed.*
> *He's really low these days.*

LOVE IS MADNESS

> *I'm crazy about her.*
> *He constantly raves about her.*
> *I'm just wild about Harry.*

LIFE IS A CONTAINER

> *I've had a full life.*
> *Life is empty for him.*
> *There's not much left for him in life.*
> *Get the most out of life.*
> *Live your life to the fullest.*

Metaphor as cognition

A naive reading of Lakoff and Johnson would be to simply note that we sure use a lot of metaphor and that your conlang ought to have some. Along the same lines, older schools of linguistics were somewhat dismissive of metaphor— it was filed under 'rhetoric', to be dealt with (if at all) only after pragmatics.

A deeper reading, however, is that metaphor is central to how our cognition works. Metaphors are not a matter of poetry or clever ways of speaking; they're necessary for any abstract thought at all. We can't get away from metaphor, we can only hide it (i.e. by using fossilized etymological metaphors, or things like the conduit metaphor that are so habitual that we forget they are metaphors at all).

For instance, the metaphor THE MIND IS A COMMUNITY allows us to use our extensive social vocabulary to talk about our own minds: *My heart tells me to do it; He is ruled by lust; She was divided on the subject; Your memory is deceiving you.* (As an exercise, try to state these sentences, or the ones on 'love' or 'life' above, without any metaphors, and without losing the implications and connotations.)

Lakoff has gone further, identifying BASIC METAPHORS said to underlie our cognition, each based on direct bodily experience. E.g. the act of categorization itself is said to be a metaphor CATEGORIES ARE CONTAINERS. For much more on this, see his *Women, Fire, and Dangerous Things.*

Grammaticalized metaphor

Some metaphor systems are so basic that it may take a mental effort to recognize them as such. Examples:

- TIME IS SPACE, which allows us to use placement in space as a stand-in for order in time, and to treat blocks of time as spaces to be traversed.

    ° Spatial prepositions (*before, after, in*) are used for location in time.

    ° Spatial dimensions can be used to measure time: e.g. periods of time can be *short* or *long.*

- EVENTS ARE OBJECTS, which extends the previous metaphor to treat actions (which would otherwise be rather intractable) as things which can be isolated and counted, and which can serve as grammatical subjects and objects. In other words, nominalization is a metaphor, which allows us to treat a *sale* as concretely as we treat *coins* or *merchandise.*

- ACTION IS MOVEMENT, e.g. *I'm going to sleep, He returned to the task.*

    The equivalent of 'go' can be used in many languages as an auxiliary.

- A QUALITY IS A POSSESSION. We use this metaphor directly, as in *She's got nerve.* But equivalents of 'have' can be grammaticalized as perfectives, among other things. The Romance future derives from *habere* 'have' plus the infinitive; e.g. *cantare habeo* 'I have to sing' → French *je chanterai* 'I will sing.'

- AN INDIVIDUAL IS A SAMPLE. This pattern allows us to talk about an indefinite individual as a stand-in for its class: *A goat has two horns.*

Metaphors this basic are hard to do without or change, but trying to do so might make for an interesting conlang.

Perspective

We can compare meaning to vision, in that words' meanings tell us what we are looking at. Many words or expressions differ not so much in what we're looking at, as in our point of view.

Leonard Talmy explains many lexical and grammatical processes as changes in perspective. To emphasize the commonality between nouns and verbs, united by metaphors such as EVENTS ARE OBJECTS and TIME IS SPACE, he proposes several new terms:

	Nouns	Verbs
CONTINUOUS / DISCRETE	mass / count nouns	action / events
PLEXITY	singular / plural	single event / habitual or repeated action

Nominalization preserves continuousness/discreteness and plexity: actions are nominalized as mass nouns (*John gave me some help*), events as count nouns (*I got a call from John*).

However, I find it more useful just to catalog some instances where we're looking at the same thing from different perspectives.

- We can mentally zoom in on a mass to see the discrete pieces, either syntactically (*rice* → *a grain of rice*) or lexically (*rain* → *raindrop*).

- We can zoom out as well (*horse* → *herd (of horses)*; *shrub* → *shrubbery*).

- We can zoom in to a smaller extent and treat the components of an object as entities: *the front of the bed.*

- If an object's plexity is changing, we can take the point of view either of the whole (*The rock broke in two*) or the pieces (*The two halves of the rock broke apart*).

- An object may be treated as an extent (*the box is 2 feet wide*) or as a point (*the box is 20 feet from the wall*). Given TIME IS

SPACE, the same applies to events: *he lived for 70 years / he lived in the Victorian era.*

- Locative prepositions are ambiguous between a static viewpoint (*the ball is across the river*) and a moving one (*throw the ball across the river*). We may take a moving perspective even if nothing is actually moving: *There are villages now and then along the road.*

- A pair of words may differ only by argument order: that is, the same situation is described from differing points of view: *I buy from you / you sell to me; Luke is Vader's son / Vader is Luke's father.*

The importance of perspective

Two monks were disputing whether one could smoke and pray at the same time. They agreed that each should write to the Pope to see who was right. But after receiving the replies, they each claimed that the Pope supported their position.

"What exactly did you ask the Pope?" asked the first monk.

"Whether one could smoke while praying. He said 'Of course not, prayer requires one's full concentration.' What did you ask the Holy Father?"

"Whether one could pray while smoking. He replied, 'Certainly, my child; prayer is always in order.'"

Perspective on verbs

It's worth looking in more detail at how we conceive of actions. The different aspects (see p. 67) can be seen as changes in perspective: at sufficient distance, an event is a pointlike INSTANCE in time, but zoom in enough and it has a perceptible extent— it becomes a PROCESS.

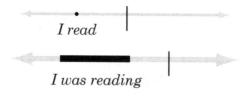

I read

I was reading

The unmarked verb in English (I read) has an instance reading; in Russian it's a progressive (*Ya čital* 'I was reading') and a prefix is added to force an instance reading (*Ya pročital knigu* 'I read a book').

The choice of article can force an instance reading for a nominalization: *Would you like a dance?* Compare *Do you like dancing?* which refers to habitual activity.

In English we often use the bare root to nominalize an instance (*a look, a dance*) rather than a process (*looking, dancing*). The choice of article can also determine the perspective: *a dance* vs. *the dance*.

We can also zoom in even closer and focus on the beginning or end of the process:

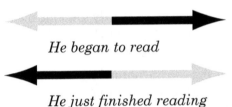

He began to read

He just finished reading

Repeated events are much like grouped objects: either instances or processes can be repeated in time, and the group of repetitions can be treated as a unit (e.g. by a habitual tense), much as we can turn nouns into collectives.

Categories and prototypes

Not all members of a class are equal. Eleanor Rosch and George Lakoff have emphasized that classes have PROTOTYPES or central members; speakers consider these typical examples of the class, list them first if asked for examples of the class, and think about the class in terms of the prototypes. The prototype *bird*, for instance, is probably a songbird— small, flying, and untamed. General statements about a class may be true only of the prototype (e.g. *birds fly*).

In our visual metaphor, we might represent this as a privileged referent within the cloud:

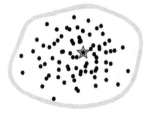

Naturally, this means that there are also untypical and marginal members of a class.

Color terms vary widely between languages in number and boundaries, but the FOCAL or prototypical colors are nearly identical, due to the shared characteristics of human vision.

Languages may provide explicit ways of indicating how far a referent differs from the prototype:

- To indicate that (say) a bird is close to the prototype, we may say *that's a real bird.* Or reduplication with emphasis: *I don't want a fish, I want a **pet** pet.*

- In English, *technically* or *strictly speaking* indicates that an item is far from the prototype but still a valid member of the class: *The penguin is technically a bird.*

- If an item is outside the normal semantic boundaries but not far, the previous expressions can be simply negated (*The whale is technically not a fish*).

Especially with abstract terms, people may not share the same prototypes, and this can lead to misunderstandings. (E.g. is the prototype of an *amateur* someone commendably unmotivated by gain, or a rank incompetent?)

Basic categories

Not all categories are alike; BASIC CATEGORIES are more perceptually salient, are learned earlier, and have simpler names. For plants and animals, for instance, basic categories nearly always correspond to the genus level: *maple, pine, rye, cod, dog, bull/cow, rabbit.*

The existence of basic categories answers Willard Quine's objection to ostension— e.g. that pointing to a rabbit cannot be used to define *rabbit*, since the speaker might be referring to rabbit noses, the act of running, or a miscellaneous collection of rabbit parts. Linguists studying language acquisition, such as Eve Clark, report that children apply some simple rules:

- use prelinguistic understanding of objects, containers, actions, and spatial relationships

- learn the basic words first

- reject synonymity: assume that each word heard has a different meaning

Quine may see rabbit parts, but children see rabbits. Presumably they have evolved to do so; we are not *tabulae rasae*, and by the time we learn language we have strategies for dealing with it, provided both by our animal inheritance and by our experience exploring the world.

Of course, these categories are basic *to humans*. This is clearest with human-oriented words like *chair*, which are defined not so much by shape as by interaction with the body. But even the taxonomic categories are not 'natural kinds' pre-existing in the world. They are natural to human minds interacting with the world with human bodies.

Register

As society grows more complex, its language will develop multiple REGISTERS. You don't speak the same way to, or about, a king, a peasant, or a thief.

There are several sources of variation:

- **Regional** variation: generally the language of the capital becomes the STANDARD— the highest-prestige variety. Indeed, its prestige becomes so overwhelming that non-linguists have a hard time accepting that non-standard varieties have any valid place at all, and may even deny that they are "languages".

   Sometimes particular lexical items are borrowed from a dialect. E.g. *one* used to rhyme with *alone*; the pronunciation [wʌn] comes from southern and southwestern England. Similarly *vixen* comes from a southern dialect where *v* replaced initial *f*.

- **Foreign** words may supplement native words; after all, it adds a certain *je ne sais quoi* to show that you're conversant with the wider world.

- **Time**: A written language has contact with its own past. Literary classics use words and constructions which have gone out of use, and as literacy may require much time and money to attain, old-fashioned forms are prestigious.

   A written standard may persist for millennia— e.g. *wényán* or Classical Chinese was the standard in China for two thousand years. Latin persisted almost as long, remaining the language of scholarship until the Renaissance; Classical Arabic is still very alive.

   It's always possible to have a literary revolution, in which the elite adopts a more recent standard instead, as happened in China after the 1911 revolution. Our own written standard is only a century or two old: we certainly don't write like Shakespeare, and not much like Samuel Johnson, but the writing style of Mark Twain or Charles Dickens is still highly readable.

If you have a parent language worked out, you can borrow from it— but only if your people's writing system is phonetic. French writers can look at written Latin and easily see that *père* was once *pater*, but Chinese speakers can't do the same with *fùqin*. In Chinese, borrowings from *wényán* are detected because they use out-of-date characters, word meanings, or syntax.

- **Jocular replacement** of words with SLANG terms. Occasionally this is done to confuse outsiders, but sometimes it seems to be sheer exuberance. Spoken French has parallel terms for a wide range of words; a very small selection:

standard	colloquial	meaning
centime	balle	1/100 franc
cheveux	tifs	hair
cigarette	clope	cigarette
cinéma	cinoche	movies
comptoir	zinc	counter
espérer	moisir	wait
fils	fiston	son
frère	frangin	brother
heure	plombe	hour
homme	mec	man
lire	ligoter	read
lit	plumard	bed
médecin	toubib	doctor
nez	pif	nose
perdre	paumer	lose
pétrol	jus	gasoline
regarder	mater	look
voiture	bagnole	car

If you studied French in school and can't understand a French movie, this is why!

Slang terms have several sources:

° Pure invention: *dweeb, nerd.*

° Abbreviations (*zine, blog, exam, prof, cab, W.C., LOL*).

° Taboo-deformation: *darn, heck;* middle English *zounds!* from *God's wounds.*

○ Re-use of other words, following any of the paths noted above (p. 101); e.g. *moisir* above means 'mold'.

○ Borrowing from a minority (e.g. *jazz, funky* from American blacks; *toubib* above from Arabic; *pal, narc* from Romani).

○ Wordplay. Almost anything can be seized on; netspeak has even adopted typos like *teh* and *pwn*. One of my favorites is Cockney rhyming slang, in which a rhyming phrase is substituted for a word. For further obfuscation you can use just the non-rhyming portion:

look → *butcher's hook* → *butcher's*

wife → *trouble and strife* → *trouble*

head → *loaf of bread* → *loaf*

mate → *China plate* → *china*

The end result is that a speaker has a choice of terms ranging from formal to colloquial to slang.

Some semantic fields

This section simply considers some common semantic fields and offers some ideas.

Divisions of time

How are the day and year divided? Don't just assume that days have 24 hours, weeks have 7 days, years have 12 months. How would your people see things?

If your people live on another planet, make sure you know the length of the day and the year.

We number days within the month, but the ancient Romans gave dates as the number of days before the three named days in a month: the kalends, the nones, and the ides. E.g. March 13 was *a.d. II Id. Mart.*, 'the second day before the ides of March'.

The early Romans didn't number years, but named them according to the Consuls who ruled that year. Some cultures name years by a major event that happened that year. Years may also be numbered according to who's in power (e.g. the 15th year of Louis XIV). The Chinese would give a block of years a name; eventually these coincided with an emperor's reign.

The Islamic year is lunar, 12 months of 29 or 30 days giving 354 or 355 days; it thus runs out of sync with the Gregorian year used in the West.

When does your year reckoning start? For the purposes of writing history, you might consider using your earliest culture's starting date, just to avoid negative years.

Directions

A four-way division of directions is natural enough based on astronomical observations.

The diagonal directions are named the opposite way in Chinese; e.g. 'southeast' is *dōngnán* 'east-south'. The Chinese also list the directions in the order E-S-W-N, where we use N-S-E-W.

The major cultures of my planet, Almea, are found in the southern hemisphere. How do we know which way is south on a planet? We can check which way a magnet points; or we could name north as the pole where the planet turns counter-clockwise. These need not coincide!

In a particular geographical situation, directions might be determined by the course of a river (e.g. the Nile in Egypt) or a seacoast.

Names and titles

Names are worth some thought, especially as they're the bit of your language that people will see the most.

Given names

Naming a child is a portentous event, and name are likely to show the values and aspirations of the culture.

Our own names are a mix of Greek, Hebrew, Germanic, and Celtic borrowings that are mostly unanalyzable except by etymologists. You can imitate this, but by borrowing from other languages, not by just making words up.

Indo-European and Hebrew names are often formed of two elements:

>*Timothy* ← Greek *Timótheos* 'honoring God'
>
>*Philip* ← Greek *Fílippos* 'lover of horses'
>
>*Henry* ← Germanic *Haimric* 'home ruler'
>
>*Alfred* ← Old English *Ælfræd* 'elf counsel'
>
>*Kevin* ← Irish *Caoimhghín* 'kind birth'

Hebrew names are often short sentences:

> *Michael* ← Hebrew *Mikha'el* 'who is like God?'

> *Joshua* ←Hebrew *Yehoshua* 'Yahweh is salvation'

Chinese given names are usually two characters; e.g. Mao's given name *Zédōng* means 'lustre east'.

Single-word names are common too, of course. Some common contenders:

- Names of virtues or valued things: *Grace*, *Joy*, *Hugh* (Germanic 'heart, spirit'), *Aurora* (Latin 'dawn'), *Irene* (Greek 'peace'), *Sophia* (Greek 'wisdom'), *Vera* (Russian 'faith'), *Luz* (Spanish 'light'), *Ruth* (Hebrew 'friend'), *Amal* (Arabic 'hope'), *Jamal* (Arabic 'beauty'), *Layla* (Arabic 'night')

- Adjectives: *Felix* (Latin 'happy'), *Asher* (Hebrew 'blessed'), *Bella* (Latin 'beautiful'), *Bonnie* ('pretty'), *Melanie* (Greek 'dark'), *Hakim* (Arabic 'wise'), *Karim* (Arabic 'noble'), *Yasir* (Arabic 'rich')

- Name of flowers and jewels: *Rose*, *Daisy*, *Violet*, *Heather*, *Jasmine*, *Jade*, *Ruby*, *Amethyst*, *Margaret* (Greek 'pearl'), *Rhoda* (Greek 'rose')

- Animals: *Raven*, *Leo* (Latin 'lion'), *Rachel* (Hebrew 'ewe'), *Ursula* (Latin 'little bear'), *Björn* (Norse 'bear')

- Actor nominalizations or past participles: *Victor*, *Benedict* (Latin 'blessed'), *Hamid* (Arabic 'praised')

- Lofty figures: *Sarah* (Hebrew 'lady'), *Rex* (Latin 'king'), *Basil* (Greek 'king'), *Malik* (Arabic 'king')

- Geographical origins: *Lydia*, *Scott* ('Scotsman'), *Francis* ('Frenchman')

Other names

Don't assume that everyone has a given name followed by a family name. Some other formats:

- family name / given name, as in Chinese, Japanese, and Hungarian.

- given name / PATRONYMIC, the old Scandinavian system, still maintained in Iceland; the name of the singer *Björk Guðmundsdóttir* means that she's the daughter of Guðmundur.

- given name / patronymic / family name, as in Russian: *Fyodor Mikhailovich Dostoevsky*. The polite form of address is not the surname but the first two elements, e.g. *Fyodor Mikhailovich*.

- given name / father's family name / mother's family name, as in Spanish: from the name *Mario Vargas Llosa* we can tell that his father's family was Vargas and his mother's Llosa. His father's name was *Ernesto Vargas Maldonado*.

- given name / clan / family, as in ancient Rome, e.g. *Gaius Julius Caesar*, where *Caesar* was a family within the Julia clan.

- Arabs have a given name (*ism*; e.g. *Karim*), but this can be either replaced or supplemented by other designations:

  ◦ a TEKNONYM, 'father of <eldest son's name>', e.g. *abu Nidal*

  ◦ patronymic, e.g. *ibn Amal* 'son of Amal'

  ◦ description, e.g. *al-Rashid* 'the rightly guided'

  ◦ occupation, origin, or descent, e.g. *al-Ajami* 'the Persian'.

Nicknames

People like to create close variants of a name. The ordinary diminutive may be used, or even several diminutives (Russian is notorious for having many of these). There may be abbreviations (*Nick* for *Nicholas*), or baby-talk (a Brazilian friend *Luis Carlos* became *Lica*).

Nicknames may be assigned in childhood or later, and even supplant the given name.

In traditional Japan, one might take a new name when entering a new field— becoming a geisha, taking up flower arranging. The American writer Liza Dalby went by the Japanese name *Kikuko* (from 'chrysanthemum'); as a geisha she was *Ichigiku* (a combination of her own name with that of her mentor).

Titles

Americans tend to refer to everyone by name— even the CEO introduces himself as Jack. Many cultures would consider this insufferably rude; they would use titles instead.

In Japanese, in fact, you almost never refer to a superior by name or even via pronouns; you use their title: *otōsan* 'father', *sensei* 'teacher', *shachō* 'CEO', etc.

Titles of **nobility** may involve a rather complex protocol. For instance, take Gerard Christian Wimsey, the aristocrat invented by Dorothy L. Sayers, whose title is Duke of Denver. Some things of note:

- *Duke* is the highest English noble title, just below royalty.

- The duke is normally referred to by his title, Denver, not his surname, Wimsey; however, this doesn't apply to other family members.

- His son Gerald has a title of his own— Viscount St. George, and he's known as Lord Saint-George.

- His brother Peter, hero of Sayers's detective stories, is in English law not a noble at all, but is entitled anyway to be called Lord Peter.

Expletives and obscenities

Writers often invent foreigners who exhibit a most amazing linguistic deficiency: they speak perfect English except for greetings, titles, "yes" and "no". Of course, this isn't modeling any real-world behavior; it's flattering the reader who can at least recognize *monsieur, bonjour,* and *oui.*

But expletives are one perfectly valid way to show off your conlang— since people are likely to resort to their native language for them. Foreign language expletives just don't seem potent enough.

The most highly charged words in English related to the body and sex, but this isn't a universal. In Catholic countries, or in older English, religious words are dirtier. In Quebec, for instance, you can string together any number of religious references— *ostie de criss de tabernac'!*

If you have a science fiction milieu, please don't make your character swear by the atoms or the spaceways. People swear by what they hold sacred, not by their technology. We don't swear "Automobiles!"

Terms relating to sex are a good place to explore multiple registers. Think of the English *vagina, genitals, sex, pussy, cunt.* It's been said that we lack a purely neutral term for sexual parts— a term neither vulgar nor medical nor euphemistic, like 'nose'.

Modern English is rather weak and predictable in the way of vituperation. Compare some of these gems from Shakespeare:

> *Thou clay-brained guts, thou knotty-pated fool, thou whoreson obscene greasy tallow-catch!*

That trunk of humours, that bolting-hutch of beastliness, that swollen parcel of dropsies, that huge bombard of sack, that stuffed cloak-bag of guts, that roasted Manningtree ox with pudding in his belly, that reverend vice, that grey Iniquity, that father ruffian, that vanity in years?

You starvelling, you eel-skin, you dried neat's-tongue, you bull's-pizzle, you stock-fish— O for breath to utter what is like thee!— you tailor's-yard, you sheath, you bow-case, you vile standing tuck!

Out of my door, you witch, you hag, you baggage, you polecat, you ronyon!

Your hearts I'll stamp out with my horse's heel and make a quagmire of your mingled brains.

Or consider some of the insults of Captain Haddock, in Hergé's Tintin books:

Anthropithecus

gang of Zapotecs of thunder of Brest

devil of a guano merchant

type of badly licked bear

big full-of-soup

freshwater pirate

type of Patagonian Zulu

bandage cream with herring sauce

devil of hydrocarbon extract

Pragmatics

In our own tradition PRAGMATICS is something of the trash bin of linguistics: anything that didn't fit into truth-conditional semantics was shoved aside into pragmatics, to be dealt with later if at all. However, many of the items put aside— utterances, speakers, conversational rules and strategies, speech acts, real-world knowledge— turn out to be pretty interesting, and close to the core of what language is.

The boundary between semantics and pragmatics is vague and disputed, though as rough guide we may say that semantics deals with the meanings of words and sentences, while pragmatics deals with the way speakers use utterances in context. A short dialog may illustrate:

> A: You're such a smart kid.
>
> B: Who invited you?

Semantics seems to fully explain both sentences, and yet it is unable to explain even the basics of the exchange. A's statement is ironic, the sentence's meaning being interpreted as its opposite (aided by the deliberate choice of a word that's insulting when applied to an adult). B's question is logically a *non sequitur*, but we have no trouble taking it as an insulting rejoinder. Neither utterance is intended to convey or query a proposition, and thus truth conditions are irrelevant.

Yet these are not marginal examples; they're typical of actual human conversation. Most broadly, pragmatics studies how language is actually used in the world.

Deixis

Expressions are DEICTIC when their referents inherently vary by context. They are so basic to language that they were discussed many pages back: personal pronouns, demonstratives, words like *now* and *there*.

They are not at all mysterious; they're interesting to logicians because they so glaringly prevent abstract evaluation of the truth of sentences. For instance,

> *Carrie is the daughter of Debbie Reynolds.*

is the sort of sentence logicians love; we can easily decide whether it's true, or with more sophistication, consider the set of possible worlds where it is true. But we can't do the same with

> *I am the daughter of Debbie Reynolds.*

This can only be evaluated as an utterance: its truth depends on whether the person who speaks or writes it is in fact Debbie Reynolds's daughter.

A related phenomenon is ANAPHORA— expressions which refer to a previously cited entity or action.

> *Debbie Reynolds was a Hollywood legend. **She** is the mother of Carrie Fisher.*

Here the logician is on firmer ground, since *she* refers back to *Debbie Reynolds*. The rules for interpreting anaphora can be complex (e.g. determining their scope— here's an actual usage for the tree diagrams we saw on p. 85), but the problems are largely technical. Note however that anaphora can be used without an antecedent— for instance, pointing at someone— and thus reduce to deixis:

> *She* [pointing] *is the daughter of Debbie Reynolds.*

Extra points to readers who speculate that *all* nouns are in some sense deictic. *Carrie* in the first example could refer to someone else— the protagonist of the movie of the same name, for instance, who certainly wasn't Debbie Reynolds's daughter.

Like name, ordinary nouns like *mother* normally refer to single individuals rather than to a class. The difference from deictics is not binary; it's a matter of how much additional informational content is provided. *She* provides only the information that the referent is singular, female, and animate; compare Mandarin *tā* which doesn't indicate gender. Words like *woman* or *human* provide little more information than these pronouns. A full noun phrase like *Debbie's fat bald neighbor* offers quite a bit of information but still may be ambiguous.

Implicature

Conversational maxims

Ordinary language is a trap for logicians: people seem to make remarks and draw conclusions that don't relate to what has been said.

> *A: Is John promotion material?*

> *B: John... well, he's pleasant, very neat.*

If A were a logician, he would complain that B's response is entirely irrelevant. Paul Grice pointed out that such replies make sense if we assume that speakers follow CONVERSATIONAL MAXIMS, and exploit apparent violations to convey subtle messages. The full maxims can be easily found elsewhere, but they can be summarized as follows:

- *Quality*: stick to the truth

- *Quantity*: be i

nformative (but not over-detailed)

- *Relevance*: be relevant to the topic

- *Manner*: be clear, concise, and orderly

B's response violates the maxims of relevance and perhaps quantity. Why doesn't B directly address John's qualifications? Most likely, because there *is* nothing better to say about him. By flouting the maxims, B makes a CONVERSATIONAL IMPLICATURE that John is in fact incompetent.

Often implicatures can be treated as adding unspoken propositions: the speakers can be taken as intending some specific statement (e.g. *John is incompetent*) but not saying it. However, as Dan Sperber and Deirdre Wilson take pains to show in *Relevance*, there is no guarantee that all the implicatures of a statement are consciously present and intended. To take a simple case, B might have responded as follows to A's query:

> B: *Well... you know how John is.*

Like the first statement, this information is strictly irrelevant, and implicates that John is not a prime candidate; but unlike it, it does not commit to a simple proposition. It appeals to common knowledge without pinning it down— B may be referring to any number of known facts about John; B may not even be able to explain what John's problem is; A's impression of John need not be the same as B's. (So much for the conduit metaphor of language (p. 105): that the speaker has a fixed meaning in her head, dehydrates it into an utterance, and passes it to the hearer, who rehydrates it into a copy of her original meaning.)

Grice was writing about English, and you should expect cultural variation. Cultures vary on how direct disagreement can be, what questions are appropriate, how honest answers must be and to whom.

Lexical implicatures

Implicatures neatly address some puzzling aspects of quantifiers, among other things. For instance, *Some Belgians are cheaters* is taken in logic to mean just that at least one Belgian is a cheater. The logician insists that the statement is compatible with all Belgians being cheaters. But in ordinary language we wouldn't say *some* if we meant *all* or *one*.

So is the meaning of ordinary-language *some* (as opposed to logical *some*) *more than one but less than all?* Not at all, because we can without contradiction say:

> *Some Belgians are cheaters, in fact all of them.*

We can say that *some* has the *meaning* of logical 'some', but has the IMPLICATURE that the quantity is more than one and less than all. (By the maxim of quantity, if the speaker knows that all Belgians are cheaters she should say so.) Implicatures can be explicitly denied without contradiction.

Similarly, *Julie has written three books* logically implies that she's written one book or two, but it implicates that she's written no more than three. Again, the implicature can be explicitly overridden: *Julie has written three books; in fact, she's written five.*

(If the implicatures are features of a word rather than deduced by the maxims of conversation, Grice called them CONVENTIONAL IMPLICATURES; I prefer LEXICAL IMPLICATURES.)

Presupposition

PRESUPPOSITIONS are classically defined as inferences that survive negation of a sentence. For instance, these sentences

> *You knew that the old lady was dead.*

> *You didn't know that the old lady was dead.*

both presuppose that the old lady was dead. So does the interrogative: *Did you know that the old lady was dead?* The presupposition is associated with a TRIGGER, in this case the word *know*.

There is a bewildering range of presuppositions, as suggested by the following list. The symbol >> stands for 'presupposes'. The **boldfaced** expression is the presupposition trigger.

> Bill **stopped** / didn't stop fighting with Susan.
> >> Bill had been fighting with Susan

*The ghost was / wasn't seen **again**.*
>> *The ghost had been seen before*

*He's (not) busy **right now**.*
>> *He is not always busy*

*Bill **accused** / didn't accuse Susan of cheating on him.*
>> *Bill believed that cheating was bad*

*I'm **proud** / not proud to be your student.*
>> *I'm your student*

***Since** we conquered Mongolia, we've had / haven't had peace.*
>> *We conquered Mongolia*

***If** Richard had finished that project, we'd still have / wouldn't have their business.*
>> *Richard didn't finish that project*

*The college's **admission** of my friend shocked / didn't shock me.*
>> *The college admitted my friend*

*Audre, **who** was born in the Islands, is / isn't a major poet.*
>> *Audre was born in the Islands*

Like lexical implicatures, presuppositions can be denied, though with restrictions. For instance, an outright denial following a positive statement is anomalous:

?You knew that the old lady was dead, and she wasn't dead.

?The ghost was seen again, but it had never been seen before.

More precisely, then, there are contexts or special circumstances under which the presupposition can be removed. E.g. *know* in the first person:

I didn't know that the old lady was dead, and in fact she wasn't.

(This sounds better with stress on *know*.)

Again takes a bit more context:

There were rumors that a ghost had been seen in the city. There was intense excitement, but nothing could be confirmed. In a few months the furor had died down. The ghost wasn't seen again.

Speech acts

In our philosophical tradition, it has sometimes been assumed that the central function of language is to inform, and that semantics deals largely with analyzing when sentences are true or not.

J.L. Austin challenged this view, first drawing attention to PERFORMATIVES, sentences which do not convey information, but actually accomplish a task:

> *You are hereby accepted as a member of the Raccoon Lodge.*

> *I bet you a hundred bucks that he'll lose.*

Performatives don't have truth conditions, but they do have FELICITY CONDITIONS— e.g. one who utters the first example must have authority to admit members to the lodge, must be speaking to a prospective member, must not have admitted the person already, etc.

Expressions like imperatives can also be seen as performatives— *Go back!*— since they perform a command.

It's a small step now to maintain, not that performatives are an unusual subclass of utterances, but that informative utterances are just one subclass of SPEECH ACTS. All utterances do something: inform, remind, disagree, complain, promise, warn, announce, propose, lie, flatter, persuade, mock, amuse, joke, threaten, praise, boast, show respect, kill time, show solidarity, express an aesthetic reaction, greet, apologize, and so on.

Speech acts should not be confused with syntactic or morphological categories. E.g. the imperative is often an order, but it may just as well be advice, pleading, or a dare; in particular expressions it can be almost anything— e.g. *excuse me* is used to apologize for an interruption. As well, orders can be expressed by questions (*Would you please go back?*) or declaratives (*If you know what's good for you, you'll go back*).

Adverbials may refer to the speech act rather than the content of the sentence.

> *Frankly, the debate bores me.*

Frankly doesn't modify the verb *bores*— it doesn't tell *how* the debate bores me. It relates to the speech act, that of informing. Even more subtly:

> *In a few words— is the girl's poem any good?*

Here *in a few words* doesn't refer to the question itself, or to the speech act of asking, but to the addressee's expected act of answering.

Similarly *please* may be attached to any utterance used as a request, whatever its surface form:

> *You will please open your books to page 23.*

Discourse structure

It's not only sentences that have structure; conversations do as well. The rules are looser than syntax, however, befitting a process worked out cooperatively by two or more people.

This section is based on the methods of CONVERSATION ANALYSIS, and focuses on the prototypical case of two people conversing face to face. Extension to multiple speakers is not difficult. Obviously speech contexts such as lectures, court sessions, electronic chat, and meetings have different rules.

Turn-taking

Conversations can be divided into TURNS— the time one speaker holds the floor. Turn-taking is remarkably efficient: overlaps are rare, and yet the average gap between speakers is less than half a second.

Again, cultural rules may differ on who is allowed to speak, and whether interruptions are allowed.

Adjacency pairs

Turns rarely occur alone; they are grouped into ADJACENCY PAIRS, an utterance and a response. Examples:

- greeting/greeting
- question/answer
- offer/acceptance
- apology/minimization
- request/fulfillment
- assessment/agreement
- complaint/apology
- objection/counter

- insult/riposte
- closing/closing.

These are the building blocks of conversation, especially as they can be **nested**. For instance, a request may have one or more nested questions:

> *REQUEST*
> *A: I'd like a beer.*
>
>> *QUESTION*
>> *B: Dark or light?*
>>
>> *RESPONSE*
>> *A: Dark, please.*
>
> *FULFILLMENT*
> *B: Here you are.*

There are PREFERRED and DISPREFERRED responses for each adjacency pair; dispreferreds are marked by pauses, more verbiage, explanations, and pragmatic particles such as *well.* Compare two responses to an invitation:

> *INVITATION/ACCEPTANCE*
> *A: Come see me later this afternoon?*
>
> *B: With pleasure.*
>
> *INVITATION/REFUSAL*
> *A: Come see me later this afternoon?*
>
> *B: Well... (pause) You're very kind. (pause)*
>
> *I can't really... I have to stay home, my mother is sick...*

Pauses are indeed so characteristic of refusals that silence may be taken as a negative response:

> *REQUEST/REFUSAL*
> *A: Would you like to read my novel?*
>
> *B: (silence)*
>
> *A: Ah... I understand; you're busy...*

Pre-sequences

From the evidence of conversations, refusals are so distressing that strategies have evolved to head them off. One is the PRE-SEQUENCE or PRE-S, an adjacency pair that sets the stage for another, heavier action— a request, an invitation, an offer, etc.

REQUEST PRE-S
A: Are you busy tonight?

B: No, what's up?

REQUEST
A I'm lost in Lecter's class, could we go over anatomy together?

Very often the pre-s questions a felicity condition of the request. For instance, felicity conditions for accepting an invitation include not being busy, being in town, being willing to come, enjoying that type of event, etc. Any of these can be queried in a pre-s, thus heading off a direct refusal.

The listener may choose to respond to the anticipated sequence rather than to the pre-s:

INVITATION PRE-S
A: Did you know that Debbie is throwing a party tomorrow?

B: Yes, I'll go to the damned party with you.

Pre-sequences are especially characteristic of a low-status person addressing a higher one— a nervous person may even have a pre-s for asking a question:

QUESTION PRE-S
Can I ask you a question?

The habit of issuing a pre-s is so ingrained that one may be given even for an insult:

INSULT PRE-S
A: You know what I call you?

B: No, what do you call me?

Long turns

A pre-s is also expected before one takes an especially long turn— e.g. telling a story or a joke, or giving news. Curiously, in this case silence is taken as assent rather than a refusal.

STORY PRE-S
A: Did you hear about Debbie?

B: No, what happened?

Stories may be followed by a contentless statement which serves to indicate that the story is over, prompts for a response, and signals that ordinary shorter turn-taking can resume.

STORY WRAP-UP
A: *So that's how it went.*

B: *Wow, what an idiot!*

Greetings and closings

Greetings in English conversations tend to consist of two adjacency pairs:

SUMMONS/ANSWER
A: *Hey, Bill.*

B: *Hi.*

POLITE QUERY/ANSWER
A: *How are you doing?*

B: *Fine.*

The second pair is not a real query— even if Bill's dog just died, he'll still respond "Fine". Real topics begin after the conventionalized opening.

There's room for cultural variation here. For instance, in my conlang Xurnese one makes two polite queries, one about the other person's institution (e.g. school, temple, company), the other about their health.

The disconnect between polite convention and raw content is nicely captured in Sholem Aleichem's 1892 epistolary novel *Menachem-Mendl*. One of his wife Sheyne Sheyndl's letters begins:

> *To my dear, learned, & illustrious husband Menachem-Mendl, may your light shine!*
>
> *First we're all well, thank God. I hope to hear no worse from you.*
>
> *Second, your lovely letters are making me spit blood. Money from boards I'll be sent! Are you working for a newspaper or a lumber yard? You can put a match to your board and all its money! I need it like last year's snow. To quote my mother: "Spare me your sting and you can keep your honey."*

The end of a conversation typically consists of at least two turns, a PRE-CLOSE which ensures that neither party has more to add, and the actual closing.

PRE-CLOSE
A: *OK, good.*

B: *OK.*

CLOSE
A: G'bye.

B: Bye.

This pattern may be extended; e.g. there is often a mutual acknow-ledgement of any action items (*"See you Tuesday." "Right."*), and greet-ings to others (*"Say hello to your wife." "I will."*).

Repair

Actual spoken sentences, as opposed to textbook examples, often look embarrassingly sloppy. Here's an instance of real speech recorded by E.A. Schegloff:

> A: An' s- an'... we were discussing, it tur-, it comes down, he s- he says, I-I-you've talked about thi- si- i- about this many times. I said, it came down t' this: our main difference, *I* feel that a government, i-the main thing, is th- the purpose of the government is, what is best for the country.
>
> B: Mmhmm.
>
> A: **He** says governments, an' you know he keeps- he talks about gov-ernments, they sh- the thing that they sh'd do is what's right or wrong.

Speaker A is constantly backing up and making REPAIRS. Here's the same dialog with the repaired material crossed out:

> A: ~~An' s- an'... we were discussing, it tur-, it comes down, he s-~~ he says, ~~I-I-~~you've talked ~~about thi- si- i-~~ about this many times. I said, it came down t' this: our main difference, *I* feel that ~~a government, i-the main thing, is th-~~ the purpose of the government is, what is best for the country.
>
> B: Mmhmm.
>
> A: **He** says governments, ~~an' you know he keeps- he talks about gov-ernments, they sh-~~ the thing that they sh'd do is what's right or wrong.

Once the repairs are made, the result is often a clear, well-formed set of utterances:

> A: He says, you've talked about this many times. I said, it came down t' this: our main difference, *I* feel that the purpose of the gov-ernment is, what is best for the country. **He** says governments, the thing that they sh'd do is what's right or wrong.

SELF-REPAIR is preferred to OTHER-REPAIR, which will be marked with hesitations and other indicators of a dispreferred response.

> A: *So you're going to Toronto in the morning.*
>
> B: *Uh, no, not Toronto, Montreal.*
>
> A: *Oh right, Montreal, very good.*

If an other-repair is necessary, it can be softened by not drawing attention to it— in effect acting as if the other person said the right thing:

> A: *So you're going to meet this girl in Toronto.*
>
> B: *I'm going to meet her in Montreal, yeah.*

Pragmatic markers

Many words and expressions have a pragmatic rather than a semantic meaning. Dictionaries often throw up their hands at these; e.g. the interjection *well* is defined as "1. Used to express surprise. 2. Used to introduce a remark or as a filler in a pause during conversation."

Pragmatics lets us be more concise and more accurate: *well,* for instance, marks dispreferreds. *Oh* acknowledges new information; *uh* prolongs a turn or marks dispreferreds; *by the way* introduces a topic jump.

Narrative

Languages generally have syntactic or even morphological means of distinguishing TOPIC (or old information) from COMMENT (new information). This has already come up in several sections:

- Topicalization
- The passive
- The obviative pronouns
- Topic-changing markers

Focusing on sentences, however, we lose track of the big picture. These are just parts of a theory of narrative. How do people agree on topics? How do they change? How do we follow a narrative? How do we know what a conversation is about?

Let's look closely at a fictional conversation, from Roddy Doyle's *The Commitments.* Jimmy, the manager of a soul band in Dublin, needs to talk with his saxophonist, Dean.

—I was thinkin' we could have a chat abou' the group.

—Wha' abou' it?

—Wha' d'yeh think of it?

—It's okay.

—Okay?

—Yeah. Okay. —Why?

Jimmy states a topic— *the group. The* has a pragmatic force; it means that the listener can identify which referent is meant. No problem here; the obvious group is their band, The Commitments.

But this doesn't get at what Jimmy is after. He probes a bit, getting a lackadaisical response, so he has to keep asking.

—How is it okay?

—Jaysis, Jimmy, I don't know. —I like— the lads, yeh know. Derek an' Outspan, an' James. An' Washin'ton D.C. An' Joey's taught me a lot, yeh know. —I like the girls. They're better crack than most o' the young ones I know. —It's good crack.

—Wha' abou' the music?

—It's okay. —It's good crack, yeh know. —It's good.

—But?

Invited to talk about the band, Dean talks about the people in it. But none of this reaches Dean's real dissatisfaction, so Jimmy presses him about the music.

Dean either hasn't formulated his ideas or is extremely reluctant to express them. But finally he responds more directly.

—Ah, Jaysis, Jimmy, I don't want to sound snobby but— fuck it, there's not much to it, is there? Just whack whack whack an' tha' fuckin' eejit, Cuffe, roarin' an' moanin'— an' fuckin' gurglin'.

—Forget Cuffe. —What's wrong with it?

Dean suggests two topics— the limitations of the music they play (soul), and his dislike of the lead singer, Cuffe. Jimmy dismisses one of them, probably on the grounds that everyone dislikes Cuffe. He presses Dean about the other topic.

—Nothin'. —Don't get me wrong, Jimmy. —It's too easy. It doesn't stretch me. —D'yeh know wha' I mean? Em, it was grand for awhile,

while I was learnin' to play. It's limitin', know wha' I mean? —It's good crack, but it's not art.

—Art!

—Well— yeah.

—You've been listenin' to someone, haven't yeh?

—No. [...]

The real topic is out in the open: Dean finds the music too limiting. As it's Jimmy's passion, Jimmy at first rejects the idea: Dean can't really think this, it must be coming from someone else.

Again, beware the conduit metaphor. Very likely Dean doesn't know exactly what the problem is till he talks it through in a conversation like this. As the old lady in E.M. Forster says, "How can I know what I think till I see what I say?"

The subject of "art" means something different to the two of them— to Dean it's liberation, to Jimmy it's an affectation.

Dean warms to his subject:

—Look, Jimmy. —I went through hell tryin' to learn to play the sax. I nearly jacked it in after every rehearsal. Now I can play it. An' I'm not stoppin'. I want to get better. —It's art, Jimmy. It is. I express me-self, with me sax instead of a brush, like. That's why I'm gettin' into the jazz. There's no rules. There's no walls, your man in the Observer said it—

—I knew it! The Observer, I fuckin' knew it!

—Shut up a minute. Let me finish. —That's the difference between jazz an' soul. There's too many rules in soul. —It's all walls.

—Joey called them corners.

—That's it. —Dead on. —Four corners, an' you're back where yeh started from. D'yeh follow me?

—I suppose so.

In an argument, people don't necessarily want agreement, they want validation— they want to know that the other person has understood. At first Dean doesn't get this from Jimmy, thus the explicit meta-communication ("shut up"). This time Jimmy echoes Dean's thought, and also offers assurance that he understands.

Note the use of metaphors, similar but with different connotations. To Dean, strict formal rules in music are "walls", things that block you in. As Jimmy's mentor Joey explains it, however, "Soul solos have corners. They fit into the thump-thump-thump." Corners imply solid, simple construction, and in this case working together with the rest of the music.

Up to now the focus of the conversation has been finding out what Dean's problem is. Now that he knows, Jimmy switches to the consequences: is this a problem for the group?

> —*Are yeh goin' to leave?*
>
> —*The Commitments?*
>
> —*Yeah.*
>
> —*No, Jaysis no. No way.*
>
> —*How come?*
>
> —*It's good crack.* —*It's good. The jazz is in me spare time. That's okay, isn't it?*
>
> —*Yeah, sure.*

The vehemence of Dean's reply offers all the reassurance Jimmy needs. (How we say something is as important as the content.)

Dean offers a compromise— he'll stay with the band, doing jazz on his own. As Jimmy only cares about the band, he has no problem with this.

They end with some mutual affirmations— e.g. they both fancy one of the girls in the band— and Jimmy reinforces the action item:

> —*But go easy on the solos though, righ'*
>
> —*Okay.*

Politeness

Languages seem to be permeated with certain notions: gender, location, time, politeness. These may affect pragmatics, morphology, even phonology. None of this is surprising— these are basic factors of human society— but they're also somewhat arbitrary. Languages are much less likely, for instance, to grammaticalize age, wealth, size, or spirituality.

Some examples of politeness in language:

- The formal and informal pronouns of Romance languages, (e.g. *tu/vous* in French) or the use of titles rather than pronouns in Japanese— examples of SOCIAL DEIXIS, words chosen to indicate social placement much as locative pronouns indicate spatial placement.

- Specific polite verb forms— e.g. Japanese *tetsudau* 'help', polite form *tetsudaimasu*. Sometimes the polite form is suppletive: *iku* 'go', polite form *irassharu*.

- The avoidance of bald imperatives for commands. As Anna Wierzbicka points out, English is striking for its wide array of ways to avoid imposition:

  > *Will you have a drink?*
  > *Would you like a drink?*
  > *Sure you wouldn't like a beer?*
  > *Why don't you pour yourself something?*
  > *How about a beer?*
  > *What if we had a little something to drink?*
  > *Aren't you thirsty?*

  We're so used to such pseudo-questions that we use them rather than a direct imperative even when actual politeness is far from our minds: *Will someone put this fucking idiot out of his misery? For Christ's sake, would you get lost?*

  In French, the infinitive or past tense can be used to avoid imperatives: *Ouvrir le paquet; Si nous allions?*

  In Polish, by contrast, a courteous host pushes his hospitality on the guest, dismissing the guest's expressed remonstrances and desires as irrelevant: *Prosze bardzo! Jeszcze troszke! —Ale juz nie moge! —Ale koniecznie!* "Please, a little more!" "But I can't!" "But you must!" An imperative can be softened by adding in one or more diminutives.

- The use of higher registers or euphemisms in certain social circumstances.

- The protocol for using titles.

- Conversational maxims, which allow speakers to avoid direct negative statements.

- Turn-taking in conversations.

- The avoidance of dispreferred responses in conversation, including the use of pre-sequences to shield participants from refusals, and the questioning of felicity conditions (*Are you busy?*) as a means of avoiding direct requests (*Will you come over?*).

- The avoidance of other-repair among peers.

- Greetings and closings.

The predominant analysis of politeness is that of Penelope Brown and Stephen Levinson. Following Erving Goffman, they emphasize the concept of FACE— itself a calque on Chinese *liǎn*. This can be divided into positive and negative face:

- POSITIVE FACE is the desire to have one's wants acknowledged and shared by others; it's threatened by disapproval, contradiction, inattention, or irreverence.

- NEGATIVE FACE is the desire to have one's wants unimpeded; it's threatened by orders, requests and threats (which limit freedom of action), offers (which may generate debts), and expressions of envy or anger.

Politeness strategies

According to Brown and Levinson, speakers can adopt one of four approaches; these are exemplified below by a speaker who wants a friend to serve as a nude model.

- BALD ON RECORD: direct and concise orders or statements, without mitigation. These are perfectly acceptable from high superiors, but highly impolite between peers, except in emergencies.

    Take off your clothes.

- POSITIVE POLITENESS, which seeks to flatter positive face: you praise, exaggerate markers of solidarity and group membership, joke around, offer reciprocity, use inclusive language.

    Susan, I'm doing so badly in this class of ours... maybe we could model nude for each other, you think?

- NEGATIVE POLITENESS, which seeks to minimize negative face: use conventionalized indirectness, assume noncompliance, minimize the request, be deferential, apologize, use impersonal forms.

    I don't want to be a bother, but if you could please do me a favor... there's a little modeling au naturel *I need done.*

- OFF RECORD, which avoids a direct request by using language that can be interpreted as not a request at all: hint, use understatement or exaggeration, use tautologies or contradictions (i.e., flout the conversational maxims), be vague or elliptic.

> *I don't know where I can find a model to sketch. I've asked everyone.*

Cultural differences

The rules for politeness vary by culture. The following points are geared at Americans to help avoid cloning American culture.

- Other cultures, especially pre-modern ones, may be much more **hierarchical** than ours. Respect for authority, and disdain for inferiors, may be more freely expressed. On the other hand, our business culture is fairly authoritarian; the Japanese, say, prefer to operate by consensus.

  Our **family** structure is relatively weak... compare ancient Rome, where the *paterfamilias* ruled the family, including adult children, till he was dead.

- Other cultures may be much more, or less, **direct**. Americans don't like to give offense— we soften commands, refusals, and hostile opinions; others (especially in Mediterranean cultures) may not have these filters. On the other hand, East Asians might consider us embarrassingly open: strong emotions and direct refusals are to be hidden.

- **Disagreement** is easier to express in America than in Japan— but we tend to see it as a negative. In Jewish culture, according to Wierzbicka, disagreement expresses sociability and is taken as bringing people closer together. Similarly, white Americans consider self-praise to be boasting, but it's good form among blacks.

- **Taboo subjects** may vary. We're wary of (say) asking someone else's salary, or why they don't have children; these may be quite acceptable elsewhere. Societies may be more open about sex or less so.

- The **leading class** in society will determine many of its values and ways of speaking: are these military men, priests, scholars, bureaucrats, businessmen, women, elves, AIs?

- We're obsessed with **time**— why isn't this done *right now*? Many other cultures just don't see the urgency.

A nation is composed of many subcultures— regions, classes, genders. Roy Miller provides an amusing example from Japanese: a female and male conversation in which a guest praises the host's garden:

Female:

> A: *Mā, go-rippa na o-niwa de gozāmasu wa nē. Shibafu ga hirobiro to shite ite, kekkō de gozāmasu wa nē.*
>
> B: *Iie, nan desu ka, chitto mo teire ga yukitookimasen mono de gozaimasu kara, mō, nakanaka itsumo kirei ni shite oku wake ni wa mairimasen no de gozaimasu yo.*
>
> A: *Ā, sai de gozaimashō nē. Kore daka o-hiroi de gozāmasu kara, hitōtori o-teire asobasu no ni datte taihen de gozaimasho nē. Demo mā, sore de mo, itsumo yoku o-teire ga yukitodoite irasshaimasu wa. Itsumo honto ni o-kirei de kekkō de gozāmasu wa.*
>
> B: *Iie, chitto mo sonna koto gozāmasen wa.*
>
> A: My, what a splendid garden you have there— the lawn is so nice and big, it's certainly wonderful, isn't it!
>
> B: Oh no, not at all, we don't take care of it at all any more, so it simply doesn't always look as nice as we would like it to.
>
> A: Oh, I don't think so at all— but since it's a big garden, of course it must be quite a tremendous task to take care of it all by yourself; but even so, you certainly do manage to make it look nice all the time; it certainly is nice and pretty any time one sees it.
>
> B: No, I'm afraid not, not at all.

Male:

> A: *Ii niwa da nā?*
>
> B: *Un.*
>
> A: It's a nice garden, isn't it?
>
> B: Mm.

Real-world knowledge

To fully understand language use, we can't avoid social interaction, emotion and intention, wordplay and rhetoric, wide realms of implicature or presupposition, and ultimately REAL-WORLD KNOWLEDGE. This isn't really controversial, except to those who hope to treat language as an isolated subsystem (e.g. Chomskyan syntax, or early attempts at AI).

As a random example, here's a passage from Kyril Bonfiglioli's *Don't Point That Thing at Me*. The narrator, Charlie, has just escaped a police tail, a certain Maurice, by taking a taxi.

> *Now, as I've already told you, Martland's men have a year's training. Ergo, spotting Maurice so easily had to mean that Maurice was there to be spotted. It took me a long time but I spotted her in the end: a burly, clean-shaven, auntlike woman in a Triumph Herald: an excellent car for tailing people in, unremarkable, easily parked and with a tighter turning circle than a London taxi. It was unfair on her not to have had a companion though. I simply hopped out at Piccadilly Circus, went in one Undergound entrance and out of another. Triumph Heralds are not all that easily parkable.*

Let's enumerate some of the real-world knowledge a reader needs to interpret this paragraph. (Much of this will be blindingly obvious, of course, but that's because you're a human being. Imagine programming an AI to translate this passage or respond to questions on it.)

- We understand the subtle insult of "a year's training": these cops are trained but not terribly bright.

- We can work out who "her" refers to. Charlie is leaving out a logical step: there was another tail besides Maurice; the reader can fill this in from general knowledge of police or police stories.

- We know that women are all pretty much "clean-shaven", so we understand Charlie's use of the adjective as another insult— the woman looks mannish. "Auntlike" is probably a P.G. Wodehouse reference; as such it reinforces the woman's formidableness.

- We understand why the specs for the Triumph are given— they relate to the idea of a possible car chase.

- We understand what kind of a "companion" the woman lacks— not a friend or a lover, but a partner who could go after a pedestrian.

- We understand that Charlie did not actually hop like a rabbit; he asked the driver to stop and got out, through the door.

- We know enough of city traffic to understand the female cop's problem— she can't follow Charlie without parking, and that's difficult in central London.

- Even if we haven't seen similar scenes in movies, we know that Charlie is talking about going into the Underground (to make it look like he's going to take the subway) and then immediately leaving by another entrance— we know that he doesn't mean to say that he took a train ride then left by the next station's exit.

It would take us far afield to consider how the brain stores real-world knowledge— and we know little— but a common analysis assumes that it's organized into FRAMES or SCRIPTS— essentially, structured chunks relating to a subject. (Marvin Minsky and Roger Schank have explored these in detail.)

The above passage invokes e.g. a script on Chases, which contains common knowledge such as that the chase is at the highest speed possible, who are the typical participants (at least one quarry and at least one pursuer), their motives (the quarry to elude, the pursuer to capture), and perhaps common strategies. Scripts on Police Detectives, Cities, and Taxis are also invoked.

It's easy to show that almost any of the information in a script is relevant to language understanding. For instance, once a script is invoked, all the participants and objects can be considered to be referenced. It would be odd for Charlie to write

> *I got into the taxi. There was a driver in the front seat.*

because the "there" construction highlights new information, and once the taxi script is referenced, we already know that there's a driver— it's not new information.

Frames and metonymy

William Croft has suggested that frames underlie common uses of metonymy. For instance, we can use an author's name to refer to his works: *I've read Plato.* A mention of reading activates the entire frame of reading. We read books, and books have authors, so mentioning the author can serve as shorthand for mentioning the book. Similarly:

- a reference to a book may invoke its contents: *This book is obscure.*

- body parts or accoutrements refer to people: *There are new faces in Congress; Our swords will be victorious; He's after some ass.*

- buildings refer to institutions or, even more indirectly, to their leaders: *The church wants to buy the lot next door.*

- *objets d'art* can refer to their creators: *That nude is competent.*

What isn't so well explained is why some metonymies fail. Since Plato was a philosopher, his ideas should be activated by references to learning or thinking; but we can't say **I've thought Plato.* If I live in a house built by Mies Van der Rohe, I can't say **I live in Mies*— though perhaps *a Mies* is OK. Body part metonymies are curiously restricted; though we can stick our nose into things, it sounds odd to say ?*My little brother's nose was a pest today.*

As we often say in linguistics, more research is needed.

Culture

We've seen a number of ways in which CULTURE is reflected in language:

- Idioms (p. 55)

- Borrowing based on the history of your culture and its neighbors; the Kebreni lexicon has examples (p. 237)

- Pronouns: T/V forms (p. 73), avoiding pronouns in favor of titles (p. 74)

- Categorization (p. 95) and metaphors (p. 103)

- Particular semantic fields: the calendar, kinship terms, names and titles

- How conversations work

- Politeness

Many linguists, after doing fieldwork with Native Americans, came to feel that even the structure of language reflected culture... or vice versa, that we think using the categories and ideas embedded in our language— LINGUISTIC RELATIVITY, to use Benjamin Lee Whorf's term. Here's a typical passage:

> We might isolate something in nature by saying 'It is a dripping spring.' Apache erects the statement on a verb *ga:* 'be white (including clear, uncolored, and so on).' With a prefix *nō-*, the meaning of downward motion enters: 'whiteness moves downward.' Then *tó*, meaning both 'water' and 'spring' is prefixed. The result corresponds to our 'dripping spring', but synthetically it is 'as water, or springs, whiteness moves downward.' How utterly unlike our way of thinking!

> —"Languages and Logic", in *Language, Thought, and Reality*

Part of the strangeness here is due to a change in glossing conventions—
Whorf tries to suggest the structure of native sentences by making
strained but evocative literal translations. Compare the convention used
in this book:

Tó-nō-ga

water-downward-uncolored

Whorf's ideas melded with 1960s liberation movements; it was commonly argued that the *he/she* distinction in English itself contributed to
sexism.

Whorf often seems to carelessly analyze his own language... e.g. he
makes much of the fact that English divides sentences into subject and
predicate, even adding dummy subjects. Well, yes, but that doesn't mean
that when we say *it rains* we picture an inanimate object which is doing
the raining. Or consider the range of people who have spoken English:
medieval peasants, Elizabethan pirates, American colonists and tycoons,
Victorian bankers, Australian ranchers, black rappers, Evangelicals,
punk anarchists— surely the range of cultural diversity is wide enough
that little can be due to the language itself?

Still, why not take a Whorfian approach to your conlang? It's another
opportunity to show what your people are like and how they think.
Some examples:

- For a people very concerned with spirituality, I created a language which grammaticalized it: matter and spirit were its noun
  classes.

- Barakhinei is spoken by a culture of warriors; one aspect of this
  is that men and women use slightly different phonologies and
  differing sets of phatic particles. Another is that words inherited
  from its parent Cadinor often changed meanings according to
  Barakhinei values:

  inges 'kind' → 'womanly'
  kebi 'brutal' → 'firm'
  kormach 'harmonious' → 'tedious'
  krêtrê 'pleasant' → 'wimpy'
  rhu 'lame' → 'useless in battle'
  simirê 'poor' → 'rabble'

  An amusing bit along the same lines from Klingon: 'like' is
  parHa', 'dislike' is **par**. The word for 'dislike' is primary—this
  emotion must come easier to Klingons.

- Another language, Eteodäole, is spoken by iliu, sentient beings who live in the oceans of Almea and have a much higher civilization than humans. The iliu can produce visions in other sentients' minds; naturally, this is used to communicate mere facts. Their language is used more for nuance, emotion, relationships, play, and style.

  An example:

  21-k$\underline{4}$7$\underline{6}$1~ 2$_{33}$-s5:$\underline{7}$·21$\underline{2}$\

  recent.love gratitude best-unexpected soft.smooth

  Great fish, thanks.

  The numbers are tones; the other symbols represent modulations such as tempo, beat, tonal color, tremolo, and intensity. The morpheme **k47617** refers to gratitude of a particular sort: domestic, egalitarian, and unsurprising. It's inflected to show that it refers to the most recent of an ongoing series of actions and that these were done out of love; the final note is omitted, conveying a certain affectionate gruffness.

  The morpheme **s57212** is a specific culinary term, difficult to convey to human palates; it's inflected to note that it's the best description of the fish (i.e. that no other term would be better) and that this quality was surprising at this time of year.

  Some of the other modulations express a willingness to reciprocate or else make love, a faint dislike for the kelp garnish, and a ruefulness that the couple has had some difficult times lately.

- Jack Vance's *The Languages of Pao* describes an experiment where, to shake up a backwards planet, new languages are developed that encourage fighting, science, or commerce.

- Suzette Haden Elgin created a language, Láadan, intended to express female perceptions. This is done a bit in the grammar (e.g. Láadan has a pejorative -**lh**, and evidentials), but mostly in the lexicon. A couple of examples:

  ramimelh— *To refrain from asking, with evil intent; especially when it's clear that someone badly wants the other to ask.*

  radíidin— *Nonholiday; a time allegedly a holiday but actually so much a burden because of work and preparations that it is a dreaded occasion; especially when there are too many guests and none of them help.*

In general: What are the preoccupations and values of your people? What distinctions are important enough to mark in every sentence? What aspects of English would they be surprised by or uninterested in?

If you're creating an auxlang, you should still keep these issues in mind— otherwise, the cultural conventions your language reflects will be your own.

Style

STYLE isn't normally considered in linguistics— linguists are generally interested only in what all the speakers of a language have in common. But that just means that conlangers need to switch disciplines at this point, and look at how the best speakers and writers use language.

Here are some examples of particular styles:. As you read, consider such questions as these:

- What makes the passages different?

- What type of vocabulary or syntax distinguishes them?

- What's a good writer doing differently from a bad writer?

- What would they sound like in your conlang?

Academic:

> Consider now how information of the sort given in (2iii) can be presented in explicit rules. Note that this information concerns *subcategorization* rather than "branching" (that is, analysis of a category into a sequence of categories, as when S is analyzed into NP—Aux—VP, or NP into Det—N). Furthermore, it seems that the only categories involved are those containing lexical formatives as members.
> —Noam Chomsky, *Aspects of the Theory of Syntax*

Bureaucratic:

> **Exception 3**. If the distribution is a qualified charitable distribution (QCD), enter the total distribution on line 15a. If the total amount distributed is a QCD, enter -0- on line 15b. If only part of the distribution is a QCD, enter the part that is not a QCD on line 15b unless *Exception 2* or *Exception 5* applies to that part. Enter "QCD" next to line 15b.
> —Internal Revenue Service, *1040 Forms & Instructions 2008*

Literary, modern style:

> Very many of the young women are exceedingly pretty and dress with rare good taste. We are gradually and laboriously learning the ill manners of staring them unflinchingly in the face— not because such con-

duct is agreeable to us, but because it is the custom of the country and they say the girls like it. We wish to learn all the curious, outlandish ways of all the different countries, so that we can "show off" and astonish people when we get home.
—Mark Twain, *The Innocents Abroad*

Literary, older style:

Human nature is so well disposed towards those who are in interesting situations, that a young person, who either marries or dies, is sure of being kindly spoken of.

A week had not passed since Miss Hawkins' name was first mentioned in Highbury, before she was, by some means or other, discovered to have every recommendation of person and mind— to be handsome, elegant, highly accomplished, and perfectly amiable; and when Mr. Elton himself arrived to triumph in his happy prospects, and circulate the fame of her merits, there was very little more for him to do than to tell her Christian name, and say whose music she principally played.
—Jane Austen, *Emma*

Colloquial:

—Jimmy, said James. —Are yeh seriously expectin' us to deck ourselves out in monkey suits?

—Yeah. ——Why not?

—Yeh can go an' shite, said Billy.

—Well said.

—Yis have to look good, said Jimmy. —Neat —Dignified.

—What's fuckin' dignified abou' dressin' up like a jaysis penguin?

—I'd be scarleh, said Derek.

—Roddy Doyle, *The Commitments*

For Children:

"Why, that's us," said the Dwarf. "We're a kind of rebellion, I suppose."

"I see," said Peter. "And Caspian is the chief Old Narnian."

"Well, in a manner of speaking," said the Dwarf, scratching its head. "But he's really a New Narnian himself, a Telmarine, if you follow me."

"I don't," said Edmund.

"It's worse than the Wars of the Roses," said Lucy.

—C.S. Lewis, *Prince Caspian*

Stylized:

During World War II a bomber crashed up the street's top end, a great tin angel with a sucking chest wound fallen from the Great Judgement. It was drawn down inexorably by tractor beams of sympathetic magic emanating from the subterranean speakeasy that's under Adam's Bakery behind the church, a marvellous forgotten space designed to reproduce the shape and seating of a buried aeroplane. Imagined engine-drone above the cold flint jetstreams, the clay strato-cumulus, like calling unto like, dragging the bomber overhead into a helpless and enraptured nosedive.

—Alan Moore, *Voice of the Fire*

Poetry

Hope is the thing with feathers
That perches in the soul,
And sings the tune without the words,
And never stops at all,

And sweetest in the gale is heard;
And sore must be the storm
That could abash the little bird
That kept so many warm.

I've heard it in the chilliest land
And on the strangest sea;
Yet, never, in extremity,
It asked a crumb of me.

—Emily Dickinson, *Poems*

What's good about good writing? There are really several kinds of goodness, which different cultures and times weight differently, and which can pull in opposite directions.

- **Education**: an impressive vocabulary; erudite allusions; mastery of idioms that belong only to the literary language or to high-prestige foreign ones. Popular genres may be filled with pop allusions instead.

- **Elegance**: From all the options, the good writer chooses the best one. (By contrast a bad writer uses words tritely, vaguely, or incorrectly.)

- **Weight**: In the 18th century, the time of Joesph Addison and Samuel Johnson, it was fashionable to write gravely and reflectively. Oliver Goldsmith commented of Johnson that if he wrote dialog for little fishes, they would sound like great whales. Jane Austen is influenced by this tradition.

- **Simplicity**: It's not as easy as it sounds to write simply and directly. Mark Twain must have sounded brash and primitive to the literary elite of the time.

- **Dazzle**. Many writers would be embarrassed to write simply. They write with wit, with surprise; their surface style calls attention to itself; their metaphors are daring.

- **Efficiency**. Technical terms are precise and save enormous time. On the other hand, it's all too possible to hide fallacies or perfect nonsense behind jargon. Academic writing should be no harder than it needs to be.

- **Realism**. A good writer is a good observer of people, places, and language. Twain carefully analyzes the oddities of both foreigners and tourists; Doyle takes care to reproduce the sass of his young Dubliners.

- **Control**. A good writer is in command— his language serves his purpose, whatever that is. A bad writer wanders off the point, leaves necessary things out, leaves stumbling blocks in, makes poor word choices that mislead readers or invite mockery rather than engagement.

You can certainly expand or revise this list, especially if you're a lit major. The point, however, is to think about good style in your conlang. Which of these goals is more important? Can you write good and poor passages in your language and make it clear which is which?

Poetry

For poetry you must consult your own Muse. However, it's worth pointing out that RHYME is not the only thing poetry can be based on:

- Old English verse was based on ALLITERATION (though with some use of stress and quantity as well). To quote an example in modern English by C.S. Lewis:

  MERCURY marches; —madcap rover,
  Patron of pilf'rers. Pert quicksilver
  His gaze begets, goblin mineral,

Merry multitude of meeting selves,
Same but sundered...

- Latin and Greek poetry was based on QUANTITY, that is, patterns of long and short vowels. A Latin example in HEXAMETER (lines of six FEET, each foot being composed of long/long or long/short/short syllables). In the first line I've separated the feet with | marks.

Cūm puer| āudā|cī coe|pīt gaū|dēre vo|lātū
Dēsseruītque ducēm, cāelīque cupīdine trāctūs,
Āltius ēgit itēr. Rapidī vīcīnia sōlis
Mōllit odōrātās pēnnārūm vīncula cērās.

When the boy began to rejoice in bold flight
He deserted the leader and, drawn by desire for the sky,
Made his way higher. Proximity to the fierce sun
Softened the fragrant wax, the binding of the feathers.

- Blank verse, of course, is based on patterns of STRESS, without having to rhyme.

Friends, Romans, countrymen, lend me your ears.
I come to bury Caesar, not to praise him.
The evil that men do lives after them,
The good is oft interrèd with their bones.

[Shakespeare, Julius Caesar]

- French verse is generally based on lines of a certain SYLLABLE LENGTH, e.g. the alexandrine, of twelve syllables, generally placed in rhymed couplets:

Que Votre Majesté, Sire, épargne ma honte.
D'un si faible service elle fait trop de conte,
Et me force à rougir devant un si grand roi
De mériter si peu l'honneur que j'en reçoi.

May Your Majesty, Sire, spare my shame.
It makes too much of a very small service
And makes me blush before such a great king
To merit so little the honor I receive from him.
[Corneille, Le Cid]

Similarly, the haiku is composed of three lines, of 5, 7, and 5 syllables each.

Furu ike ya
kawazu tobikomu
mizu no oto

Old pond—
a frog jumps in
sound of water   [Bashō]

- Ancient Hebrew poetry was based on PARALLELISM, the near
  repetition of an idea ("But let justice roll down like waters, and
  righteousness like an ever-flowing stream."), or on successive
  sentences or verses each beginning with a different letter (notably Psalm 119).

Poetry may be tied to song— one reason why poetic forms often emphasize meter or number of syllables.

Language families

You can add enormous depth to a fantasy language by giving it a history and relatives. Verdurian and its sister languages Barakhinei and Ismaîn derive from Caðinor, as French and Spanish derive from Latin. Caðinor, Cuêzi, and Xurnese, in turn, derive from Proto-Eastern, and thus are related in systematic ways, much as Latin, Greek, and Sanskrit all derive from proto-Indo-European.

What can you do with such relationships?

- Most obviously, easily create **neighboring languages**.

- Create DOUBLETS of words to enrich the language: one that derives from the ancient language and is worn down by millennia of sound change, one that has been borrowed more recently in its ancient form. Verdurian has doublets such as these:

  feir 'hurl' / *pegeio* 'force'
  sönil 'saddle' / *asuena* 'seat'
  žanec 'coming' / *ctanec* 'future tense''
  elut 'fair play' / *aelutre* 'virtuous'

- You can BORROW from nearby languages, e.g. Verdurian *kenek* 'camel' ← Barakhinei *kêntek* ← Cað. *kentos* 'plain', which has also come down into Verdurian as *kent*. Or compare *çişte* 'guitar', borrowed from Ismaîn, and cognate with native *sista* 'box', both going back to Cað. *cista* 'box'. Verdurian *ruzbideš* 'hard cider' is borrowed from Xurnese *rus bídeš* 'apple wine'; *rus* 'apple' is a distant cognate of Verdurian *luom*.

- Legal, scientific, medical, literary, and theological terms in Verdurian are often REBORROWED (i.e. back-borrowed) from Caðinor: e.g. *vocet* 'summons'; *gutia* 'epilepsy' (from a Caðinor word meaning 'shaking'), *menca* 'style, school'. Verdurian has also borrowed educated terms from Cuêzi: *avisar* 'school', *deyon* 'matter', *risunen* 'draw'. Moreover, some terms were borrowed direct from Cuêzi; others were borrowed from Cuêzi into Caðinor in ancient times, and then inherited in Verdurian: e.g. *risunen* ← *risunden* ← Cuêzi *risonda* 'drawing', ultimately from *risi* 'reed pen'.

People sometimes make false reborrowings. E.g. *island* is a native English term, from Old English *īegland*, but it's been contaminated by *isle*, an early borrowing from French. Similarly *debt* is a straight borrowing from French *dette*; the *b* was inserted in a misguided bow to Latin *debitum*.

Words often **change meaning** as they're borrowed. Some cute examples from Verdurian:

- *čayma* 'tent' ← Western *chaimba* 'shelter' because the shelters of the Western barbarians were in fact tents

- *dalu* 'king' ← C. *dalu* 'prince'— because when the Cadinorian empire fell, its princes each became independent rulers

- *garlo* 'sorcerer' ← C. *garorion* 'wise or clever man'

- *kestora* 'natural philosophy' ← C. *kestora* 'the categories (of study)'

- *minyón* 'cute' ← C. *mingondul* 'beggar' ← *mingonda* 'large mat', i.e. all that a beggar possessed

- *nočula* 'together' ← C. *nodatula* 'tied up'

- *ponyore* 'baritone' ← Cuêzi *pomioro* 'manly'

More on historical linguistics

There are some great, readable books on this— I recommend Larry Trask's *Historical Linguistics*, and there's more in the bibliography.

And as usual, see the web resources page.

Sound change

When I created the first version of the Eastern languages, I assumed that a sister language would just unpredictably distort all the words, and that daughter languages would wear them down. Then I learned better, and had to redo them all.

The main, surprising thing to learn is the REGULARITY OF SOUND CHANGE. Words don't change randomly; a given SOUND CHANGE is like a function that applies to all the words it can.

For instance, Latin *-ct-* changes to *-it-* in French:

nocte → *nuit* 'night'
octō → *huit* 'eight'

> *bīs coctu* → *biscuit* 'biscuit'
> *lacte* → *lait* 'milk'
> *lactuca* → *laitue* 'lettuce'
> *strictu* → *étroit* 'narrow'
> *dīrēctu* → *droit* 'right'

Most sound changes are CONDITIONAL, and the conditions can be quite precise. For instance, Latin **c** [k] changes to /ʃ/ in French, but only before [a], and not between two vowels:

> *capra* → *chèvre* 'goat'
> *caru* → *cher* 'dear'
> *scala* → *échelle* 'ladder'
> *piscāre* → *pêcher* 'fish'
> *caballu* → *cheval* 'horse'
> *vacca* → *vache* 'cow'
> *cambiāre* → *changer* 'change'
> *manica* → *manca* → *manche* 'sleeve'

Sound changes tend to act on similar sounds in a similar way. For instance, Latin **g** + **a** becomes French /ʒ/ (*gaudia* → *joie* 'joy', *gallīna* → Old French *geline* 'hen')— this is exactly parallel to **c** + **a**, only with voiced sounds on both sides.

+---
| **Really regular?**
|
| Full disclosure: not all sound changes *are* completely regular. Sometimes a word just fails to be affected. (And sometimes we just haven't figured out a more complicated condition.)
|
| How much should this worry you as a conlanger? Not much. Make your sound changes regular; but if you have an exception or two, fine.
+---

Notation

Linguists write sound changes briefly; e.g. the second example would be

> c → ʃ / (#,C)_a

The condition is on the right, after the slash. # means "the beginning or end of the word"; C is any consonant; the underscore _ refers to the thing being changed, in this case *c*. Another useful abbreviation is $ for a syllable break.

Using feature notation, several rules can be consolidated. For instance, the C and G rules could be combined:

> [+velar +stop] → [+fric] / (#,C)_a

A language family

Apply a different set of sound changes to a parent language, and you get a family. For instance, some of my languages:

Caḍinor	Verdurian	Ismaîn	Barakhinei	gloss
prosan	*prosan*	*prozn*	*proza*	'walk'
molenia	*mólnia*	*moleni*	*molenhi*	'lightning'
ueronos	*örn*	*ŕone*	*feron*	'eagle'
aestas	*esta*	*eşte*	*âshta*	'summer'
laudan	*lädan*	*luẓn*	*laoda*	'go'
geleia	*želea*	*jeleẓe*	*gelech*	'calm'

From such a short list you can't see all the changes— you can find the full set of sound changes on my website— but note the following:

Verdurian:

- unstressed middle vowels lost

- ae → e, au → aa (spelled ä)

- g becomes ž before a front vowel

- Final -s lost

Ismaîn:

- vowel before final n is dropped (the n is syllabic)

- vowels or diphthongs + r turn into a syllabic r

- medial consonants are voiced

Barakhinei:

- final -n is lost

- s before a stop becomes ∫

- n before a semivowel i is palatalized

- an intervocalic semivowel i becomes /t∫/

As an exercise, try rewriting my informal descriptions in formal notation.

Proto-languages

Historical linguists can compare existing, related languages via the COMPARATIVE METHOD, reconstructing their ancestor, which is called a PROTO-LANGUAGE. For instance, Latin, Greek, Sanskrit, Albanian, and the ancestors of the Germanic, Slavic, Baltic, and Iranian languages are compared to reconstruct Proto-Indo-European.

For instance, suppose we had only the descendant forms in the table above:

Verdurian	Ismaîn	Barakhinei	gloss
prosan	prozn	proza	'walk'
mólnia	moleni	molenhi	'lightning'
örn	ŕone	feron	'eagle'
esta	eşte	âshta	'summer'
lädan	luẓn	laoda	'go'
želea	jeleẓe	gelech	'calm'

(And suppose we had very many more words. Brief examples like this may suggest that historical linguists only look at half a dozen words; in fact they examine hundreds. It's tedious work and takes years.)

The goal would be to suggest plausible forms for the proto-language and regular sound changes for each daughter language. Reconstructions are always tentative, because we could be wrong. For instance, it's a good guess that 'calm' began with g- (since the ž- and j- can be derived from fricativization, a common process). But it's certainly not clear what the initial vowel for 'summer' should be, or whether the initial f- in Barakhinei feron 'eagle' is an innovation or a retention.

A RECONSTRUCTED form is marked with an asterisk, e.g. *snora 'daughter-in-law'. (This is related to the use of asterisks to mark ungrammatical senses; think of the underlying meaning as 'unattested'.)

You can invent a proto-language, use it to derive ancient languages, then use those to create modern ones. Of course you, unlike terrestrial linguists, know what the proto-forms are. But you might use asterisks anyway to simulate the uncertainty of actual proto-languages.

How do you invent a proto-language? Just as you invent any other language; there's nothing special about it, except that its lexicon should reflect the technology of its time— if it's prehistoric, it shouldn't include words like 'steel' or 'ship' or even 'city'.

Dialects

You can use the same technique to create DIALECTS for your language. Linguistically, dialects are simply a set of language varieties which haven't diverged far enough apart that their speakers can't understand each other. Dialects can be created simply by specifying a smaller number of less dramatic sound changes.

For instance, the Verdurian dialect of Avéla is characterized by the following changes:

- Unstressed vowels are reduced to **i** (front vowels), schwa (back vowels), or vocalic **r** (before r)

- Consonants between vowels become voiced: standard **epese** 'thick' becomes **ebeze**

- Where Cad̂inor *c* changes to **s** in standard Verdurian, in Avéle it changes to **š**

- Where Cad̂inor *ct* changes to **ž** in standard Verdurian, in Avéle it changes to **š**

Dialects can also have their own lexical terms, of course, perhaps borrowed from neighbors or previous inhabitants of the local territory.

People often suppose that the dialect of the capital city (or whatever other place has supplied the standard language) is more 'pure' or more conservative than provincial speech. In fact the opposite is as likely to be true: the active center of a culture will see its speech change fastest; rural or isolated areas often preserve older forms. (However, language changes everywhere; don't invent pockets that speak ancient tongues.)

If you're inventing an interlanguage you may of course want to do everything possible to *prevent* the rise of dialects. This is probably an expression of the authoritarian streak common to language tinkerers. Why not *design* your interlanguage with dialects, reflecting the phonology of various linguistic regions? The resulting language, with varieties close to the major natural languages, might achieve more acceptance than uniform interlanguages have.

Americans, whose language is remarkably uniform, may underestimate the amount of dialectal variation in languages that have occupied a region for millennia. For instance, here's the variation of the word *cheval* 'horse' in French, within an area less than the width of Texas:

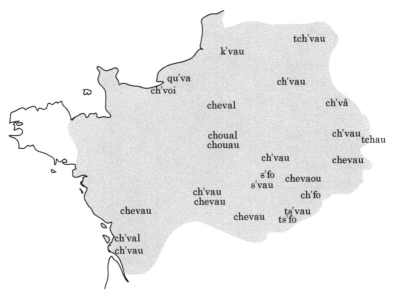

Dialectologists can draw lines (ISOGLOSSES) around common features—
e.g. the eastern dialects with initial [tʃ], the northern ones with [k]. Isoglosses for different words may be strikingly different.

The Sound Change Applier

My site offers a Sound Change Applier, SCA^2, to help make modified
vocabulary lists. It works in your browser, so you can use it from any
operating system.

> http://www.zompist.com/sca2.htm

An example

I find generating changes using SCA^2 to be a pleasure and an art; it's a
kind of magic to generate a particular feel in the words of a language
merely by carefully adjusting the rules.

This is a iterative process, so let's work through an example. Say I have
the following wordlist, which happens to be from Wede:i.

> *beda* 'sister'
> *bika* 'fir'
> *de:i* 'people'
> *dowogu* 'nobody'
> *gala:i* 'walled town'
> *gauji* 'fruit'

iteru 'shine'
jo:na 'cat'
kulana 'cod'
la:ŋu 'marry'
ma:ngu 'nobleman'
ma:nzi 'noblewoman'
naka 'hemp'
ŋa:una 'street'
papa 'mother'
rada 'seed'
ruŋa:i 'kingdom'
sukwen 'dagger'
tinbu 'yesterday'
wata 'year'
yok 'two'
yona 'language'
zu:ru 'get'

I would work with a much larger list, of course. But for the first few iterations, I mostly look at the first page of results anyway. Once they look OK, I look farther down the list.

I enter the words above in the Input Lexicon field. You can press IPA to get a display of phonetic symbols to copy and paste. To keep things simple I change the digraphs a: e: i: o: u: to ā ē ī ō ū.[2]

How to start? Well, how about an old Romance standby, deleting intervocalic voiced stops. I add these rules to the Sound Changes field:

    b//V_V
    d//V_V
    g//V_V

The first rule means "b becomes nothing (is deleted) between two vowels". To make these work, we have to define the categories, like V, so they can be used in the conditions for sound changes. I add these definitions to the Categories field:

    C=ptkbdgjszmnŋlrwy
    V=aeiouāēīōū

Here's the output of the SCA, highlighting words that changed:

---

[2] Or I could use rewrite rules to handle the digraphs. Press the "Help me!" button on SCA[2] to learn about advanced features.

beda → **bea**
bika → *bika*
dēi → *dēi*
dowogu → **dowou**
galāi → *galāi*
gauji → *gauji*
iteru → *iteru*
jōna → *jōna*
kulana → *kulana*
lāŋu → *lāŋu*
māngu → *māngu*
mānzi → *mānzi*
naka → *naka*
ŋāuna → *ŋāuna*
papa → *papa*
rada → **raa**
ruŋāi → *ruŋāi*
sukwen → *sukwen*
tinbu → *tinbu*
wata → *wata*
yok → *yok*
yona → *yona*
zūru → *zūru*

Not much change so far. Let's fricativize stops before high vowels—

T=tdkg
Q=cjcj
Y=uiü
T/Q/V_Y
T/Q/#_Y

The change T/Q means that any sound in the category T (that is, t d k g) is replaced by the corresponding sound in Q. This is easier than writing separate rules for each sound.

Plus, let's front back vowels before liquids:

R=rl
o/ö/_R
ō/ö/_R
u/ü/_R
ū/ü/_R

We've created some new phonemes here— /c j ö ü/— and these should be added to the definitions of V and C.

The results:

> beda → **bea**
> bika → bika
> dēi → dēi
> dowogu → **dowou**
> galāi → galāi
> gauji → gauji
> iteru → iteru
> jōna → jōna
> kulana → **cülana**
> lāŋu → lāŋu
> māngu → māngu
> mānzi → mānzi
> naka → naka
> ŋāuna → ŋāuna
> papa → papa
> rada → **raa**
> ruŋāi → ruŋāi
> sukwen → sukwen
> tinbu → **cinbu**
> wata → wata
> yok → yok
> yona → yona
> zūru → **zūru**

I like some of these words, but we're far from done— most words are still unchanged. OK, let's add some monophthongization—

> au/ö/_
> āu/ò/_
> ei/ī/_
> ēi/è/_
> āi/à/_
> ai/ē/_

and voice unvoiced stops between vowels:

> P=ptks
> B=bdgz
> P/B/V_V
> P/B/V_w

Results:

> *beda* → **bea**
> *bika* → **bia**
> *dēi* → **dè**
> *dowogu* → **dowou**
> *galāi* → **galà**
> *gauji* → **göji**
> *iteru* → **ieru**
> *jōna* → *jōna*
> *kulana* → **cülana**
> *lāŋu* → *lāŋu*
> *māngu* → *māngu*
> *mānzi* → *mānzi*
> *naka* → **naa**
> *ŋāuna* → **ŋòna**
> *papa* → **paa**
> *rada* → **raa**
> *ruŋāi* → **ruŋà**
> *sukwen* → **sugwen**
> *tinbu* → **cinbu**
> *wata* → **waa**
> *yok* → **yok**
> *yona* → *yona*
> *zūru* → **züru**

Wait a second, didn't I say I wanted unvoiced stops voiced? I expected *biga*, not *bia*. Ah, I added the voicing rule *before* the rule that drops voiced stops. So, *bika* became *biga*, then the dropping rule applied, producing *bia*. (SCA[2] has a "Report which rules apply" checkbox which shows all the intermediate steps, making it easier to find out exactly what's going on with your rules.)

I don't like *dowou* either— I'd like to see my fricativization apply to -*g*-, and it never applies because the -*g*- is dropped first. So I'll move the fricativization rule up.

With these order corrections, we get:

> *beda* → **bea**
> *bika* → **biga**
> *dēi* → **dè**
> *dowogu* → **dowoju**

> *galāi* → **galà**
> *gauji* → **göji**
> *iteru* → **ideru**
> *jōna* → *jōna*
> *kulana* → **cülana**
> *lāŋu* → *lāŋu*
> *māngu* → *māngu*
> *mānzi* → *mānzi*
> *naka* → **naga**
> *ŋāuna* → **ŋòna**
> *papa* → *paba*
> *rada* → **raa**
> *ruŋāi* → **ruŋà**
> *sukwen* → **sugwen**
> *tinbu* → **cinbu**
> *wata* → **wada**
> *yok* → *yok*
> *yona* → *yona*
> *zūru* → **züru**

We're getting there... most words are changed, now. Let's remove some final vowels

> H=ae
> H//VC_#

and replace V + n syllable endings with nasals:

> n/~/_#
> n/~/_C
> m/~/_#
> m/~/_C

The results:

> *beda* → **bea**
> *bika* → **big**
> *dēi* → **dè**
> *dowogu* → **dowoju**
> *galāi* → **galà**
> *gauji* → **göji**
> *iteru* → **ideru**
> *jōna* → **jōn**
> *kulana* → **cülan**

lāŋu → lāŋu
māngu → mā~gu
mānzi → mā~zi
naka → nag
ŋāuna → ŋòn
papa → pab
rada → raa
ruŋāi → ruŋà
sukwen → sugwe~
tinbu → ci~bu
wata → wad
yok → yok
yona → yon
zūru → züru

The coverage is pretty good now— almost all words are affected. Time to check the larger wordlist to see if that's true globally.

As it happens, this is about half the rules I actually used to develop Cuolese from Wede:i. Here's the complete set of categories and rules for Cuolese:

C=ptkbdgjszśźmnŋlrwyc
V=aeiouāēīōūüöòéáíóúàè
M=aeiou
L=āēīōū
K=áéíóú
J=szśźj
T=tdkg
Q=cjcj
H=ae
D=tdc
P=ptksś
B=bdgzź
R=rl
Y=uiü
X=aeouöò

And here are the sound changes, with annotations:

* monophthongization
au/ö/_
āu/ò/_
ei/I/_
ēi/è/_

āi/à/_
ai/E/_
yu/ü/_
yo/ö/_
* fricativize dental/velar stops before high vowels
T/Q/V_Y
T/Q/#_Y
* drop voiced intervocalic stops
b//V_V
d//V_V
g//V_V
* voice the remaining (unvoiced) intervocalic stops
P/B/V_V
P/B/V_w
* umlaut before liquids
o/ö/_R
ō/ö/_R
u/ü/_R
ū/ü/_R
* back i after sibilants
i/u/J_C
* raise a before ng
a/o/_N
* raise e before liquids + i
e/i/_Ri
* soften final k
k/w/_#
* palatalization
p/py/_i
ky/c/_
gy/j/_
* drop vowels in middle syllables
M//VC_CV
* diphthongize o if it's the only vowel
o/ou/#C(C)_#
* nasalization
n/~/_#
n/~/_C
m/~/_#
m/~/_C
* drop final a, e (unless they're the only vowel)
H//VC_#
o/u/VC(C)_#

* **drop liquids before a consonant**
R//_C
* **replace long vowels with stress**
L/K/_
* **initial ng becomes g before back vowels**
ŋ/g/#_X
* **assimilation of remaining nasals**
ŋ/m/_[wmb]
ŋ/n/_D
n/m/_w
* **unround o if it follows u**
ö/o/u_
* **spelling rules**
a~/ã/_
e~/ẽ/_
i~/ĩ/_
o~/õ/_
u~/ũ/_

Careful readers may wonder why we still have nasal consonants (see the third-to-last rule): didn't we nasalize them all before? Yes, but we added *another* rule that dropped vowels in middle syllables, and that reintroduced consonant-final nasals.

And the final results applied to the wordlist above:

beda → bea
bika → big
dēi → dè
dowogu → dowju
galāi → galà
gauji → göji
iteru → idru
jōna → jón
kulana → cüna
lāŋu → láŋu
māngu → má~gu
mānzi → má~zi
naka → nag
ŋāuna → gòn
papa → pab
rada → raa
ruŋāi → ruŋà
sukwen → sugwẽ

> *tinbu* → *cîbu*
> *wata* → *wad*
> *yok* → *öw*
> *yona* → *ön*
> *zūru* → *züru*

Every word is affected, with just 46 total rules. (Many of them could be combined with clever use of categories, but it's fine to implement similar sound changes with separate rules.)

If you need to use Unicode combining characters, you'll need to add rewrite rules. E.g., we can get rid of the makeshift á~ above with this rule:

> ã|á~

Morphology

To start out your morphology, run a set of morphological forms through SCA². Let's start with these Wede:i forms. Wede:i is agglutinative and doesn't indicate number on the verb; the *-ok-* is the past tense morpheme.

> *yoniŋ*   I speak
> *yonil*   you speak
> *yon*   he speaks
> *yonokiŋ*   I spoke
> *yonokil*   you spoke
> *yonok*   he spoke

The Cuolese sound changes give these results:

> *yoniŋ* → *öniŋ*
> *yonil* → *önil*
> *yon* → *ö̌*
> *yonokiŋ* → *ö̌ciŋ*
> *yonokil* → *ö̌cil*
> *yonok* → *önow*

As if by magic, an agglutinative paradigm has become fusional— there is no longer a separable past tense morpheme. Indeed, the endings have partially fused with the root— *ön-* 'to speak' becomes *ö̌-* before a consonant. In fact this is a pretty good model for how fusional languages are formed.

The SCA² output may suggest simplifications. Some distinctions might be merged together and lost. (E.g. if there were a sound change that dropped final -*ŋ* and -*l*, the first/second person distinction in the above paradigm would be lost.)

Or perhaps the whole system would become more regular if a couple of forms were slightly changed. In the above paradigm, nasalization *almost* serves as a marker of past tense. Maybe it becomes interpreted as such, resulting in a regularized paradigm:

> *öniŋ*
> *önil*
> *ön*
> *őciŋ*
> *őcil*
> *őow*

That last form is hard to pronounce; perhaps it just becomes *őw*.

Alternatively, looking at other verbs, this nasalization might be perceived as so rare that it disappears— the original root *ön-* is restored by analogy:

> *öniŋ*
> *önil*
> *ön*
> *önciŋ*
> *öncil*
> *önow*

If you look at the Cuolese grammar online, you'll see that I adopted this last idea, but only for the 3s *ő*. So the final paradigm is:

> *öniŋ*
> *önil*
> *ön*
> *őciŋ*
> *őcil*
> *önow*

Another alternative would be to preserve the agglutinative nature of the verbal system, perhaps by generalizing the most common or clearest reflex. We might take -*ow*- (from the 3p) as the descendant of -*ok*-, leading to the agglutinative paradigm

> *öniŋ*
> *önil*
> *ön*
> *önowiŋ*

önowil
önow

The bottom line: don't just copy the SCA^2 output to your grammar. Look hard at it, look for ways lazy speakers would knock it around and make it a little easier.

After using SCA^2

If you use SCA^2, or apply sound changes manually, you won't be creating a phonetic inventory or a set of phonological constraints by hand— you'll be letting one develop. The inventory is whatever set of sounds you ended up with once all the rules apply. The phonological constraints can be deduced from the wordlist.

For the final run of SCA^2, I choose the following output format option, suitable for a lexicon entry with etymology:

bea [beda]
big [bika]
...

After applying SCA^2, I go through the entire wordlist manually, and adjust words I don't like or that are too hard to pronounce. If an edit affects a lot of words, probably it should be added to SCA^2; but a few quirky changes are naturalistic. See also *Irregular changes*, p. 171.

Sort the output; this not only produces a useful lexicon, but reveals MERGERS. There's nothing wrong with mergers: an *ear* of corn isn't called that because it looks like an ear; these were two separate Old English words, *ær* and *ēare*. But if two words in the same semantic field merge, one is likely to be replaced. For instance, Spanish *coser* 'sew' and *cocer* 'cook' merged in Latin America where both are pronounced /koser/; *cocer* has been replaced with *cocinar* there. So check your mergers and decide which would be annoying enough to prompt replacements.

You can include **English glosses** in the input; see the SCA^2 documentation for how. But remember to apply semantic changes! (See the semantics chapter for ideas.)

Think about the **history** of the people who speak these daughter languages. What specializations do they have? If one becomes an empire, the others are likely to borrow military and administrative terminology from it. Similar story with inventions or religions.

And don't forget borrowing and reborrowing (p.149).

Finally, remember that the daughter languages are supposed to be languages, not just lexicons. They shouldn't all have the same morphology or syntax.

Cheap 'n easy language families

Perhaps you want a convincing language family, but only for naming languages, perhaps to fill out a remote area of your map. It would be tedious to make a set of sound changes for half a dozen languages. and run them all through SCA^2. Is there a shortcut?

There is! It takes advantage of the fact that the first phoneme in a word counts the most in how different it looks.

For instance, for an Almean family called Proto-Western I started with the following table. The top row are the phonemes in the proto-language. The next rows show what happens to that initial consonant in each daughter.

P-W	p	t	k	kw	b	d	g	gw	kš	f	s	x	xw	w	r	l	m	n	ñ	ñw
Nan	p	t	ty	k	b	d	ty	g	ts	f	s	ȟ	ḧ	-	r	l	m	n	ny	y
Ome	p/b	t/d	k/g	gu	b	d	g	gu	č	f	s	š	šu	-	l	l	m	n	y	u
K'ai	p	t	k'	k	p	t	k'	k	č	v	z	f	p	p	r	r	b	d	g	n
Moa	f	s	ȟ	w	v	z	ɣ	w	ş	-	h	h	w	w	j	n	p	t	ñ	ñ

- Nanese keeps most of the sounds as is (but the velars are palatalized, while the labiovelars take their place).

- Omeguese voices initial stops in closed syllables and retains the labiovelars.

- K'aitani devoices the stops, glottalizes the velars, voices fricatives, merges r/l, and denasalizes the nasal stops.[3]

- Moa fricatives the stops and lenits the fricatives, and both denasalizes and devoices the nasal stops.

Proto-Western has a seven-vowel system, which also changes in systematic ways:

- Nanese lowers most vowels.

---

[3] Oh dear, did I use apostrophes in a conlang? Yes, but they're used with the IPA value, to mark ejectives.

- Omeguese and K'aitani raise them. In Omeguese the highest vowels change to diphthongs; in K'aitani the same happened but the offglide was lost.

- Moa keeps the vowels as is.

P-W	i	e	ê	a	ô	o	u
Nan	e	ê	â	a	ô	ô	o
Ome	ai	i	e	a	o	u	au
K'ai	a	i	i	e	u	u	o
Moa	i	e	ê	a	ô	o	u

I specified some actions for the final consonant:

- Nanese changes final labials and labiovelars to -u, others to -i; but final nasals all become -m

- Omeguese simply loses the final consonant (except nasals); but final labiovelars become -t

- K'aitani fricativizes final stops and retains nasals, and changes final -ŋ to -a

- Moa generally retains the final consonant, but nasalizes -V + nasal, and metathesizes the labiovelars (e.g. kw → wk)

Finally, some rules for two-syllable words:

- Nanese collapses the first syllable (and simplifies the resulting cluster)

- Moa loses the middle consonant and second vowel

- K'aitani loses the final consonant

- Omeguese loses the second syllable

Here's the results applied to a set of sample words:

P-W	Nanese	Omeguese	K'aitani	Moa
bêk	bâi	be	pih	vêk
dôčw	dôi	dot	tuč	zôş
kap	tyau	ga	k'ef	ȟap
kul	tyo	gau	k'or	ȟul
kwim	kem	guaim	kam	bũ
kwôk	kôi	guo	kuh	bôk
gekš	tyêi	git	k'iç	ɣeş
lak	lai	la	reh	nak
mêrê?	mrá → trâ	meu	biri	pêr
mogw	môu	mut	bug	pog

nêkwa	nyâu	nega	dike	tewka
nôk	nôi	no	duh	tôk
ŋap	nyau	ya	gef	ñap
ŋwop	yôu	wu	nuf	ŋop
ŋwan	yam	wan	nen	ŋã
sik	sei	sai	zah	hik
tan	tam	dan	ten	sã
tugw	tou	daut	tog	sug
waku	ko	a	peko	wak
wan	am	an	pen	wã
xuro?	ȟrô → rô	šau	foru	hur
xwañ	ȟa	šuan	pea	waŋ
xwêk	ȟâi	šue	pih	wôk

The main idea here is to use a small number of sound changes, but fairly spectacular ones that affect the whole phoneme inventory. Thus, without too much work we get a set of derived words that look quite different; that's quite sufficient for a set of naming languages.

Sound changes to get you started

You're sitting in front of SCA^2 but coming up blank: what sound changes do you apply? Well, as an idea bank, here are some actual sound changes. Mix and match freely!

I've included sample SCA^2 rules for each.

- LENITION. The most basic tool in your workshop— very many sound changes involve sounds getting weaker (Latin *lenis* 'soft'). Examples:

  ° stops become affricates: Latin *vōcem* /woːkem/ 'voice' → Italian *voce* /voče/

  ° stops become fricatives: Latin *cēra* /keːra/ 'wax' → French *cire* /sir/

  ° Unvoiced consonants are voiced: Latin *amīcus* 'friend' → Spanish *amigo*

  ° Stops erode into glottal stops, or h. E.g. English *bottle* → dialectal /baʔl/; Old Japanese *pa* → Japanese *ha*.

  ° The ultimate lenition is loss; e.g. Latin /h/ simply disappeared; Latin /b, d, g/ usually disappeared inter-vocalically in French (*rūga* 'furrow' → *rue* 'street').

The intervocalic position is especially prone to change.

S/Z/V_V

- PALATALIZATION. Consonants can palatalize before or after a front vowel *i e* or /j/, perhaps ending up as an affricate or fricative; e.g. Middle Chinese **kjɐŋ* → Mandarin *jīng* 'capital' as in *Běijīng*.

  k/č/_F

- MONOPHTHONGIZATION. Diphthongs tend to simplify, as in Southern American English *I* /aj/ → /a/. This rule is fun to apply *after* letting the vanished sounds affect adjoining consonants.

  W=yw
  W//CV_C

- ASSIMILATION. Consonants change to match the place or type of articulation of an adjoining consonant, e.g. Japanese *donburi* 'rice dish' → *domburi*.

  D=td
  m/n/_D

- NASALIZATION. A nasal consonant can disappear, after nasalizing the previous vowel; e.g. Latin *bene* 'well' → French *bien* /bjɛ/.

  Â=âêîôû
  N=mn
  V/Â/_N
  N//Â_

- UMLAUT. A vowel changes to match the rounding of the next vowel in the word; e.g. Old High German *hōhiro* 'higher' → German *höher*.

  u/ü/_C(C)i

- VOWEL SHIFTS. One vowel can migrate into a free area of the vowel space, perhaps dragging others behind it. An example is English's Great Vowel Shift, in which low long vowels raised (*meet* → /mit/) and /i:/ and /u:/ diphthongized; that's why our vowels are out of step with the 'Continental' ones.

  a/æ/_

o/a/_
u/o/_

- TONOGENESIS. One way tones can originate is for voiced consonants to induce the next vowel to be pronounced in a low pitch.

  Z=bdgzvmnlr
  V=aiu
  L=àìù
  V/L/Z_

- LOSS of unstressed syllables; e.g. Vulgar Latin *apicula* 'bee' →
  Spanish *abeja*.

  A=āēīōū
  V//AC(C)_

- Loss of final sounds, as in Latin *bucca* → French *bouche* /buʃ/
  'mouth'. This can wreak delightful havoc on your carefully
  worked out inflectional system.

  V//_#

Irregular changes

Some changes are inherently irregular.

- DISSIMILATION takes one of two identical sounds and changes
  it. For instance, Latin *arbor* becomes Spanish *arbol*. The near-
  adjacent nasals in Proto-Germanic **heman-* 'heaven' seem to
  have been problematic; English changed the first (*heaven*), German the second (*Himmel*).

  The consonant need not change *much*; e.g. both changes to
  *heman- just remove the nasality, leaving the place of articulation unchanged.

- METATHESIS is the switching of two sounds. E.g. Latin *miracu-
  lum* became Spanish *milagro*; Old English *frīst* became English
  first.

- REANALYSIS involves reinterpreting, or misinterpreting, how a
  word or phrase is parsed.

  ° Often articles are the culprit. English *apron* was originally
    napron; but *a napron* was reanalyzed as *an apron*. Similarly

Italian *una narancia* 'an orange' (from Arabic *naranj*) became *una arancia*.

° *Peas* was originally a mass noun, deriving ultimately from Latin *pisa*. But it was reinterpreted as a plural, giving us a new singular *pea*. Similarly, *kudos* is a singular noun in Greek, but sounds to English speakers like a plural; they are therefore tempted to grant someone a *kudo*.

° Reanalysis affects derivational morphology too. For instance, *alcoholic* simply derives from *alcohol* plus the adjectivizer *-ic*. But popular coinages like *chocoholic* or *shopoholic* reanalyze *-oholic* as an affix meaning 'addict'.

- FOLK ETYMOLOGY is a form of reanalysis: an unfamiliar word is taken as if it was made of native roots. E.g. Algonquian *oček* sounded to English speakers like *woodchuck*.

- BACK-FORMATION reanalyzes what looks like a compound form, producing a simple but unhistorical 'root'. Examples are *laze, emote, burgle* from *lazy, emotion, burglar*.

- LEVELLING is the reduction of irregularities by generalizing one of multiple variant forms. Consider this Germanic paradigm:

	Old English	English	Old High German	German
pres.	*cēozan*	*choose*	*kiosan*	*küren*
past sg.	*cēas*	*chose*	*kaus*	*kor*
past pl.	*curon*	*chose*	*kurun*	*koren*
past part.	*ge-coren*	*chosen*	*gi-koran*	*gekoren*

Both languages had an alternation between /s/ and /r/, and in Old English also /z/. English has generalized /z/ and German /r/ in all forms.

- ANALOGY replaces an irregular form with a regular one based on some other, more common, set of forms. For instance, consider 'stone' and 'cow' and their plurals in Old English:

stān   stānas
cū   kyn

Plurals with *-n* were common in Old English. We've inherited a few of them (*children, brethren*), but mostly we've generalized the *stān : stānas* pattern. The natural development of the above in Modern English would be

stone   stones
cow   kine

but for most purposes we've replaced *kine* with *cows*, by analogy.

- A related change is CONTAMINATION, where a word is modified to resemble a related word. For instance:

  ° French *mâle* / *femelle* has been borrowed into English as rhyming *male* / *female*.

  ° Proto-Indo-European *newn* / *dekm* 'nine, ten' should have become Latin *noven* / *decem*; but 'nine' became *novem* instead to match 'ten'.

Going backwards

I strongly advise starting with the ancestor language and deriving daughters from it. It's easier and produces a more coherent family.

But very possibly you'll want to go the other way as well— in fact that's just what happened with Verdurian; I had to back-derive its parent Cađinor and its grandparent Proto-Eastern.

Ideally you should still use SCA^2 and have regular sound changes for each daughter. Take the Verdurian *mólnia* 'lightning'. Where might this have come from?

- *mólnia*— possible but dull

- *molenia, molinia, molunia*, etc.— that is, an unstressed vowel was lost, and working backwards we're restoring it. But make sure that other unstressed vowels get reduced too!

- *molenga* — i.e. Ver. /nj/ derives from an earlier cluster.

- *maulnia, molneia*— i.e. the parent vowels were more complex

- *monelia*— i.e. the consonants were switched

- *molnida, mirolnia*— i.e. entire consonants or syllables were lost

Working backwards is something of an art; you have to consider multiple possibilities, and yet avoid inventing rules just for one word. E.g. if you decide on *ng* → *ny*, make sure other examples of *ng* also change to *ny*. I had a Cađinor lexicon and Verdurian sound changes, and kept modifying the input words, the rules, and occasionally the outputs until it all fit together. (But this is why the Cađinor to Verdurian sound changes are so extensive, much more so than if I was working forwards.)

What if you just can't get a plausible parent for a word? You can try several strategies:

- Change the daughter form. (In fact I did this with *mólnia*; the old form was *äzt*, which I no longer liked anyway and which didn't produce nice ancestral forms.)

- Derive it from an alternate ancient form. E.g. for *süro* 'cheese' I didn't like the most likely ancestral form *suiro*, so I decided the Caďinor was *siuro*, and the Verdurian derived from a metathesized variant.

- Maybe the standard language borrowed it from a different dialect. E.g. the -*uo*- in *luom* 'apple was hard to explain. I decided the original was just *lomos*, but that *luom* derived from a dialect that tended to diphthongize certain vowels.

- It's a reborrowing— e.g. I decided that *alcalë* 'treasure' was a reborrowing of *alcalie*, largely because -*alc*- was hard to derive, since I had a sound change $l \rightarrow u$ / _[+stop].

- It's a borrowing from another language.

- Leave it for later! I still have an "underivables" file for Verdurian. This is perfectly naturalistic; we don't know where some English words come from either!

Look for patterns, even if you hadn't considered them such when creating the target language. For instance, I had a few Verdurian nouns inexplicably ending in -*ta*: *šrifta* 'knowledge, *oresta* 'truth'. Then I noticed that words like *nurža* 'food' could derive from Caďinor *nuricta*. I decided that -*ta* marked collective nouns; e.g. *scrifta* 'was 'all that is known', *nuricta* was 'all that is provided'. I liked this so much that I altered other words to match— e.g. I changed Verdurian *falahno* 'army' to *falata* so it could be the collective of Caďinor *falañ* 'soldier'.

As with working forward, don't stop with the lexicon. Were there major typological distinctions— e.g. the parent is SVO and agglutinative, and the daughter SOV and fusional, or vice versa?

What distinctions in morphology and syntax might have been lost? Which might have been innovated? As a rule of thumb, whatever is most regular is a good candidate for an innovation. E.g. the Verdurian conditional, based on a constant suffix -*cel*, suggested that this was developed since Cadinor— unlike (say) the personal verb endings, which were too quirky to be innovations.

Writing systems

Historically, writing systems first appear as LOGOGRAPHS, then SYLLABARIES, CONSONANTAL ALPHABETS, TRUE ALPHABETS, and FEATURAL SYSTEMS. I'll discuss each of these below.

Preliminaries

First let's consider some topics that apply to all writing systems.

Bits of writing

I'll use the word GLYPH to refer to one of the basic graphic elements of the system— e.g. letters, in an alphabet; characters, in a logographic system.

Brackets can be used to make it clear we're talking about glyphs as glyphs— e.g. the letter <b>, or <α> for the Greek letter alpha, or <中> for the Chinese character *zhōng* 'middle'. Sometimes it's convenient to use the transliteration instead of the original character, so we might write <zhōng> for <中>.

Glyphs can often be decomposed into smaller parts which have meaning as part of the script; these can be called GRAPHEMES. Diacritic marks are examples; the umlaut ¨ can be applied to various other letters. Chinese characters are almost all composites of simpler characters.

Medium

What's the prototypical way your culture writes? This will affect the look of the script.

Most of us learned to write using **pens and pencils**, which produce a line of uniform thickness. You can certainly design your glyphs this way, but you may not be aware that the medium is imposing a certain aesthetic.

The quintessential form of our upper case letters are Roman inscriptions **carved in stone**. The SERIFS or widened areas at the ends of a stroke are artifacts of this.

SENATVSPOPVLVSQVEROMANVS

Carving also favors straight lines— even more so rough carving in wood; thus the linearity of runes.

ᚠᚾᚦᚨᚱᚲ

Our lower case letters were formed by and for writing with a bias-cut **quill pen**, held at a low angle. A calligraphic pen produces similar results. Such pens produce a natural variation between thick and thin strokes.

Calligraphy

The angle at which the pen is held has an effect— for standard Hebrew letters, the pen is held such that pure horizontals are the thickest.

רבי משה בן מימון

Writing with a pen is a fast process which encourages running the glyphs together, forming a CURSIVE hand.

Марк Розенфельд

Traditionally Tamil was written with a **stylus on palm leaves**. This encouraged the use of curves, as angular strokes tended to rip the leaves.

சிற்றில் நற்றூண் பற்றி நின் மகன்

Chinese calligraphy is done using a **brush**, which is correctly handled by moving the whole arm rather than the wrist and fingers. This encourages a curvy, flowing calligraphy with great variations in stroke size.

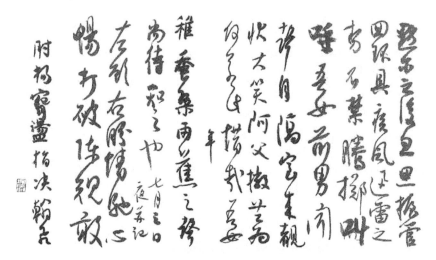

The Sumerians formed letters with a CUNEIFORM (wedge-shaped) stylus **pressed into clay**. (The other end was a circle, and numbers were written using the circular impressions thus formed.) They started by incising lines in the clay, but as you may remember from grade school, this is a fairly awkward process— pressing the stylus is much faster. To speed it up even more, the range of angles was highly limited.

Egyptian hieroglyphics were **painted**, which allowed fairly elaborate little pictures in color. For everyday use they wrote much simplified forms in ink on papyrus.

The development of **metal type** allowed standardized shapes; these first imitated handwriting, but the process has few limitations, and FONTS could be produced that would be quite difficult to draw. For that matter, aesthetics were no longer dominated by the quill pen; to many people a uniform SANS-SERIF font looked particularly modern.

Helvetica

Courier

Playbill

Curlz

Tekton

Computer fonts allow even more possibilities, many yet untried: fonts with embedded colors, for instance, or animated shapes (e.g. all those ads with slowly moving or expanding letters). Very early fonts were made with small numbers of pixels, and some fonts imitate this look.

Ultra modern

Venice

New York

Direction

We're so used to writing left to right, top to bottom that we may forget that there are alternatives. Right to left, for instance. Chinese was traditionally written top to bottom, right to left.

Some people wrote alternate lines right to left and left to right— reversing the characters so you could see what direction each line went in. The process has a cute name— BOUSTROPHEDON, as an ox plows.

Variation

Like speech, writing varies by person, by region, and over time.

Consider all the variants that we can easily recognize as instance of the letter U:

We very likely have a prototype U that we compare these to— perhaps something like a sans-serif U. Like Saussurian words, letterforms are constrained by their relationship to other glyphs— e.g. U has to be rounded on the bottom so it's not confused with V, or at least wider; it has to be more open at the top lest it become an N; the two sides can't be too different in height or else it'll start looking like a J or L.

The nature of the prototype can change over time. Consider the early development of the Brāhmī glyph *ṇa* in India over more than two millennia:

First the letter was written with two curves rather than three straight lines. The northerners then joined the two curves, allowing the letter to be written in one stroke. This produced a squarish form in the middle which seems to have been reinterpreted as part of the prototype of the glyph— in later centuries it's accentuated, and then re-simplified into a prong.

In the south the glyph was simplified differently— the top developed separately from the bottom, which developed a little loop. Finally the whole letter was replaced with a single complex curve.

There seems to be some tendency for each language to develop its own writing system— there are over a dozen derivatives of Brāhmī script, for instance. Even in Europe, Germany had very distinctive letters (Fraktur) till the last century. In the West the process may have been arrested by the development of printing, which encouraged standardization.

Conservativism

Writing systems encourage retention of old forms in language. When the classics are written down their lexicon and syntax are readily available as standards, perhaps for thousands of years.

The process applies to the writing system itself. For instance, in 12th century French 'they have' was [tiɛnənt] which was written, perfectly reasonably, as *tiennent*. But it's written the same way today, when the pronunciation is [tjɛn].

Such conservativism isn't always a bad thing, since it preserves spellings of a root across morphological changes. E.g. *photograph, photography* keep the root <photograph> though none of the vowels are the same: ['fotəgræf] vs. [fə'tagrəfi]. Similarly Italian *dico, dici* 'I say, you say' keep the root <dic> though the pronunciations are [diko, ditʃi].

Such an orthography is called MORPHOPHONEMIC, recognizing that it reflects morphology as well as phonemics.

Completeness

Designing a writing system, you're well advised to represent all the phonemic contrasts in the language... at the least, this is what you need to pronounce the words correctly yourself! But historically, writing systems don't always match this ideal.

The first writing system used to represent Greek, for instance, Linear B, didn't represent the voiced/unvoiced or aspirated/unaspirated distinctions of Greek consonants, nor the length of Greek vowels. And to boot, it tended not to write final consonants. E.g. the word *ant^{h}rōk^{w}ōi* 'man (dat.)' was written with the glyphs <a-to-ro-qo>.

Prosodic features like stress and tone are often omitted: though stress accent is phonemic in Italian and Russian and English, it's not indicated in the orthography. Swedish and Japanese don't indicate their pitch-accent systems, and though pīnyīn romanization of Chinese does represent tone, the tone marks are often omitted.

Even if a writing system captures the phonology, it leaves out other aspects of speech— loudness, tempo, intonation, pauses, the modulations that allow us to infer sarcasm or anger or teasing.

On the other hand, writing systems can indicate things that aren't part of the spoken language— distinguishing homonyms, adding punctuation to clarify clause structure or the meaning of sentences, indicating word boundaries. Sumerian writing enclosed each sentence in a little box, while Egyptian hieroglyphics drew one around proper names.

Producing fonts

So how do you show your pretty scripts to the world?

One way is to draw them and scan them. This is probably the best bet for logographic systems, or ones with a heavy emphasis on calligraphy, but it's awkward for extended use.

Or you can produce a computer font (such as the Verdurian one below). This is the easiest way to produce large blocks of text. Available programs change too quickly to recommend one in a book; I'll maintain some current suggestions on the web resources page.

Another option is to use a vector graphics program such as Illustrator, which I've used for some of the examples in this section. This is more work than drawing, but the results are much neater, and can easily be cut and pasted into a document.

Alphabets

ALPHABETS are easy— just create a glyph for each phoneme! Since your conpeople use their own alphabet, not ours, the orthography you've used till now becomes a TRANSLITERATION of the native writing system.

Here's the alphabet I came up with for Verdurian:

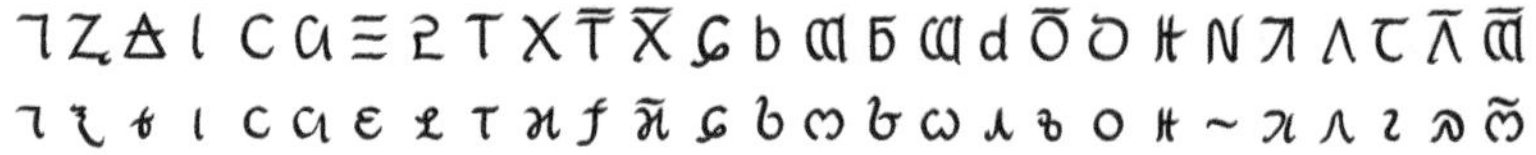

u a o e i y k ř p c b g d s š z č t d̂ r h l m f n v ž

There's a one-to-one correspondence between the Verdurian alphabet and the standard English transliteration. This isn't entirely naturalistic— transliteration schemes are not usually this straightforward— but it's a good place to start. Once you can fluently read your own alphabet, feel free to add complications.

A good alphabet can't be created in a day. This one took shape over a period of weeks, as I played with various letterforms.

Keep the letters looking distinct. The best alphabets spread out over the conceptual graphic space, so that letters can't be confused for one another. Tolkien is a bad example here: the elves must have been tormented by dyslexia. If letters start to approach each other too closely, users find ways to distinguish them, in the way that computer programmers, for instance, write zeroes with a slash. Europeans write <1> with an elaborate introductory swash— impossible to confuse with <I>, but looking much like a <7>, which has therefore acquired a horizontal slash!

 17

Remember that letters are written over and over again, over the life of an individual or a civilization. Elaborate letters are likely to be simplified. You can simulate this process by writing the letter over and over yourself; the appropriate simplifications will suggest themselves automatically.

Verdurian has UPPER and LOWER CASE forms, as in the Roman and Greek alphabets. The lower case forms are all cursive simplifications of the upper case forms (which are the ancient forms— e.g. <𝔁> c is a worn-down form of <X> C). In retrospect I probably shouldn't have imitated the mixed-case system, which on our world is basically limited to Western alphabets. I should have kept the 'upper case' forms for ancient times, the 'lower case' forms for modern times.

The letters have individual histories, as with our alphabet. The letter <d> t, for instance, derives from a picture of a cup ☌, *touresiu* in Cuêzi; <Ϲ> n was originally a picture of a foot ☋ (*nega*). I have to admit that I did this backwards— I invented pictographs that could have developed into the letters, which I had devised years before!

In upper case, the voiced consonants are simply the unvoiced forms with a bar over them (this is a bit obscured with <Ō> d and <d> t), and the letters <ɑɑɑɑ> č š ž are all transparent variations of each other. This slightly violates my 'maximally distinct' rule, but I think it adds interest to the alphabet.

You'll also notice both c and k in the alphabet. This is the sort of ethnocentrism it's all too easy to fall into. Why would another language duplicate the convoluted history of our alphabet's c and k? I've reinterpreted these symbols to refer to /k/ and /q/.

On starting with alphabets

If you have a pedantic nature, be aware that alphabets don't come out of the ether; they develop from one of the earlier systems. If you think you'll eventually develop the ancestral system, you might avoid future headaches by making your characters the worn-down versions of pictographs. For instance, our M derives from the early Semitic letter *mēm* which seems to depict *majim* 'water', by means of a stylized wave still preserved in our letterform.

> **Reading about writing**
>
> Before creating anything fancier than an alphabet, I recommend reading more on the subject. Geoffrey Sampson's *Writing Systems* is an excellent overview. Peter T. Daniels and William Bright's *The World's Writing Systems* is huge but authoritative.

Consonantal alphabets

The earliest alphabet, that of the Semitic peoples of around 1250 C.E., represented only consonants. Peter T. Daniels suggests the term ABJAD for this type of writing.

𐤘 𐤙 ∧ △ 𐤀 𐤲 Y I 𐤒 ⊕ 𐤊 𐤉 𐤁 𐤋 𐤼𐤼 𐤉 ‡ O 𐤂 𐤔 𐤟 𐤟 𐤟 W +

א ב ג ד ה ו ז ח ט י כ ל מ נ ס ע פ צ ק ר ש ת

ʔ b g d h w z ħ ṭ j k l m n s ʕ p ç q r š t

The top row shows an early form of the abjad; the second shows modern Hebrew forms, and the third is a transliteration. If bits of the order seem familiar, it's because this alphabet— with intermediate stops among the Greeks and Etruscans— was adapted to become our Roman alphabet.

The system is used today for writing Hebrew and Arabic— though this statement requires immediate caveats. Arabic and classical Hebrew did find ways of representing the long vowels, and for teaching purposes there are ways to represent the short vowels.

An abjad fits the Semitic languages rather neatly, because roots are consonantal— e.g. Arabic KTB represents a wide range of forms referring to writing and books (p. 54). (This is preserved by the optional representations of short vowels in both languages: the additional marks are placed above or below the consonants, not between them.)

The Semitic abjad was adopted by the Greeks. Greek has a very different linguistic structure where vowels are more important. Nonetheless it may have developed letters for vowels by a sort of misunderstanding. The Semitic letters follow the ACROPHONIC principle: their names begin with the sound in question, e.g. *bēt* for ב <b>. Some of the letters adopted by the Greeks for vowels have Semitic names that begin with non-Greek sounds— e.g. א *ʔālep* begins with the glottal stop ʔ. One can imagine a Greek hearing a Phoenecian trying to explain the system, understanding the acrophonic principle, but simply not recognizing [ʔ] as a sound. It would be easy to understand the letter as referring to [a], and indeed the letter became Greek <α> *alpha*.

Abugidas

A variant of the consonantal alphabet is the ABUGIDA (taken from the initial four letters of Geʿez script). Here there is a separate glyph for each consonant, and a diacritic is added for each vowel.

For instance, here are the glyphs for pV syllables in Devanāgarī, the script used for Hindi:

प पि पु पृ पा पी पू पॄ पे पो पै पौ
pa pi pu pr pā pī pū pr̄ pe po pai pau

A curious feature of many of these scripts is that a bare symbol includes a following vowel; to indicate a consonant with no following vowel (e.g. word-finally) a diacritic must be used: bare p is written प्.

Like a syllabary, an abugida has a separate glyph for each CV combination (and often for CCV syllables as well), but the glyphs are composed of two or more graphemes, one per phoneme.

Logograms

The earliest writing systems— Egyptian, Sumerian, Chinese, and Mesoamerican— were all LOGOGRAPHIC— i.e. a glyph represents a single word.

Early reports suggested these systems are IDEOGRAPHIC— that they somehow directly represent ideas. This is quite wrong! All of these writing systems represent **words** in specific languages.

All four systems start with PICTOGRAPHS— glyphs which represent the word pictorially.

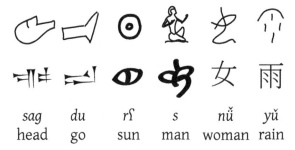

sag	du	rſ	s	nǔ	yǔ
head	go	sun	man	woman	rain

The pictures don't stay pictorial for long. The illustration shows early and late forms of the same glyph.

- The left two examples are Sumerian, showing the progression from drawings incised in clay to cuneiform symbols stamped with a stylus.

- The next two are Egyptian: the top row shows HIEROGLYPHIC, the middle is the cursive HIERATIC script. The Egyptian words had vowels, but we don't know what they were.

- The final two are Chinese— still in use today.

Pictures may be abstractions; e.g. Chinese <上> shàng 'above' started out as a picture of a dot above a line. The Sumerians used the picture of a foot both for 'foot' and 'go'.

Extending the system

Not everything is easily pictured. But once you have a repertoire of pictographs, they can be extended in several ways:

- Highlighting or emphasizing part of the picture. E.g. Sumerian *ka* 'mouth' was represented by a drawing of the head with hash marks over the location of the mouth.

- Combining signs by meaning. E.g. Sumerian < ⊢ > *munus* 'woman' + < 𝍏 > *kur* 'mountain' formed < ⊢ 𝍏 > *geme* 'slave girl', since female slaves were taken from the mountains. Chinese <東> *dōng* 'east' is a picture of the sun <日> *rì* seen behind a tree <木> *mù*.

- The REBUS PRINCIPLE— using homonyms (or near-homonyms). E.g. Sumerian < ⊢⊨‖ > *su* 'body' made do for *su* 'replace'; Chinese <来> *lái* 'wheat' was used for *lái* 'come'.

Most of these writing systems included at least two-syllable words: e.g. Sumerian *dingir* 'god', Egyptian *mṣḏr* 'ear', and Maya *kawaw* 'helmet'. However, all three had a large store of one-syllable words that allowed a wide range of homonymic substitutions, and Chinese seems to have always represented a single syllable with a single glyph.

You could easily develop a syllabary from this principle— and in all four systems it's been done, in derived systems at least. However, none of them were entirely replaced by syllabaries. Chinese <失> *shī* 'lose', <十> *shí* 'ten', <石> *shí* 'stone', <市> *shì* 'market', <世> *shì* 'life, world', and <事> *shì* 'matter', for instance, are represented by entirely different characters. As a result John deFrancis proposes the term MORPHOSYLLABIC for Chinese, reflecting the fact that in almost all cases a single character (*zì*) represents a single syllable and a single morpheme.

Clarifying signs

The extension principles above can produce a good deal of ambiguity. This can be reduced by adding additional signs.

- A DETERMINATIVE, or a RADICAL as it's called in Chinese, selects a class of meanings. For instance, Sumerian had determinatives for gods, male names, female names, places, and so on. Chinese has over two hundred radicals.

- A PHONETIC COMPLEMENT (or just PHONETIC) adds a phonological clue. For instance, Sumerian < ⊬ > could represent *dingir* 'god' or *an* 'sky'. To ensure the correct reading, a scribe might add a glyph whose phonetic reading corresponded to the final consonant of the intended word: <*ra*> for *dingir*, <*na*> for *an*.

The vast majority of Chinese characters consist of two graphemes, a radical giving the overall meaning class, and a phonetic indicating the rough pronunciation— rough because rhymes were acceptable.

For instance, <中> by itself refers to *zhōng* 'middle', as seen in 中国 *Zhōngguó* 'the middle country, China'. Add the <禾> *hé* 'crop' radical and you get <种> *zhòng* 'grow'. Note that the *meaning* of <中> contributes nothing to <种>; it's used only for its pronunciation *zhōng*.

<国> *guó* 'country' has the traditional form 國, which has the radical < □> *wéi* 'enclosure' and the phonetic <或> *hùo* 'region'.

"If English was written like Chinese", on my website, explores how a logographic system could be devised for English. See the web resources page, or go directly to:

http://www.zompist.com/yingzi/yingzi.htm

Syllabaries

A SYLLABARY contains a glyph for each possible syllable. A good example is *hiragana*, one of the *kana* systems of Japanese (next page).

Syllabaries are very appropriate for languages like Japanese with simple syllable structure; they'd be quite inconvenient for English or Russian.

In a true syllabary, the glyphs for (say) initial **k**- or final -**a** have nothing in common. In fact each *hiragana* glyph developed from a Chinese character used for its sound. <い> *i*, for instance, derives from <以> 'by', from Chinese *yǐ* 'use'.

あ	a	い	i	う	u	え	e	お	o
か	ka	き	ki	く	ku	け	ke	こ	ko
さ	sa	し	shi	す	su	せ	se	そ	so
た	ta	ち	chi	つ	tsu	て	te	と	to
な	na	に	ni	ぬ	nu	ね	ne	の	no
は	ha	ひ	hi	ふ	fu	へ	he	ほ	ho
ま	ma	み	mi	む	mu	め	me	も	mo

や ya		ゆ yu		よ yo
ら ra	り ri	る ru	れ re	ろ ro
わ wa				を o
ん -n				

Note the sound changes in the **s-** and **t-** rows (and a few other places).

Featural systems

A FEATURAL script encodes not phonemes but phonetic features. For instance, there might be a symbols for **p t k**, which are systematically modified by graphemes to form voiced **b d g** and fricative **f s x**.

Korean Han'kul is essentially a featural system.

	labial	dental	palatal	velar	glottal
nasals	ㅁ m	ㄴ n			ㅇ ŋ
lax stops	ㅂ p	ㄷ t	ㅈ c	ㄱ k	
aspirated stops	ㅍ pʰ	ㅌ tʰ	ㅊ cʰ	ㅋ kʰ	
tensed stops	ㅃ p'	ㄸ t'	ㅆ c'	ㄲ k'	
fricatives			ㅅ s		ㅎ h
			ㅉ s'		
liquid		ㄹ l			

The basic forms are < ㅁ ㄴ ㅅ ㄱ ㅇ > **m n s k ŋ**, one per place of articulation. The forms evoke the phonetics: < ㅁ > **m** is a picture of the mouth, < ㄴ ㄱ > **n k** picture the tongue touching different points along the inside of the mouth, < ㅅ > **s** represents a tooth, and < ㅇ > **ŋ** is a circle representing the throat.

The general rule is to add a horizontal line for the lax stops, two lines for the aspirated stops, and to double the symbol for the tensed consonants.

< ㅇ > only has the value /ŋ/ at the end of a syllable; at the beginning it has no value at all— it marks syllables that begin with a vowel. There's a reason for this, but it's a long story— see Sampson's *Writing Systems* for more.

The vowels were originally abstract symbols: a dot · for /ʌ/, a horizontal line — for /ɯ/, and a vertical line | for /i/. The other vowels were combinations of dots and lines. This system has been graphically simplified (the dots are now little strokes) and somewhat distorted by sound change.

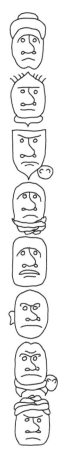

For my conlang Elkarîl, I invented a featural system using columns of faces, such as those at the right, which represents the sentence

Ruch phimqebat tul-kugg p-têt-jênat lek.

I climb the mountains, but I have no feet.

Each face represents a syllable. The shapes of the top and bottom of the face give the initial and final consonants (e.g. a pointed shape is /p/; a square one is /q/). A hat or neckpiece is used for nasals; a soft turban or cravat for liquids. Voicing is represented with an additional line above the brows or below the mouth; implosives by doubling the line; fricatives by adding hair.

The vowels are indicated by the facial expression— e.g. /u/ in the top face has a sad expression; /i/ in the next one down is neutral.

The suffix *–at* (seen in two words here) marks pronominal reference and has a special representation (the little circle to the bottom right). The ear on one face is the prefix *p-*.

For a full explanation see

http://www.zompist.com/elkwrite.htm

Punctuation

Some scripts have or had no punctuation at all, not even spaces for word boundaries.

We mark off several kinds of sentences— statements, questions, exclamations. You could extend this to other speech acts. How about signals of evidentiality or importance?

Very roughly, commas mark pauses. What other aspects of intonation or sentence structure could be captured?

We use boldface and italics in various ways. Think about alternatives... e.g. Russian typography instead d r a w s   o u t words for emphasis.

Comics often play with the way words are represented— e.g. Walt Kelly used black letter to suggest one character's stentorian speech style, and drew a huckster's speech balloons to resemble circus posters.

Kebreni

This chapter contains the complete reference grammar of one of my conlangs, Kebreni, with director's commentary. I'll explain where some of the ideas came from, some linguistic highlights, and why I made the choices I did.

To cut down on bulk I've removed all but a sample of the lexicon, and some of the details of Meťaiun, Kebreni's ancestor.

Why Kebreni? Well, unlike Verdurian, it's short enough to fit in the book; and Kebreni was sort of a playground for trying out non-Indo-European features, so it makes an interesting example.

The Monkhayic family of languages, though now restricted to Kebri and the southwestern corner of Dhekhnam, was once spoken throughout the Plain, and indeed has left its linguistic traces heavily on the map of the Plain. The Mišicama ocean, the Ctelm mountains, the Svetla, Menla, Vesi, Meuna, and Efrat rivers, the nations of Ismahi, Azgami, Koto, Melináe, and Érenat, lake Como, the Arosd delta, and the cities of Kebropol, Lädau, Avéla, Ydamai, Raizumi, Nuveta, Kereta, Mituré, Gödo, Mogör, Melahdo, Trežda, Mabola, and Pelym all have Monkhayic names.

> A grammar customarily places its language in context: where is it found, what family does it belong to, why is it important.

> Though Kebreni is a living language, its ancestor forms a SUBSTRATE LANGUAGE in the Plain: the later invaders (themselves the ancestors of the Verdurians) took many place names and other words from the people they conquered.

The first states of men in the Plain were Monkhayic: **Como** and **Metaiu** on the upper Svetla. By the time they appeared, men had lived in the Plain for twenty thousand years, and the Monkhayic peoples were divided into dozens of mutually incompatible languages.

Civilization and trade spread the prestigious dialects of the cities, and just before the Eastern invasion we are aware of three major speech varieties: that of **Okiami** and **Metaiu** in the south, that of **Davur** along the lower Svetla, and that of **Ažimbea** and **Newor** along the Serea and the Mišicama littoral.

The Easterners pushed the Monkhayic peoples (those who were not absorbed) north and east (-375). Refugees from Davur established the kingdom of **Davrio** on Kebri.

Most of these lands were then conquered by Munkhâsh (440), except for the littoral (reorganized as **Leziunea**) and Kebri.

The continental Monkhayic peoples (and, for about two centuries, even Kebri) were incorporated into the Cadinorian empire as it pushed back and ultimately destroyed Munkhâsh, and though the Monkhayic languages persisted throughout the entire classical area, colonization and Cadinorization eventually replaced Monkhayic languages everywhere except two areas, **Kebri** (plus some regions of Érenat and, till recently, the island of Koto) and **Monkhay**, the mountainous southwestern corner of Dhekhnam.

> None of this will be on the test; but it's worth emphasizing that Kebri is an island. This both isolated it from mainland influence, and led to it becoming a maritime, commercial nation, both of which influenced its vocabulary.

The relationship between Kebreni and Monkhayu (both the languages and the peoples) has been obscured by long isolation. In addition, Kebreni has been highly influenced by Caðinor, Ismaîn, and Verdurian, and has borrowed from languages further afield, the Kebreni being great seafarers; while Monkhayu is heavily influenced by Dhekhnami, Caizuran, and Sarroc.

> All of these historical details provide hooks for conlanging: borrowings, the creation of dialects or variants.

> The relationship between the advanced Kebreni and the isolated Monkhayu recalls that between the Hungarians and the Khanty or Mansi.

Monkhayu, which has given its name to the language family, simply means "the people"; compare Kebreni *nehada*.

> Many people call themselves The People. The Quechua, for instance: *runa*. And the Germans: *Deutsch*.

Phonology

The **consonants** of modern standard **Kebreni** are as follows.

	labial	dental	palatal	velar	glottal
stops	p	t	c	k	
	b	d		g	
fricatives	f	ŧ s	ħ ś		h
	v	z	ź		
nasals	m	n		ŋ	
liquids		l r			

> The main items of interest here are the palatal series (none of these corresponding to any English sounds) and the six-vowel system. Looking at this years later, I'm a little sorry I didn't provide a palatal ń.

Kebreni is written using the Verdurian alphabet. The orthographic representations of the above sounds are as follows. The non-Verdurian sounds ŧ ħ ś ź [θ ç ç ʑ] are written ø ʋ ɷ ɷ̃.

> Why not use IPA ç ç ʑ? Because they mean nothing to non-linguists; at least h s z will be taken as "something like ħ ś ź". Plus, using h refers to the fact that the Kebreni letter actually is the Caðinor <h>.

	labial	dental	palatal	velar	glottal
stops	τ	⅄	ʮ	Ɛ	
	ʃ	⸂		ʮ̃	
fricatives	⅄	ø ɓ	ʊ ᴄᴏ		ⱪ
	ℛ	ɮ	ᴄᴏ̃		
nasals	ʮ	ɩ			ɿʮ̃
liquids		~ o			

> Leverage previous creations if you can. I already had the Verdurian alphabet, so it was easy to adapt to Kebreni.

c (ʮ) is a true palatal stop /c/, and should not be confused with any sort of affricate.

> I add explanations of any non-obvious transliterations and non-English sounds. If you want to save time, just give the IPA values.

ś, though it's written using the Verdurian š (ᴄᴏ), is an alveolo-palatal fricative [ɕ], the same as the Polish ś or Chinese x. One recipe for producing it is to start with an š and add more palatal friction to it— say š, think [ç]. ꝥ̃) is the voiced equivalent.

h (ⱪ) is pronounced as in English (and Old Verdurian), while **ħ** (ʊ) is a palatal fricative /ç/, as in German *ich*.

k (Ɛ) is pronounced like a Verdurian ʮ /k/, not a Ɛ /q/. Kebreni has sensibly used Cadinor's two back stop symbols for two places of articulation, but they are moved forward one step.

> All right, this is a rationalization of a noob mistake: using both c and k in a language. For Verdurian I reinterpreted these as /k q/, for Kebreni as /c k/. This violates my general advice to avoid transliterations that are pitfalls for English-speaking readers... on the other hand, if you're reading this, you're an advanced student who can handle the information!

> Reinterpreting alphabetic values like this does happen. Pinyin, for instance, uses the two labial stops in the Roman alphabet (p b) for its two labial stops— though these are [pʰ p] rather than [p b]. This was a wise decision— much better than writing pʰ p or p' p, which are ugly and easy to confuse.

ng (ᴢᴕ), pronounced [ŋ], is a fairly marginal phoneme, occurring only between vowels. Some dialects lack it, saying [ŋg] instead.

Doubled consonants (as in **linna** 'lord') are drawn out, as in English *pen knife*, not *penny*.

The **vowels** are these:

	front	back	front	back
high	i y	u	c	cₗ ꓶ
mid	e	o	ι	ϯ
low	a		ⳑ	

y is a high central vowel, partially rounded— a medium between **i** and **u**.

Long **aa** is often written **ä** (ꚃ), as in Verdurian.

> When borrowing an alphabet, a language is likely to borrow its quirks as well.

Stress is placed on the last syllable if it ends in a consonant, otherwise on the second-to-last vowel: **Kébri, Kebropól, pahár, Leléc, śaída, nizýru, Raazám, mýgu, paúśte, kulséu, ingaréi**. Since stress is completely predictable, it is never indicated orthographically.

Kebreni is a SYLLABLE-TIMED language— one where each syllable takes up an equal amount of time— rather than a STRESS-TIMED one like English, where stresses occur at roughly equal intervals. Unstressed syllables in Kebreni retain their clear vowel sounds.

> I think I say that a lot. But that's because English is unusual in its large vowel system which goes heavy on the lax variants. It's what gives English its distinct sound, and makes English speakers sound so bad speaking a multitude of languages.

Morphology

Only verbs (including predicate adjectives) have a true inflectional morphology; nouns and attributive adjectives are not inflected, and the remnants of inflection among the pronouns are not synchronically salient. However, there is a productive derivational morphology.

Verbs

Kebreni verb inflection is quite different from that of the Eastern languages such as Verdurian. Verbs are not inflected for person, number, or tense. Rather, the chief categories of inflection are **aspect**, **politeness**, **volition**, and **effect**.

In addition, inflection is accomplished by vowel interchange, vowel change, and infixing, not by affixation.

> As I've made plenty of fusional languages, Kebreni was a chance to explore features not found in Indo-European languages. If you do multiple languages on a single planet, make sure they show the same variety as earthly languages.

Aspect (imperfective and perfective)

The citation form of the verb is the **imperfective**:

kanu	I see, you see, he was seeing...
diru	I work, you work, he was working...
sudy	I am called, you are called...

> The CITATION FORM of a word is the one that appears in the dictionary. Ideally choose a form which allows all the forms of the word to be generated. In Romance languages, for instance, the citation form for verbs is the infinitive; but for Latin it's the 1s present indicative.

The final **-u** is not part of the root; it's a grammatical ending. It dissimilates to **-y** when the last vowel of the root is **u**, as in *sudy*.

To form the **perfective** you switch the last two vowels. (This relationship holds for all the other forms described below, as well.)

kuna	I have seen, I saw...
duri	I have worked, you worked...
sydu	I was once called...

Perfective forms are used for **completed** actions, no matter what time they occur. Thus you'd use the imperfect **diru** for "I was working", because you weren't done yet; and the perfective **kuna** for "I will read it", if you mean you'll read it and finish.

> Thus Kebreni verbs are modified by ASPECT not time— like Chinese, among many other examples.

An explicit time may always be indicated with adverbs:

> **Pahar kanu pol.** *Tomorrow you will see the city.*
> **Pahar kuna pol.** *Tomorrow you will have seen (everything in) the city.*

Note that Kebreni transitive or ditransitive verbs, used with one less noun phrase, express a passive meaning. Thus

> **Melah <u>kuna</u> neku.** *The king saw the cat.*
> **Neku <u>kuna</u>.** *The cat was seen.*
>
> **Nyne <u>houźi</u> aisel.** *The girl lost the key.*
> **Aisel <u>houzi</u>.** *The key is lost.*
>
> **Gymu <u>sudy</u> kulseu 'Hulo'.** *We call the commander 'Idiot'.*
>
> **Kulseu <u>sudy</u> 'Hulo'.** *The commander is called 'Idiot'.*

> The emphasis (underlining here; I use color on the Web) helps highlight what we're talking about. While you're writing the text you remember what words are what, but the reader doesn't know them.

Schematically:

> NP V_o NP = S V O
> NP V_o = O V
> NP V_{oo} NP NP = S V O O
> NP V_{oo} NP = O V O

Some English verbs work this way as well; but all Kebreni verbs do.

> **Falte śenen <u>truśe</u> lyh.** *Your boy broke the window.*
> **Lyh <u>truśe</u>.** *The window broke.*

> You may have specified whether your language is SVO or OVS or whatever; but can one argument be omitted, and if so what happens to the sentence?

Volition

To form the volitional, add an initial **e**, voice the initial consonant (if any), then switch the first two vowels (that is, the added **e-** plus what was the first vowel of the root). A final **-y** returns to **-u**.

agenu	I intend to see, I will see, see!, ...
agune	I intended to see, I will have seen...
ideru	I intend to work, I will see, work!

idure   I intended to work, I will have worked...

uzedu   I intend to call, I intend to be called...

uzude   I intended to call / no longer be called...

The volitional forms emphasize that the agent consciously **intends** the action (imperfective) or the result (perfective).

> **Pucso** mabu. *I kicked the dog (perhaps accidentally).*
> **Obucse** mabu. *I kicked the dog (on purpose).*

> Japanese has volitional verb forms (though the usage isn't identical to Kebreni). Morphology by vowel interchange is borrowed from Hebrew and Arabic; again, not slavishly.

It is frequently used for a future event (**lahu** 'come' → **alehu** 'I will come'), and by extension as an imperative: **alehu** 'come!' Neither of these extensions is permitted with non-sentient subjects.

> You can always create a special verb form called the "imperative", but don't imagine that this meets all your speakers' needs. More naturalistic is a range of options matching politeness strategies (p. 135).

There is no word for 'want' as an independent lexical item; some volitional expression must be substituted. Often in fact this is **agenu** 'want to see', but other verbs are used as appropriate:

> **Impuźeu agenu bonnezi!** *The publisher wants (lit. wants-to-see) the story!*

> **Linna ezeḣepu gembadi?** *Does His Lordship want (lit. want-to-eat) breakfast?*

> To put it another way, Kebreni GRAMMATICALIZES volition, which we express lexically. In every sentence a Kebreni must be conscious of volition, as we're conscious of person and number.

If the verb begins with a vowel, insert an **h** before the vowel switch: **adnedu** 'I added it' → **ahednedu** 'I added it on purpose'. (**Eśu** 'to not be', discussed later, inserts **v** instead, for historical reasons.)

> You've probably noticed the pseudo-academic tone here. I describe these languages exactly as if they were unknown natural languages. This is a straightforward approach, but you can certainly do something different— a phrasebook, or lessons, for instance.

I wrote a Caďinor grammar in the same style, but the one I posted on the web is something different— a translation of a Verdurian grammar of the language. That allowed me to parody the nationalism, linguistic naivete, and metaphysical concerns typical of our own tradition a couple of centuries ago.

Polite forms

karynu	I see, you see, he sees
kurina	I have seen, you've seen, he's seen
agerynu	I intend to see, I will see, see!
agurine	I intended to see, I will have seen

Polite forms express **deference** toward a superior, or politeness to an equal. They are used with nobles and royalty, employers, military superiors, parents, in-laws, teachers, and so on. In addition the middle and upper classes use it with each other; but man and wife, siblings or cousins, or very close friends do not.

Ḣem <u>cyryru</u>? *Do I know you, sir?*

<u>Alerihu</u>! *Please come!*

Note that the politeness applies to the listener, not to the referent.

Kulseu, falaute mabu <u>furina</u>; neḣat <u>obucrise</u>.

commander / you-SUB dog die-PERF-POL / man kick-PERF-POL

Commander, your dog is dead; a man kicked (it).

Polite forms are made by inserting -**ri**- within the verb root, before the last consonant; -**ry**- if the vowel in the next syllable is a **u**. The infix may divide a consonant cluster: **kulsu** 'command' → **kulrysu**.

In addition there are a few suppletive forms; e.g. **badu** 'eat' has the polite form **seḣepu**; **tasu** 'do' has the polite form **soru**, and so on. (Do not add -**ri**- to the suppletive forms; they are already polite.)

The ideas of polite forms, politeness applying to the listener not the referent, and suppletive polite forms, are all borrowed from Japanese.

Positive effect

The **benefactive** implies that the given action **benefits the speaker** in some way:

keni	someone sees, to my benefit

deri	someone works for me
sidi	someone is called, and it helps or flatters me
syti	someone provides to me

It is formed by fronting the stem vowel (a → e, o →e; u → y, y → i, i → e, e unchanged) and changing the final -u to -i. The perfective, volitional, and polite forms are formed according to the usual rules.

The stem vowel is the last vowel of the root; e.g. **pansyru** 'someone kisses' → **pansiri** 'someone kisses me'. (Verbs with stem **y**, like this one, have identical perfective and imperfective.)

> This would be a flaw in an auxlang; but natural languages do have such mergers. E.g. Spanish *dudamos* 'doubt' (and the corresponding 1p form for all *-ar* verbs) can be either present or past indicative.

To indicate that the action was performed for the benefit of the **listener**, the infix -**ni**- is added before the final consonant of the root:

kenini	someone sees, to your benefit
deniri	someone works for you

Compare:

> Ḣazum diru keda. *Hazum is working on the house.*
>
> Ḣazum <u>deri</u> keda. *Hazum is working on my house.*
>
> Ḣazum <u>deniri</u> keda. *Hazum is working on your house.*
>
> **Kulseu nuzi melaḣ.** *The commander spoke to the King. (from nizu, speak)*
>
> **Kulseu <u>nize</u> melaḣ.** *The commander spoke to the King on my behalf.*
>
> **Kulseu <u>ninize</u> melaḣ.** *The commander spoke to the King on your behalf.*

> The idea of a benefactive comes from Quechua. It also provided a neat way of avoiding having to mark arguments on the verb or with pronouns (this *isn't* modeled on Quechua).

Negative effect

The **antibenefactive** implies that the given action **harmed the speaker** in some way. It's very common in the mouths of Kebrenis and essential for mastering colloquial speech.

kona	someone sees, to my loss
dyra	someone works against me
soda	someone is called, and it harms or insults me
suta	someone provides at my expense
kano	someone saw, has seen, to my loss
dary	someone worked against me
adery	someone purposely worked against me
oseda	they purposely call him that to spite me
loriha	someone is coming to harm me (polite form)

> I think the amount of meaning packed into these words is pretty neat. As always, it's not that we can't express the same thing in English. But compactness of expression, I think, has an effect. Since it's so easy to express whether an action is beneficial or not, the Kebreni would do so much more often than we do.

It is formed by backing the stem vowel (a → o, e → o, i → y; y → u, u → o, o unchanged) and changing the final -u to -a. The perfective, volitional, and polite forms are formed according to the usual rules.

Mabu fano. *The dog went and died on me.*

Hem dyra. *I'm killing myself by working.*

Kona hem. *He watched me (in order to hurt me); he's spied on me.*

Obeka. *Oh, fuck me.*

Again, -ni- can be infixed to indicate that the action was performed to the harm of the **listener**.

Kulseu nyniza. *The commander is speaking against you.*

Lelec pocnisa? *Is Lelec kicking you?*

Subordinating form

The **subordinating** form is used when there is another verb in the sentence. It's formed by moving the final vowel of the verb before the final consonant and adding -**te**. A labial stop becomes dental and a voiced stop becomes unvoiced before the -te (so **m** → **n**, **p/b/d** → **t**, **g** → **c**, **z** → **s**, etc.).

> How are such irregularities created? In this case, they're simply sound changes. These are all examples of assimilation.

kanu 'say' → **kaunte** 'saying'
diru 'work' → **diurte** 'working'
kulsy 'command' → **kulyste** 'commanding'
mimu 'deal' → **miunte** 'dealing'
cihcu 'praise' → **cihucte** 'praising'

> The form and function are more or less borrowed from the Japanese -te form.

> Turning a verb into something more like an adjective is very useful; our participles are instances of the same idea, though the details differ.

This form has several uses. One is with **auxiliary verbs**, which in Kebreni are verbs which can take another verb as a possible object, such as **lecu** 'be able to', **maru** 'probably', **lahu** 'come in order to'. The -**te** form appears before the main verb, and after its objects:

> **Melah kaunte elecu.**
>
> king seeing VOL-able
>
> *The king is able to see you.*

> **Kulseu gorkreha kaunte maru.**
>
> commander ledger seeing be.probable
>
> *The commander is probably reading the ledger.*

> **Tarautte hilu?** *Do you like to dance?*
> **Hem diurte luha.** *I came (in order) to work.*

The **negative** in Kebreni is an auxiliary verb, **esu** (polite **natu**):

> **Hem Hazum cyurte esu.** *I don't know Hazum.*

> **Hazum kulseu kriuhte use.** *Hazum won't kill the commander.*

> **Pahar lauhte natu?** *Aren't you coming tomorrow? (polite)*

> Finnish has a negative auxiliary, *ei.*

Note that volitional, politeness, and aspect inflections normally apply only to the main verb. One can make such finicky distinctions as the following—

diurte lahu	was/is coming to be working
diurte luha	came to be working
duirte lahu	was/is coming to work (and finish)
duirte luha	came to work (and finish)

diurte alehu	is intending to come to work
iderute lahu	is coming intending to work

—but these are rare even in writing; normally only the base form (i.e. **diurte**) is used, and inflections are applied only to the auxiliary. Semantically, they are considered to apply to the auxiliary + verb combination— e.g. for **diurte alehu** the intention is taken to apply to both the coming and the working; while for **diurte luha** the entire action— coming to work— is taken as being completed.

> It's a nice touch to have features that support stylistic variation.

Another usage of the -**te** form is as a *gerund* or modifier. The subordinated verb suggests the manner in which the main action was performed, or simply names a following or resulting action.

Kulseu <u>kaunte</u> nuzi. *The commander spoke watchfully (or, while watching).*

Nyne <u>pabautte</u> taradu. *The girl was laughing and dancing.*

Ťaza mabu <u>krihute</u> pucso.

they dog killing kick-PERF

They kicked the dog to death.

Ḣulo cihucte <u>diurte</u> eśu.

fool praising working not-IMP

The fool works without praising (God).

> This is somewhat like the Mandarin resultative, though once I had the subordinating form it was easy to multiply uses for it.

Finally -**te** is used to form *relative clauses*. In this usage volitional, aspect, and effect inflections (but not those relating to politeness) can be applied to the subordinating form. Note that the clause precedes the modified noun.

Neḣat duri keda. *The man worked on the house →*

[Diurte keda] nehat alehu pahar.

[work-SUB house] man come-VOL tomorrow

The man [who worked on the house] will come tomorrow.

Kulseu nazy nehat. *The commander spoke against me to the man*
→

[Kulseu nayste] nehat sudy Kalum.

[commander spoke-ANTIB-SUB] man name Kalum

The man [the commander spoke to against me] is named Kalum.

Melah baku nyne. *The king is fucking the girl* →

[Melah baukte] nyne hilu hente mabu.

[king fuck-SUB] girl likes my dog

The girl [the king is fucking] is fond of my dog.

There is no relativizing pronoun. Note that if the subordinated verb is preceded by a subject, as in the last two sentences, the head of the clause must be taken as a direct or indirect object; if the verb begins the clause, as in the first example, the head must be the subject of the clause. Schematically:

NP Vte NP = [S V] O
Vte NP NP = [V O] S

If the head noun refers to a place or time, the phrase is equivalent to a **when** or **where** clause in English— again, these pronouns do not appear in Kebreni:

[vaac mygu moiutte] hahc

[blue ox find-SUB] valley

the valley [where the blue ox was found]

[pocuste melah] re

[kick-SUB king] day

the day [when I kicked the King]

Conjugation table

For complex forms, form the (anti)benefactive first, then the volitional, then the perfective, then (if there's no suppletive form) the polite **-ri-**, then the subordinating **-te**.

Ellipses indicate that variations (the imperfective and the two volitional forms) are being left out.

	see	*work*	*call*	*kick*	*command*	*not*
imp	kanu	diru	sudy	pocsu	kulsy	eśu
perf	kuna	duri	sydu	pucso	kylsu	uśe
vol imp	agenu	ideru	uzedu	obecsu	ugelsu	eveśu
vol perf	agune	idure	uzude	obucse	ugulse	evuśe
polite imp	karynu	diryru	suridy	pocrysu	kulrisy	natu
polite perf	kurina	duriri	syrydu	pucriso	kylrysu	nuta
vol pol imp	agerynu	ideryru	uzerydu	obecrysu	ugelrysu	anetu
vol pol perf	agurine	idurire	uzuride	obucrise	ugulrise	anute
benef imp	keni	deri	sydi	pecsi	kylsi	eśi
benef perf	kine	dire	sidy	picse	kilsy	iśe
vol ben imp	egeni	ederi	yzedi	ebecsi	ygelsi	eveśi
vol ben perf	egine	edire	yzide	ebicse	ygilse	eviśe
ben polite	kerini...	deriri...	syridi...	pecrisi...	kylrisi...	neti...
ben 'you'	kenini...	deniri...	synidi...	pecnisi...	kylnisi...	eniśi...
ant imp	kona	dyra	soda	pocsa	kolsa	ośa
ant perf	kano	dary	sado	pacso	kalso	aśo
vol ant imp	ogena	ydera	ozeda	obecsa	ogelsa	oveśa
vol ant perf	ogane	ydare	ozade	obacse	ogalse	ovaśe
antib polite	korina...	dyrira...	sorida...	pocrisa...	kolrisa...	nota...
sub imp	kaunte	diurte	suytte	pocuste	kulyste	euśte
sub perf	kuante	duirte	syutte	pucoste	kyluste	ueśte
sub vol imp	ageunte	ideurte	uzeytte	obecuste	ugeluste	eveuśte
sub vol perf	aguente	iduerte	uzyette	obuceste	uguleste	evueśte
doer	kaneu	direu	sudeu	pocseu	kulseu	
partic	kaina	diera	suida	pocisa	kulisa	
action	kani	deri	sodi	pacsi	kolsi	

> Kind of intimidating, huh? But any actual reference grammar is likely to contain huge verb charts. Humans seem to like complicated verbs.

Pronouns

Personal pronouns

	pejorative		ordinary		deferential	
person	sing	plural	sing	plural	sing	plural
1 (I, we)	cin	źum	ȟem	gymu		
2 (you)	kuȟ		fal		falau	
3 (he, she, it, they)	vuȟ		taȟ	taza	vep	vybu

There are three sets of pronouns in Kebreni, which imply contempt, neutrality, or deference toward the referent.

The **pejorative** first person forms (**cin, źum**) are humilifics, used to refer to oneself when speaking with a superior; the remaining pejorative forms (**kuȟ** and **vuȟ**— one does not bother with any number distinction) are used to refer to those of lower classes (or, of course, to insult someone by referring to them as inferiors).

> For added flavor, think not just what a form is for; think about how people will extend or abuse it.

The **deferential** second person form **falau** is an honorific, used to refer to a listener or listeners who are social superiors; its use roughly correlates with the use of the polite forms of verbs. Note that the third person forms (**vep, vybu**) express deference to the person referred to, not (unlike polite verbs) to the listener. There are no deferential first-person pronouns.

For all of these pronouns, possessive forms can be made by adding -**te** (which forces a preceding labial stop to assimilate): **ȟente** 'my (ordinary)', **falaute** 'your (deferential)', **vuȟte** 'his/her/its/theirs (pejorative)'.

It must be emphasized that pronouns are optional, and indeed to be avoided, in Kebreni. They are used only when necessary for clarity. For direct address, in fact, it's preferable to use honorifics and titles:

Linna, agenu gembadi? *Lord, [do you] want [your] breakfast?*

> Polite forms of pronouns are found in the Romance languages as well as Japanese. Japanese used to have humilific pronouns at least in the 1s— e.g. *boku* 'I' once meant 'your servant', though *boku* is now seen as overbearing!

Demonstratives

'This' and 'that', as adjectives, are **gem** and **kuri** (the relation to 'one' and 'two' is obvious, but the direction of semantic borrowing is not!): **gem nyne** 'this woman', **kuri palaźnu** 'that thorn-bush'.

> The relation of the early numerals to deictics is found in Proto-Indo-European, where **oinos* 'one' is related to **ʔey-* 'this'; Winfred Lehmann proposes that 'two' and 'three' are related to **dew-* 'farther' and **ter-* 'even farther'.

As standalone pronouns these become **gente** 'this one' and **kurite** 'that one'. (This is actually a standard nominalizing use of the clitic **-te** with adjectives.)

Myra 'here', **tomo** 'there', **źada** 'now' and **bada** 'then' function as adverbs.

Interrogative pronouns

The standard interrogative anaphora are:

śava	who, what
śete	which (of what quality)
aśeve	why (a volitional form of *śava*: i.e., 'wanting what?')
ciźe	how, in what way
śanu	where (locative verb)
śere	when
bigynte	how much, how many

Unlike in English, the interrogative anaphora cannot be used in relative clauses. Subordinated clauses usually have no explicit subordinator at all. See *Complex sentences* below for examples.

Quantifiers and indefinite pronouns

Quantifiers are ordinary adjectives, and like any adjectives are nominalized with **-te**.

fyn	none	**fynte**	nothing, no one
biha	some, any	**bihate**	something, someone, anything, anyone
kum	many, much	**kunte**	many things, many people
orat	all, every	**oratte**	everything, everyone

There are no words meaning "everywhere", "sometime", and so on; instead one uses expressions like **biha re** 'some day', **orat hami** 'every land', **fyn haȟcte zani** 'in every valley', etc.

> I like Esperanto's tables of correlatives, but I avoid simply filling it in for each language. Not all languages have a neat, fixed set of indefinite pronouns based on the quantifiers.

Numbers

The Metaiun counting system was based on counting on fingers and toes— the 10 fingers and 8 toes of an Almean.

1	*grem* (related to 'this')
2	*kuri* (related to 'that')
3	*dama*
4	*yakaȟ* ('almost (a hand)')
5	*amua* ('hand')
6	*migrem amua* ('with-one hand')...
9	*yakaȟ kuri* ('almost two (hands)')
10	*kuramua* ('two hands')
11	*poc pinaȟ* ('down to the feet')
12	*mikuri kuramua* ('two hands with two')
14	*mipoc kuramua* ('two hands with a foot')
15	*migrem mipoc kuramua* ('2 hands with a foot with 1')
18	*oranda neȟad* ('entire man')
324	*dikumi* (related to *kumi* 'many')
5832	*telei*

> Almeans have only four toes per foot; as most counting systems are based on counting on the fingers and feet, this suggested a base 18 system.

> Don't assume that number names are unanalyzable! The obvious way to name them is by reference to the finger- and toe-counting method. I like the word for 11 here, which is based on Unalit *atkahakhtok* 'it goes down = 11'.

> If you've counted to the full number of fingers and
> toes you've got a whole man's worth. Similarly Shasta
> *tsec* '20' is the word for 'man'.

Under the influence of Cuêzi and Cadinor, a decimal system was
adopted; but the Kebreni numbers from 1 to 19 still show their origins in
the Meiaiun system:

1	gem	11	pinaħ
2	kur	12	migram
3	dam	13	midakram
4	hak	14	mipoc
5	amma	15	mipokemai
6	migem	16	mipokurai
7	migur	17	hakraida
8	midam	18	raida
9	hakur	19	raigemai
10	kram	20	kur kram

The numbers from 21 to 99 are formed on the model *[tens]* **kram** *[dig-its]*-**ai**: 21 = **kur kram gemai**, 37 = **dam kram migurai**. In fast counting, *kram* is omitted.

It's still possible to count by 18s: **raida, kuraida, dam raida**...

Dygum (from *dikumi*) has become the word for 100, while **myga** '1000'
was borrowed from Cuêzi. The same basic model is followed:

487 = **hak dygum midam kram migurai**

    four hundred eight ten seven-and

3480 = **dam myga hak dygum midam kramai.**

    three thousand four hundred eight ten-and

There are two ways of numbering noun phrases: by inserting the number before the noun, or by subordinating the noun and following it with
the number:

    <u>dam</u> kyr laħ *or* kyr laħte <u>dam</u>   *three green fields*

The subordinated form is more formal, and is preferred in writing, or
with very long numbers.

The suffix -**eħ** (-**ħ** after vowel) forms ordinal numbers: **gemeħ** 'first',
raidaħ 'eighteenth'.

A fraction is named by infixing -**i**- before the last consonant, removing
the final vowel if any, and adding -**nu**: **kuirnu** 'half', **dainnu** 'third',
etc.

Derivational morphology

> You'll always find a section with this name in my grammars. I'm a great believer in multiplying your lexicon with a few simple changes.

Nominalizers

With adjectives, nominalizations with **-gu** name the abstract quality; with nouns and verbs, they generally name a countable action, result, or associated entity.

> **kanu** 'see' → **kangu** 'vista'
> **botynu** 'fight' → **botengu** 'battle'
> **syh** 'strong' → **sygu** 'strength'
> **śen** 'honorable' → **śengu** 'honor'

With nouns and verbs, **-au** (Met. *-adio*) is an abstract nominalizer, comparable to our *-tion*; with adjectives it names an object with the given quality.

> **adnedu** 'add' → **adnedau** 'addition'
> **kanu** 'see' → **kanau** 'vision'
> **maru** 'be probable' → **marau** 'probability'
> **melah** 'king' → **melahau** 'royalty, kingship'
> **ty** 'round' → **tyau** 'tube, pipe'

For simple actions, a name for an instance of the action can be formed by lowering the last root vowel (**i, y** → **e; e, o** → **a; u** → **o, a** unchanged) and adding **-i**:

> **rihu** 'count' → **rehi** 'count, counting'
> **pocsu** 'kick' → **pacsi** 'kick'
> **taradu** 'dance' → **taradi** 'dance'
> **żynu** 'go' → **żeni** 'departure'
> **kulsy** 'command' → **kolsi** 'command'

The suffix **-nu**, usually accompanied by raising of the last root vowel (**a** → **e, e** → **i, o** → **u**, others unchanged) names a concrete thing related to the root object or action.

> **gyru** (Met. *ger-*) 'rise' → **hernu** (Met. *gerno*) 'stair'
> **kam** 'oak' → **kamnu** 'acorn'
> **muk** 'new' → **muhnu** 'news'

> Note how sound change has made the regular Met. forms *ger/gerno* irregular in Kebreni.

To **pluralize** a noun, you follow the formula $(X)V_1C(V_2) \rightarrow (X)V_1C[+vcd]V_1$. The status of pluralization in Kebreni is quite different from languages such as Verdurian and English, where it is obligatory and grammaticalized. It is an optional derivation in Kebreni; it can be thought of as forming a collective noun— 'a unit formed by more than one X.'

> **hami** 'land' → **hama** 'lands, large area, nation'
> **nehat** 'man' → **nehada** 'people'
> **cai** (Met. *kiodi*) 'mountain' → **cadu** (Met. *kiodo*) 'mountain range'
> **beź** 'grape' → **beźe** 'bunch of grapes'
> **lore** 'horse' → **loro** 'team of horses'

-na is an augmentative; **-ih** is a diminutive.

> **hir** 'long' → **hirna** 'very long'
> **siva** 'sand' → **sivana** 'desert'
> **lezu** 'forest' → **Lezyna** 'Leziunea = big forest'

> **zeveu** 'friend' → **zevih** 'little friend'
> **tada** 'father' → **tadih** 'dad'
> **nyne** 'maiden' → **nynih** 'little girl'

> > Diminutives are so useful (and widespread) that it's odd that English doesn't have one (except -y for names and kinship terms).

-eu names a **person** who does the action, comes from a place, or has a certain quality:

> **kulsy** 'command' → **kulseu** 'commander'
> **taradu** 'dance' → **taradeu** 'dancer'
> **Verdura** 'Verduria' → **Verdureu** 'Verdurian'
> **zev** 'loyal' → **zeveu** 'friend'

The Metaiun equivalent was formed by replacing the final root vowel of the verb with **-u-** and suffixing **-i**. This formation is found in a few old words:

> *γis-* 'cure' → *γusi* (**hus**) 'doctor'
> *brin-* 'watch' → *bruni* (**brun**) 'shepherd'

> > Some derivations are made in the parent language instead. This offers more naturalism and depth and avoids making all the derivations look the same.

-ec has about the same meaning, but specifically names a feminine referent. Kebreni is usually not concerned to do so (e.g. **melah** means both king and queen), but may use -ec in a few cases where the occupation is chiefly female (e.g. **mahec** 'prostitute') or where it's desired to refer to a couple without awkwardness— e.g. a dance manual describing a duet may refer to the **taradeu** and **taradec**. The suffix is most commonly used to form girls' names.

> Melah is a borrowing from Hebrew.

> **lele** 'cute, pretty' → **Lelec**
> **lezu** 'forest' → **Lezec**

Metaiun -(y)umi, whose Kebreni reflex is -**um**, named someone who lives in a particular place; it's related to *yami* 'land': thus *limiyumi* 'highlander'. As a productive prefix, it has been replaced by -**eu** in Kebreni; but -**um** is still found in personal names and in inhabitant-names of very old cities:

> **kal** 'bee' → **Kalum**
> **sogu** 'ridge' → **Sogum**
> **Laadau** → **Laadum** 'person from Laadau'
> **Katinah** 'Cadinas' → **Katynum** 'Cadinorian'

A manufacturer of something is named with -**teu** (a reduced form of **taseu** 'maker'):

> **nabira** 'ship' → **nabirateu** 'shipwright'

> That's a lot of 'person' nominalizations, isn't it? But compare English *maker, actor, watchman, cutie, Italian, Hellene, Pakistani, Chinese.*

Given a verbal root CVX^n, the formula $VC[+vcd]VX^ne$ names a **tool** which accomplishes the action, or a substance which exemplifies it (contrast -**eu**, which is always a person):

> **pazu** 'cut' → **abaze** 'knife'
> **tanu** 'harm' → **atane** 'weapon'
> **treh** 'black' → **etrehe** 'ink'

The suffix -**esa** creates a concrete nominalization of an adjective: an object having the quality named by the adjective:

> **gem** 'one' → **genesa** 'primacy (among interested parties), lien'
> **hir** 'long' → **hiresa** 'street'

-**arei** names a **place**:

> **suty** 'provide' → **sutarei** 'store'
> **lore** 'horse' → **lodarei** 'stable' (with dissimilation)
> **nizu** 'speak' → **nizarei** 'forum'

The proprietor or manager of such a place is named with the suffix –**areu** (unless there already exists a simple form with -**eu**, e.g. **suteu** 'provider, storekeeper'):

> **ingarei** 'tavern' → **ingareu** 'tavernkeeper'

From toponyms and nobles' names we learn of a vowel-harmonizing **honorific** prefix **me-** in Metaiun: *Monȟado* (Monkhayu), *Mičiayama* (Mišicama), *meneula* (Menla), *melekh* 'king', *myvun* 'leader'. It's also seen in Metaiu, Meuna, Mevost, Metōre. The prefix is not seen in modern Kebreni, and usually disappears in cognates: *Šahama* 'Mišicama', *neȟada* 'the people'.

> I didn't name the places based on this bit of morphology— I noticed a number of M- names, decided they were survivals from Metaiun, and derived the honorific from them. I often work this way: I notice a pattern in words that I invented earlier, and abstract it into a feature.

Adjectivizers

The subordinator -**te**, attached to a single word, in effect turns it into an adjective.

> **keda** 'house' → **kedate** 'domestic'
> **neȟada** 'people' → **neȟadate** 'popular'
> **diru** 'work' → **dirte** 'relating to work'

Attached to expressions referring to people, including pronouns, it serves as a genitive:

> **falau** 'you' → **falaute** 'your'
> **nyne** 'maiden' → **nynete** 'maiden's'
> **Verdureu** 'Verdurian' → **Verdureute** 'Verdurian's'

An adjective related to a geographic expression is formed with -**en**:

> **Kebri** 'Kebri' → **kebren** 'Kebreni'
> **Ernaituȟ** 'Érenat' → **ernaituȟen** 'Érenati'

> I invented the terms Kebri and Kebreni years ago; when actually working out the language I added this bit of morphology which explains the variation.

The infix -**n**- + final -(**y**)**r** gives an adjective meaning 'having the quality of X' or 'liable to X':

> **boȟtu** 'water' → **bontur** 'wet'
> **men** 'hill' → **mennyr** 'hilly'

ħulo 'idiot' → **ħunlor** 'idiotic'
zeveu 'friend' → **zevenur** 'friendly'
kriħu 'kill' → **krinħyr** 'murderous'
pabadu 'laugh' → **pabandyr** 'amusing'

The infix -**su**- gives an adjective meaning 'made of X':

siva 'sand' → **sisuva** 'sandy'
ħeda 'stone' → **ħesuda** 'stony'
kam 'oak' → **kasum** 'oaken'

> One thing I like about infixes is that they create words that look and sound different from the roots. *Kasum* is interestingly divergent from *kam*.

The meaning of an adjective may be intensified by infixing -**u**- before the last consonant, or diminished by infixing -**i**-:

ħir 'long' → **ħiur** 'very long', **ħiir** 'not long'
śaida 'beautiful' → **śaiuda** 'breathtakingly beautiful'
śe 'small' → **śei** 'tiny'

A similar process can be seen in Meṫ. *nauni* 'young man', *niune* 'young woman' (but it's obscured by sound change in Kebreni: **nen, nyne**).

-*iCa* where -*C* is the final consonant of the root, or -*eCa* after **i**, means 'that has been Xed'. This sounds like a past participle, but it is never a verbal form, nor can it even be used predicatively; it can only be used to modify a noun, or as a nominalization.

nizu 'say' → **nieza** 'spoken'
suṫy 'provide' → **suiṫa** 'provisions'
kulsy 'command' → **kulisa** 'what is commanded', lexicalized as 'fleet'
nabru 'sail' → **nabira** 'what is sailed', i.e. a ship

The suffix -**lecsu** (from **lecu** 'can'), added to a verb, means equally 'that can be verbed' or 'that can verb'; context generally indicates which.

badu 'eat' → **badlecsu** 'edible'
źaiźigu 'marry' → **źaiźiglecsu** 'marriageable, nubile'
treśu 'break' → **treślecsu** 'breakable'

The infix -**at**-, used to produce antonyms in Meṫaiun, is no longer productive:

zewi 'loyal' → *zatewi* 'disloyal, treasonous'
čiam- 'aproach' → *čatiam*- 'move away from'

An adjective can be negated with **bu**- (borrowed from Caḋinor):

doĥt 'correct' → budoĥt 'incorrect'
gauryr 'pure' → bugauryr 'impure'

Bu- 'not' is stolen from Mandarin.

Verbalizers

Nouns can be fairly freely converted into verbs by adding -**u** (replacing a final vowel):

dyrĥi 'credit (entry)' → dyrĥu '(enter as a) credit'
nabra 'sail' → nabru 'sail'
alat 'silver coin' → aladu 'spend money'

A syntactic alternative, to use the verb **tasu** 'do', is extremely productive, especially for vague nonce forms:

sutarei 'store' → sutarei tasu 'shop'
zeveu 'friend' → zeveu tasu 'be friendly'
tiron 'market' → tiron tasu 'go to market'

This is similar to Japanese *suru*.

The infix -**s**- forms verbs with the meaning 'to use X (in the obvious way)' or 'to act like X':

poc 'foot' → pocsu 'kick'
bry 'eye' → brysu 'keep an eye on'
śemu 'fish' → śemsu 'swim'
mygu 'ox' → mycsu 'haul'

The infix -**ma**- means 'to make X' or 'to acquire X':

syl 'dark' → symalu 'darken'
hazik 'proud' → hazimaku 'make proud'
kur 'two' → kumaru 'split'
śemu 'fish' → śemamu 'fish'
alat 'silver' → alamatu 'scrounge up cash'

Locative verbs can be prefixed to verbs, often with the effect of specifying a direction or purpose for the action. Often an abbreviated form of the locative is used.

ebu 'be away from' + diru 'work' → ebdiru 'take off work'
dynu 'be above' + riĥu 'count' → dyrĥu 'count as a credit'

These expressions derive from a subordinated verb: *eupte diru* → *ebdiru*.

Syntax

Though you can systematically work out phonology and morphology, it's hard to move straight ahead through syntax. But you don't have to. Work out the basics— sentence order, NP order, how to form questions and negatives. Then work on translating some texts. You'll inevitably run into syntactic questions (how do I subordinate a clause? how do I say "There's an X"?), and you can fill in that part of the syntax section.

Parameter order

Kebreni, lacking case marking or articles to signal case relationships, uses word order instead. The basic word order is SVO:

Linna Kalum, gem boteneu ażeiżirygu falaute nyniħ.

lord Kalum / this soldier VOL-marry-POL your-DEFER daughter-DIM

Lord Kalum, this soldier wants to marry your daughter.

Ħazum, linna agenu hus.

Hazum / lord see-VOL doctor

Ħazum, the Lord needs a doctor.

I've added glosses to most of the examples in this edition. Glosses allow readers to grasp the structure of the language without knowing the vocabulary.

How do you write glosses? Just provide a word-for-word translation. Some useful conventions:

- Separate morphemes with a hyphen. E.g. VOL-marry-POL indicates that *ażeiżirygu* is composed of separate morphemes VOL, marry, and POL.

- If a gloss for a single morpheme requires additional words in English, use dots. E.g. the suppletive verb *natu* could be glossed not.POL to indicate that there are not separate morphemes for 'not' and POL.

- Grammatical morphemes are glossed in CAPITALS; this helps show the structure of the language.

To mark **focus**, a constituent is moved to the front of the sentence. With compound sentences, the constituent in focus may have a different case role in each sentence; context usually serves to keep the meaning clear, without any unusual syntax or the insertion of pronouns.

Muk boteneu sudy Kamum, ehc kulseu hilu.

young soldier name Kamum / and commander like

The young soldier, [he] is named Kamum, and the commander likes [him].

Linnate nyne gegeu miźynu gembadi.

lord-SUB daughter servant bring breakfast

As for the lord's daughter, the servants are bringing breakfast [to her].

> Topicalization was little studied in traditional grammar, but it shows up in some form in every language.

Note that when there are two noun phrases before the verb and no object after it, the first must be the object. If there's just one noun phrase before the verb (underlined below), it's both subject and focus.

Hus nynete baba agenu źe.

doctor girl-SUB mother VOL-see also

As for the doctor, the girl's mother wants to see him too.

Nynete baba agenu hus źe.

girl-SUB mother VOL-see doctor also

As for the girl's mother, she wants to see the doctor too.

Nehat guma mabu. *Man bites dog.* (focus unmarked or on 'man')
Mabu guma nehat. *Dog bites man.* (focus unmarked or on 'dog')

Nehat mabu guma. *As for the man, the dog bit him.* (focus on 'man')

Mabu nehat guma. *As for the dog, the man bit him.* (focus on 'dog')

Schematically:

    NP V = S V
    V NP = V O
    NP V NP = S V O
    NP NP V = O S V

Indirect objects

Kebreni makes no morphological distinction between direct and indirect objects. One or both can appear after the verb, or be fronted for emphasis. The indirect object follows the direct object if both are given.

> **Kulseu ħuvy veźa <u>taradeu</u>.**
>
> commander give-PERF bottle dancer
>
> *The commander gave the bottle to the dancer.*
>
> **<u>Nyne</u> mugeu ħuvy śemu.**
>
> girl youngster give-PERF fish
>
> *The girl was given a fish by the young man.*
>
> **Śemu nyne muħa.** *As for the fish, the girl sold it.*

Another way of putting this is that verbs like **ħyvu** 'give' are *ditransitive* in Kebreni, like **sudy** 'call (someone) (something)'.

Schematically:

> NP V NP = S V O
> NP NP V = O S V
> NP V NP NP = S V O O
> NP NP V NP = O S V O

Verbs of movement

The destination of a verb of movement is not morphologically marked in Kebreni; it's treated as a second object.

> **Linna, źyrynu <u>Laadau</u>.**
>
> lord / go-POL Laadau
>
> *Lord, we're going to Laadau.*
>
> **Kuri taniħte neħat lahu <u>źumte keda</u>?**
>
> that annoying man come we-SUB house
>
> *Is that annoying man coming to our house?*
>
> **Imeźynu śemu <u>tada</u>.** *Bring a fish to your father.*

However, the source of a movement is indicated using a locative verb (discussed below):

> **<u>Laaven eupte</u> lahu eħc bohru.**

Laaven from-SUB come and stink

They're coming from Laaven and they stink.

Noun phrases

Order

Modifiers— including adjectives, numbers, relative clauses and locative expressions— always precede the noun:

> **kur mabu**   *two dogs*
>
> **gem śaida hazigai nyne**   *that beautiful and proud maiden*
>
> **taniħte neħat**   *an annoying man*
>
> **kaunte melaħ mabu**   *a dog that looks at a king*
>
> **sivana śaunte turgul**   *the battalion near the desert*

> There's a tendency for languages to be consistently head-final or head-initial. This is easy to neglect since English is a mess. English NPs, for instance, can have material before or after the noun.

Kebreni's strong modifier-modified order would lead a linguist to suspect that it was once an OV language, which has changed, perhaps, under the influence of Verdurian. The evidence is equivocal; we do not have many actual texts in Meṭaiun. However, they do seem to be predominantly SOV.

The -te relativizer

The root meaning of **-te** is to reduce an expression to an attribute. It reduces a noun or noun phrase to an adjectival expression, a verbal expression to a subordinate clause.

With a single noun (or pronoun), a **-te** expression has an adjectival or possessive quality:

> **falaute gem**   *one of you*
> **tadate zevu**   *father's friend*
> **neħadate nizarei**   *the people's forum*
> **kedate zivan**   *the inside of the house (lit. the house's inside)*

The same can be said of longer expressions that are themselves **-te** expressions:

> **falaute gente mygu**   *the ox belonging to one of you*
> **Kalunte tadate zevu**   *Kalum's father's friend*

<u>nehadate nizareite</u> dirau   *the work of the people's forum*

With more complex expressions **-te** functions like a relative clause:

<u>dama rete</u> ebdiru *a three-day holiday; a holiday that's three days long*
<u>hulo tauste</u> melah   *a king who acts like an idiot*
<u>keda ziunte te</u> mygu   *the ox that's in the house*

Finally, a **-te** clause can stand on its own, meaning 'the one(s) which...':

Fal buda Kazumte beźe ehc hem buda <u>Lelecte</u>.

you eat-PERF Kazum-SUB grape and I eat-PERF Lelec-SUB

You ate Kazum's grapes and I ate Lelec's.

Ruhi <u>Avelah eupte lauhte</u>? Ťah miry.

count-PERF Avéla from-SUB coming / 3s rich

Did you count the one who comes from Avéla? He's rich.

> The behavior of *-te* with nouns (as opposed to verbs) is borrowed from Mandarin *de*.

Existence and equivalence

There is no verb 'to be' in Kebreni; the closest equivalent is **zaru** 'exist, be there'.

Dama gegeu <u>zaru</u>, ehc dama veźa <u>zaurte eśu</u>.

three servant exist / and three bottle existing not

There are three servants and three missing bottles.

Botengu ziunte cihica ingarei <u>zura</u>.

Boggola being.in praised tavern exist-PERF

In Boggola there used to be a praiseworthy tavern.

> Messing with very basic verbs like 'be' is a good way of making your language unlike English.

There is no verb 'have' either; **zaru** with effect inflections serves for this.

Keda, kur gegeu, ehc śemu <u>zeri</u>.

house two servant and fish have-BENEF

I have a house, two servants, and a fish. (Lit, they exist for my benefit.)

Leule leule nyne <u>zeniri</u>.

cute-AUG cute-AUG girl have-YOU-BENEF

You have a very, very cute daughter. (Lit., she exists for your bene-fit.)

> I could have invented an entirely new idiom to replace 'have', but it's neater to use already created features, in this case the benefactive.

Negative effect inflections are used when the possession is disadvantageous.

Keda eupte symanlur kangu <u>zora</u>.

house from-SUB boring view have-ANTIB

I have a boring view from my house.

Paru ziunte cuka <u>zonira</u>.

lip being.in pimple have-YOU-ANTIB

You have a pimple on your lip.

Third-person possession can only be indicated by possessive expressions, e.g.:

<u>Kulseute</u> pabandyr lore zaru.

commander-SUB amusing horse exist

The commander has an amusing horse.

> Ever since reading the Humez brothers' *Latin for People*, I've been addicted to making frivolous sample sentences. Hopefully it somewhat counters the dryness of the linguistic explanations. Samples are also a chance to explore your culture— they can feature characters, professions, and opinions that would be found there.

There is no attributive 'be' at all; to say that X is Y you normally simply adjoin the two noun phrases.

Hente tada beżarei eħc baba taradeu.

I-SUB father vintner and mother dancer

My father is a vintner and my mother is a dancer.

To say that X belongs to the class Y, you can use **sudy** 'be called':

> **Ebrankraħ sudy kraħ.**
>
> cinnabar name mineral
>
> *Cinnabar is a mineral.*

To reveal that X is actually Y, one can use the expression X Y**ai gensu** 'X and Y are one'; the opposite can be indicated with **kursu** 'be two, differ':

> **Linna, kriħu loreai <u>genrysu</u>.**
>
> lord / killer horse-AND be.one-POL
>
> *My lords, the killer is— the horse.*

> **Falte tada eħc taradeu <u>kursu</u>.**
>
> you-SUB father and dancer be.two
>
> *Your father is no dancer.*

> Getting rid of 'to be' required working out what happens to each of the major uses of 'be'.

Adjectives

Attributes

Adjectives used attributively appear before the noun, without modification: **śaida set** 'a beautiful jewel'; **taniħte żem ħulo** 'an annoying old idiot'.

Predicates

As predicates they are a bit more complicated; in effect they are partially converted into verbs. No copula is used. In the simplest form, the adjective simply appears after the noun, in verbal position:

> **Kriħeu <u>żem</u>.** *The killer is old.*

The politeness infix -**ri**- must be used in the same situations it would be used on a verb:

> **Falte nyne śaida.** *Your daughter is beautiful. (ordinary)*

> **Falaute nyne <u>śairida</u>.** *Your daughter is beautiful. (polite)*

The predication is negated using the auxiliary **eśu** and the subordinator -**te**, as with verbs, and other auxiliaries may be used as well:

> **Gem mabu <u>żente eśu</u>.** *This dog is not old.*

> **Melaħ <u>miryte maru</u>.** *The king is probably rich.*

Adjectives which already end in -**te** do not add it again:

Falau <u>**taniħte eryśu!**</u> *You are not annoying, sir!*

A perfective can be formed by appending -**u** (replacing a final vowel if any) and interchanging it with the previous vowel. Use -**y** instead if the latter is also a -**u**-.

Kriħeu śaudi. *The killer is no longer beautiful. (Cf.* śaida *'beautiful')*

Falte nyne mycu. *Your daughter is no longer young. (Cf.* muc *'young')*

Predicate adjectives are not inflected for volition or effect.

> The idea of adjectives being simplified verbs is taken from Japanese.

Substantives

An adjective can be used as a substantive by suffixing -**te**: **syhte** 'the strong (ones)', **kyrte** 'the green (ones).'

The subordinated form may also appear attributively; in this form and position it can be interpreted as a one-word relative clause.

Note the difference between:

nyyl nabira	*a slow ship*
nyylte nabira	*a ship that is slow*
nyylte	*a slow one*

Comparatives

There is no morphological comparative. A comparative "X is more Q than Y" is formed using an expression that literally means "As opposed to Y, X is very Q."

Cadec ceuste polte nyne leule.

hill-girl opposing city-SUB girl cute-AUG

A city girl is cuter than a hillbilly girl.

Bodu ceuste śemu bontuurte eśu.

frog opposing fish wet-AUG-SUB not

A fish is not wetter than a frog.

Instead of **bontuurte eśu** 'not very wet' we could say **bontuir** 'little wet'; but the negative expression is preferred in speech, where the difference from **bontuur** 'very wet' is not marked.

Where we use comparative forms Kebreni often uses the augmentative or diminutive forms: **nyul lore** 'slower horses', literally 'very slow horses'. Reduplication is also found, especially in speech: **kasus kasus re** 'a windy, windy day'.

> Consider providing alternative ways of implementing a feature; this gives you opportunities for stylistic variation.

Adverbs

Before a verb, the -**te** form of an adjective serves as an adverb:

> **Nyne nyylte taradu.** *The girl was dancing slowly.*
> **Linna hazikte nuzi.** *The lord spoke proudly.*

This form can follow the verb if it would not be confused with an object: **nuzi hazikte** is all right, but **taradu nyylte** would mean 'danced a slow one'. It can be fronted for emphasis, but only by placing it in its own subclause with **tasu/soru** 'do':

> <u>Hazikte tauste</u> linna nuzi.
>
> proud-SUB doing lord speak-PERF
>
> *Proudly the lord spoke.*

> We form adverbs with -ly, but German gets by fine without distinguishing adverbs from adjectives.

Conjunctions

Kebreni has two ways of saying *and*, with slightly different meanings: **eħc**, which appears between the conjoined constituents, and -**ai**, which attaches to the second constituent, voicing a final consonant and replacing the final vowel of a diphthong.

Applied to two (or more) modifiers, -**ai** forms an intersection, **eħc** a union, of the meaning of the modifiers. For instance, **muk syhai neħat** and **muk eħc syh neħat** both mean "the young and strong men"; but **muk syhai neħat** means the men who are both young and strong (the intersection of 'young men' and 'strong men'), while **muk eħc syh neħat** means the young men and the strong men (the union of 'young men' with 'strong men').

> It occurred to me one day to make this distinction. I scrawled it on a notepad and eventually it made its way into Kebreni. I guess it just struck me as interesting that "the young and strong men" doesn't mean the same thing as "the young men and the strong men".

The third logical possibility is a disjunction— the men that are young or strong but not both— and this corresponds to **ga** 'or': **muk ga syh neħat** 'the old or the young men (but not both)'.

Similarly, applied to separate words, -**ai** implies that both conjoints describe the same referent(s) or action, **eħc** that they are separate, and **ga** that only one applies:

> **Ħem falaai inezu.** *You and I (as a unit or team) will speak.*[4]
>
> **Ħem eħc falau inezu.** *You will speak, and I will speak.*
>
> **Ħem ga falau inezu.** *Either you will speak, or I will speak.*
>
> **nyne taradeai**   *the girl and the dancer (who are the same), the girl dancer*
>
> **nyne eħc taradeu**   *the girl and the dancer (two separate people)*
> **nyne ga taradeu**   *the girl or the dancer (but not both)*
>
> **Palec symalu taniħuai.** *Palec bores and she annoys (all at once, simultaneously).*
>
> **Palec symalu eħc taniħu.** *Palec bores and she also annoys (two different attributes).*
>
> **Palec symalu ga taniħu.** *Either Palec bores, or she annoys (not at the same time).*

Ga is thus an exclusive or. There is no conjunction that has the meaning of inclusive or (X or Y or both, X and/or Y), but, as in English, one can add the 'and' case explicitly:

> **Melaħ pabadu ga fanu <u>ga kur soru</u>.**
>
> king laugh or die or two do
>
> *The king will laugh or die or both.*

---

[4]   Here the referents are not the same. When the conjoints are obviously distinct, the meaning is that they form an indissoluble team, acting together.

There is no conjunction 'but'— which, linguistically, is an 'and' with a built-in implication of surprise or contrast. These must be explicitly indicated in Kebreni.

Locative verbs

What we would express with prepositions is expressed using **locative verbs** in Kebreni, such as **zinu** 'be in or on', **nevu** 'be in the middle of'. These can be used as regular verbs:

> **Mygu zinu keda!** *The ox is inside the house!*
> **Raazam neryvu hałc.** *Raizumi is in the middle of the valley (polite).*

Most of them in fact *are* regular verbs— e.g. **foru** 'follow', used as a locative verb with the meaning 'be behind', **mitu** 'use' or 'be with'. The others were also once regular verbs, but are no longer used in their original meanings.

More frequently a locative expression is used as a modifier or an adverbial; these are subordinate clauses in Kebreni. The locative verb conventionally ends the expression, although its parameter is technically a direct object (more evidence, perhaps, for Metaiun's OV nature):

> **ingarei ziunte** *inside the tavern*
> **re neuvte** *in the middle of the day*

> **[hir zeveu eupte] lyr muhnu**
>
> [old friend from-SUB] sad news
>
> *sad news [from an old friend]*

> **[keda fourte] lim men**
>
> [house behind] high hill
>
> *the high hill [in back of the house]*

> **[melah miutte] linna**
>
> [king supporting] lord
>
> *the lords [who support the king]*

> **[[kaldu ziunte] gem bakte kal fuuste] hulo**
>
> [[hive being.in] one fucking bee lacking] idiot
>
> *an idiot [without one fucking bee [in his hive]]*

The basic idea of locative verbs is borrowed from Mandarin. But again, I worked out the idea without specifically copying Mandarin.

These expressions are so frequent that they are phonetically degraded. The -u- is often lost, or combines with a preceding -i- or -e- to form -y-, and the final -e may be lost as well, yielding such forms as **zynt'** 'inside' or **fort'** 'in back of'.

English has at least one verb that acts like a locative verb— 'contain'. Kebreni locative verbs all act like 'contain'. Compare:

Kona zinu ciħta	→ **ciħta ziunte**
The money is in the box	*in the box*
Ciħta zadinu kona	→ **kona zadiunte**
The box contains money	*containing money*

The most common locative verbs, and the abbreviations used in derivations from them, are shown below, with some examples:

brynu	**bry**	facing, before, about	*keda bryunte* 'in front of the house', *kriidi bryunte* 'about books'
dynu	**dy**	up, on top of, over	*cadu dyunte* 'over the mountains'
ebu	**eb**	out (of), off, (away) from	*Kebri eupte* 'outside Kebri'
cezu	**cez**	against, despite	*żaiżega ceuste* 'against the marriage'
foru	**for**	behind, in back of	*keda fourte* 'behind the house'
fuzu	**fu**	without	*śemu fuuste* 'without a fish'
mitu	**mi**	with, using; supporting	*abaże miutte* 'with a knife'
nevu	**ne**	in the middle of, among, through, during	*nabira neufte* 'in the middle of the ship', *mur neufte* 'for an hour'
ponu	**po**	below, under	*broga pounte* 'under the table'
śadamu	**śada**	far (from)	*pol śadaunte* 'far from the city'
śamu	**śa**	around, surrounding, near	*turgul śaunte* 'surrounding the battalion'
vekru	**vek**	as, like	*gauryr vekurte* 'like a virgin'

zinu	**zi**	in, inside, at, on (general locative)	*lah ziunte* 'in the field', *men ziunte* 'on top of the hill', *tiron ziunte* 'at market'
zadinu	**zadi**	containing, including	*set zadiunte* 'containing a jewel'

Time metaphorically flows not forward but downward in Kebreni:

> **mur dyunte** 'an hour ago' (lit., up an hour)
> **mur pounte** 'an hour later, after one hour' (lit., down an hour)

> Even if you don't produce a full Lakoff & Johnson analysis of your language's metaphors, it's a good idea to think about some of the basic ones— such as those covering time. Otherwise you're likely to unconsciously reproduce the metaphor systems of English.

One can flow with a **river** or against it; expressions of support work the same way.

> **Tama miutte** *with (down) the Serea*
> **Tama ceuste** *against (up) the Serea'*
> **melah miutte/ceuste** *for/against the king*

Finally, note that interrogative 'where' is a locative verb:

> **Syna śanu?** *Where is the waterfall?*

Questions

Yes-no questions

Yes-no questions are indicated with intonation alone:

> **Lahu?** *Are you coming?*
> **Hulo, miźyunte hitane eśu?** *Idiot, you didn't bring your sword?*

A positive question is answered by repeating the verb or by contradicting it with the negative auxiliary **eśu**; there are no words for 'yes' or 'no'.

> **Lahu.** *Yes, I'm coming.*
> **Eśu.** *No, I'm not coming.*

To agree with a negative question, you again repeat the verb, which of course is the negative auxiliary **eśu**; to disagree with it you use the main verb:

> **Eśu.** *Yes, I didn't bring it.*

Miżynu. *No, I did bring it.*

Tag questions are formed with **eśu** (polite **natu**), without subordinating the main verb:

Laadum śenuste lecu, eśu?

Laadau-MAN swimming know.how / not

Someone from Laadau knows how to swim, doesn't he?

Melah karynu hem, natu?

king see-POL I / not.POL

The King will see me, won't he?

It should come as no surprise that a negative tag-question is formed by appending the non-negative main verb:

Fal fuuste kona eśu, fuzu?

you lacking money not / lack

You don't have any money, do you?

Question words

Unlike in English, question words are not fronted; they remain in the syntactically appropriate spot:

> I often explain technical terms in my grammars, as a way of spreading understanding of linguistics. But here's a case where I didn't— "FRONTED".

> Technical terms are used for brevity. If you understand the term, just this short sentence will do. If not, I'd need to explain it (fronting is a transformation that moves a constituent to the front of a sentence) and maybe give an English example.

Fal cyru śava?

you know who

Who do you know?

Muha śava loreai?

sell-PERF what horse-and

You sold the horse and what else?

Oteurte lore zeveu śanu?

VOL-acquire=SUB horse friend where

Where's this friend of yours who wants a horse?

Kuna śete śemu?

see-PERF what.kind fish

What kind of a fish did you see?

Kylsu bigynte ladu?

order-PERF how.many olive

How many olives did you order?

> I figure the more examples the better. It helps make this particular point since we can see interrogatives in several positions; and the more examples, the more chances to develop the language.

Complex sentences

See also the section on *Subordinating form* under *Verbs*.

Sentences as objects

Verbs such as *say* or *know* can take sentences as objects. If the object is in its usual place, after the verb, no special syntactic marking is employed:

Cyru [Verdureu amehu baba].

know [Verdurian VOL-sell mother]

We know [that Verdurians would sell their mothers.]

commander say [battalion be.at that ridge]

Kulseu nizu [turgul zinu kuri śogu].

The commander says [the battalion is on that ridge.]

If it's desired to front the sentential object, it should be followed by **gente** 'this one' or **kurite** 'that one':

[Verdureu amehu baba] gente cyru?

[Verdurian VOL-sell mother] this.one know?

That Verdurians would sell their mothers, do we know this?

Adverbial conjunctions

The conjunctions **eħc** and **ga** can be used for entire sentences:

Melaħ zinu ingarei eħc ingareu zinu ħyr.

king be.in tavern and tavernkeeper be.in castle

The king is in the tavern, and the tavernkeeper is in the castle.

Ħilu inga ga ingarei ziunte śaida nyne diru.

like wine or tavern being.in beautiful girl work

Either he likes the wine, or a beautiful girl works in the tavern.

Other relations between sentences are expressed by more specialized conjunctions. These are often expressed by adverbial clauses in English. Thus English *adverb X (adverb) Y* becomes *X (conj) Y* in Kebreni:

Melaħ kaurira pema falau yħeryvu ħitane.

king return-PERF-POL when you VOL-give-POL sword

When the king returns, you will give him your sword.

Melaħ kaurte natu heź falau oteryru ħiitiru.

king returning not.POL if.then you VOL-take-POL sash

If the king does not return, (then) you will take his sash.

Ħem ħouźi gemeśate kriida immi konarei mengu.

I lose-PERF mortgage-SUB paper because bank whine

Because I lost the mortgage document, the bank is whining.

The conjunction is considered to modify the first (X) clause. The second clause can however be fronted if a demonstrative is left in its place:

Konarei mengu, ħem ħouźi gemeśate kriida immi kurite.

bank whine / I lose-PERF mortgage-SUB paper because that.one

The bank is whining, because I lost the mortgage document.

"To do X in order to Y" is expressed by placing X in the volitional and subordinating Y:

Alamaute aeladu.

get.money-SUB spend.money-VOL

In order to get money, you must spend money.

Żyunte Kebropol ħem oteru lore.

go-SUB Kebropol I acquire-VOL horse

I want to get a horse in order to get to Kebropol.

Relative clauses

As noted under Pronouns, interrogative pronouns cannot be used as relative clauses (that is, to form subordinate clauses).

Where English would use 'what', 'who' 'where', or 'when', Kebreni uses the subordinating form of the verb:

[Żaiżiute kulseu] taradeu ħiulte eśu.

[marry-PERF commander] dancer liking not

The dancer [who married a commander] doesn't like him.

[Cuka miute] gente eveśu.

[pimple having] that.one VOL-not

I don't want to see the one [who has a pimple].

Yżenu [hamaida nyne tarautte] ingarei.

VOL-go [stripped girl dancing] tavern

I want to go to the tavern where the naked girls dance.

An English sentence with relative 'why' will be expressed using **immi** 'because' in Kebreni:

[Żyunte Laadau immi] cyurte eśu

[going Laadau because] knowing not

I don't know [why he's going to Laadau].
(Lit., I don't know because he's going to Laadau.)

> The use of brackets derives from transformational grammar, and emphasizes that the bracketed portions are entire clauses. See my Axunašin grammar online for a more thorough use of transformations.
>
> I didn't include semantics or pragmatic sections in my earlier languages. See my Xurnese grammar for a fuller treatment. If I were extending the Kebreni grammar today, I'd address semantic fields like polite formulas, the calendar, kinship terms, titles, and cursing. I'd think about what metaphor systems are peculiar to them, and how they mark dispreferreds.

Example

This selection, from a newspaper article by Śenum Polyr, shows the typical romantic, slightly defensive Kebreni patriotism. It is given in Kebreni script, then in transliteration with interlinear translation, then in a free English translation.

In the interlinear translation, for brevity, I've used the English possessive or gerundive to represent subordinating forms of nouns and verbs, respectively. However, I've used verbal forms to translate locative verbs; prepositions would misrepresent the structure of Kebreni.

Writing addressed to the world in general (stories, essays, textbooks, news articles) generally does not use the polite forms. When the writer has a specific audience in mind (speeches, petitions, personal letters, sermons), polite forms are used. They are not used in religious language or in legal documents— not signs of disrespect for gods or negotiation partners, but of the age of such language, predating the grammaticalization of politeness.

> You can translate the Babel Text or "The horse and the sheep", of course; but why pass up an opportunity to show off your culture?

> These days I feel bad if I have less than three sample texts, of different styles and registers. The more you do, the more you will develop your language.

bcᴀ͢ ιυᴎ ιʃ͢

ꓛιcᴧbꓞ Ξιʃoc= ꓚꓞᴧbc ᴏᴣᴀᴣ⇋ Ꞁᴛυᴎ bcꓞᴧι bᴀ~ᴎꓞ~ ~ꓞ͢
єᴛᴎꓞᴄιᴧι ᴣιꓞ~ ʃꞀυᴧꓞᴣιᴧι ᴎιᴄoᴣ ᴓꓞᴛᴧι ᴄᴀᴀᴄιoι= ꓚꓞᴄᴧꓞ bcꓞᴧι єᴣꓞ
Ꞁᴣbcє ꓔⅎ~~ ᴣᴜʃᴄoᴣᴧꓞ ιυᴎ єⅎꓞᴏιᴄ ιυᴎ ᴄᴣᴎᴏιᴄ ᴣᴄꓞᴧᴧι~ ᴎιoꓞ
єιʃoᴄᴧι ᴎιᴄoᴣᴧι ~ᴄιᴄιo bꓞᴎᴎꓞᴄ~ ᴣbꓞ ᴏᴣᴄ͢ єιʃoιᴣ ᴣᴄᴣᴧᴧι υᴄo ᴣⅎᴀᴣ
ᴄιʃoꓞ ᴧᴣ~ᴧι Ꞁᴛυᴎ ᴎᴣ ᴧᴣ~ᴧι ᴣⅎυᴣ bcꓞᴧι ᴧᴣꓞbᴧι c ᴓι~ι~ Ξιʃoc bc·
ꓞᴧι ᴄιᴄιᴄιo= Ʌᴣ~ єιʃoιᴣ cᴀᴀc ᴣꓞᴄᴧbꓞ ⅎoᴣ єᴛoᴄᴧι=

ꞏιoᴄᴛoιꓞ ᴣꓞᴄᴧbꓞ~ єιʃoc bᴄєᴣꓞ ᴎιᴣᴧι~ cᴣᴎꓞ~ ~ᴣᴄᴣᴧι ᴎιbꓞ~ ᴣᴜʃᴄoᴣ~
ιυᴎ bᴣᴧιᴎꓞᴄ= Ⱶᴄᴀᴣꓞ υᴄυꓞᴧι Oꓞυᴧᴄιoᴧι oιᴣᴣ Ꞁᴣᴄ~ ᴧⅎoᴄιᴀᴀᴧι
Oιυᴣᴣᴣ Ꞁᴣᴄ~ ᴣⅎoιⅎ ᴣᴏᴣᴄᴧι ᴣι~ᴣ ʃoᴄιᴣᴧι ~ιᴄιꓞ= Δoᴣᴧι ᴎιꓞbᴧι~
ᴣᴣᴣ ᴣᴄꓞᴧᴧι~ ᴧᴣbꓞ ⅎoιᴣᴣᴣ bcꓞᴧι ᴄιᴄιᴄιo cᴣᴎꓞ~ Ξι~ιᴣⅎo Nꓞᴄᴏⅎoᴣᴄ
ᴎιꓞbᴧι υꓞᴣᴀ ᴣᴄꓞoᴄᴣᴄ=

Ⱶιᴣbc ιυᴎ ᴎιᴣᴣcbc= Ξᴣꓞ ᴎᴄιᴣꓞ ⅎoιᴣᴣᴣ ᴀιєᴛoᴧι~ ʃᴣᴎꓞ~ιᴀbꓞ ᴎᴄι·
ᴣᴣᴧι єᴣᴀʃιⅎbꓞ ᴣιᴎ~ᴣꓞ= ιʃᴣᴣι єᴣꓞ ʃιᴣᴣᴏ ᴣᴄꓞᴧᴧι~ ᴎιᴣᴧι ᴎιꓞbᴧι~
ᴎᴄιᴣꓞ єᴣᴣᴧι ιꓞoᴧι ᴓᴣᴄᴧι ᴓᴣᴣ єᴣꓞ= ꓔⅎʃʃιꓞ ᴣꓞᴄᴧbᴧι ιᴏꓞ υᴄιᴣꓞ

ε⁊⁊⁊ʕᴑ⁼ Ξ⁊ʕᴑıc ᷉ℶ⁊ᴧıυ ₲⁶υᴧᴧı ıᴑ⁊⁻ ε⁊ᴑıυ ₲⁶υᴧᴧı ıᴑ⁊⁻ ⁊ıυ⁊ᴧı ᷈ᴑ
⁊cᴧı ⁊c⁊ᴧᴧı⁻ ⁊ıⁿε⁊ʕᴄıᴑ ε⁊ʕᴑıc ᵬ⁊⁊ᴑᴧı ıᴑ⁊⁼

Zivan ehc eban

Uneitsu Kebri. Nuutsi śava?

> think-VOL Kebri. think-PERF what?

Hahc ziunte sylgu, luda kuguynte men, bohtunate geira taupte yvyre.

> valley being-in shadow, olive-tree filling hill, sea's sound lapping boats.

Nuitu ziunte kanu hazik pol, nabirateu ehc konarei ehc ingarei miutte,

> mind being-in see proud city, shipbuilder and bank and tavern using,

geru kebrite ceirate lyyr zauguai, ansu śaida kebren nynete hir mova,

> hear kebri's song's sadness glory-and, feel beautiful kebreni girl's long hair,

debru falte hahc ga falte noha ziunte tauste iźele, Kebri ziunte dynyr.

> taste your valley or your island being-in making cheese, kebri being-in top.

Fal kebren immi nuitsu orat kurite.

> you kebreni because think all that-NOM.

Verdureu nuitsu, kebri zikanu gente: ingu, ladute gezu, nabira ehc zateuguai.

> verdurian think, kebri mean this-NOM: wine, olive's oil, ship, and enmity.

Gymu hihunte Ruhtyrte rema hami, toryuvte ˇehnam hami, moreo aścaite melah bryunte ledeu.

> we burning arcaln's bridge land, trading dhekhnam land, moreo aščai's king facing rival.

Oratte ceuste, nana miutte, tasu oradam ziunte dynyr ingu,

> all-NOM opposing, methods using, make world being-in top wine,

Kelenor Luiśorai ceuste hauv miuryai.

> celenor luyšor-and opposing good-AUG rich-AUG-and.

Gensi ehc gennisi. Kanu gymu oradam vekurte:

same-for-me and same-to-you. see us world seeming:

bucuelecsu cynaute kumbehsu meclau.

irreducible experience's miscellaneous mixture.

Ebaneu kanu bemaś miutte— gente ceuste, gymu kaunte euśte źaite taza kanu.

outsider see caricature with— this-NOM opposing, we seeing not-SUB things they see.

Bobabeu nuituste eśu ħymu kunnar.

drunkard thinking not-PRES drinks too-much.

Kanarei gemeħ doħtte eśu, kureħ doħtte eśu:

viewpoint first right-SUB not, second right-SUB not-PRES :

neħatte źaite miutte, nenkanyr kanarei zaurte eśu.

man's thing having, objective viewpoint existing not.

Inside and outside

Think of Kebri. What do you think of? You think of the shadows on the valleys, the hills carpeted by olive trees, the sound of the sea lapping against boats. You see in your mind the proud cities, with their shipbuilders and banks and taverns, hear the sadness and glory of Kebreni songs, feel the long hair of beautiful Kebreni girls, taste the particular cheese made in your own valley or island— the best on Kebri. You think all this because you are Kebreni.

To the Verdurians, Kebri means these things: wine, olive oil, ships— and enmity. We are the land which burned the Arcaln Bridge, the land that trades with Dhekhnam, the rival before the king of Moreo Aščai. And at the same time, somehow, we make the finest wine in the world, better and richer than that of Célenor or Luyšor.

It is the same way with each one of us. We see ourselves as a world— a jumbled mixture of irreducible experience. Outsiders see us in caricature— but may also see what we do not see: the drunkard never thinks he drinks too much. Neither point of view is the correct one; with human things, there is no objective viewpoint.

Sound changes

The following sound changes can be postulated between Meṫaiun and Kebreni.

Remember how to read these: e.g. the second rule means "a fricative changes to a non-fricative in the environment preceding a liquid."

Rule	Environment	Examples
CC → C		treggeur → trehyr
[+fric] → [-fric]	/ _[+liquid]	Davrio → Dabru, ȟras → kraȟ
e → y	/ {C,#}_Cu	keruna → kyruna
i → y	/ {C,#}_C^nu	kijur → kyźur
g → ȟ	/ _F	geilas → ȟilaȟ
g → ɣ	/ _C	mogdo → moɣdo → mohdu
r → i	/ g_	grem → giem → gem
{s, z} → [+velar]	/ _[+stop], _#	ɣask → haȟc, girilas → ȟirilaȟ
k → c	/ _i	vaiki → vaac, kiodi → cai
ai → aa		Laita → Lädau
oi → e		Awoilas → Avelaȟ
au → e		saumi → sem
Fu → y		briu → bry, neuli → nyl
io → a	/ _C	kiodi → cai
o → u	/ _(C^n)#	mog → muk, arosd → ruȟt
w → v		Newor → Nevur, Awoilas → Avelaȟ
ȟ → ȟ		ȟ am → ȟam
[+vcd+stop] → 0	/ V_F	kiodi → cai, Dobauron → Do-erun
i → 0	/ _V	lesio → lezu
[-vcd+obs] → [+vcd]	/ V_V	sifa → siva, Gutein → Gudin, Laita → Lädau
e → 0	/ _ {i, a}	geilas → ȟilaȟ, Leziunea → Lezyna
i → 0	/ C_#	raisi → raas
r → 0	/ C_#	godri → godr → god → got
č → ś		Čengo → Šengu
j → ź	/_	jindor → źindur
ɣ → h		ɣask → haȟc, mogdo → moɣdo → mohdu
k → c	/ by {x, ś}	ɣask → haȟk → haȟc
n → i	/ _[+dental]	čanda → śaida
m → n	/ by [+dental]	admettan → adnedan, ȟamsifa → ȟansiva
h → 0	/ _x	moggeur → moɣxyr → mohxyr → moxyr
n → 0	/ _s	tanso → tasu
[+stop] →	/ _#	vaiki → vaaci → vaac, mog →

[+vcd]   muk

> This is all that appears on the surface of an extensive preparatory work: creating a set of sound changes to go from Meṭaiun to Kebreni. As I had only a few Kebreni words (e.g. *Kebri*), I could do this right, working forwards.
>
> At the cost of a little additional work, I have two lexicons for the price of one— Meṭaiun and Kebreni— and the latter has some morphological variation naturally arising out of sound changes, just as in 'real' languages.

Curiously, the voicing of medial consonants (e.g. *demettan* → *demedu*) seems to be an areal feature, shared with Ismaîn and the Avélan dialect of Verdurian.

> AREAL features cross family boundaries; earthly examples include tone in Southeast Asia and the avoidance of the infinitive in the Balkans.

Lexicon

The first column gives the Kebreni word; the second is the Meṭaiun equivalent, if any; the third gives the part of speech.

Kebreni and its ancestor Meṭaiun have been in close contact with Cuêzi and the Caḍinorian languages for close to four millennia, and there has been extensive borrowing in both directions.

Meṭaiun borrowings **into Cuêzi** include *geōre* 'castle', *nîdo* 'wheel', *nêsei* 'parley', *auōni* 'treaty', *navera* 'sail', *ancua* 'sea serpent', *girin* 'ibis', *sêori* 'octopus', *buras* 'sponge', *crinu* 'papyrus', *execu* 'lentil', *ladu* 'olive', *mexera* 'type of herb', *ciotīro* 'type of flower', *talāuas* 'orange', *xariu* 'luck', *trîgo* 'soot'.

Meṭaiun borrowings **from Cuêzi** include *aviza* 'university', *numygur* 'hermit', *kriida* 'paper', *eri* 'map', *ris* 'pen', *gunaħ* 'hero', *eklura* 'sensual abandon', *kelun* 'bronze', *mardaħ* 'iron', *lidaħ* 'steel', *fadora* 'fountain', *myga* 'thousand', *nidawas* 'machine', *pery* 'flaid', *yra* 'type of flower', *alaṭ* 'silver coin'.

Meṭaiun borrowings **into Caḍinor** include *Agireis* 'the sea goddess', *Meneu* 'the star Meme', *evranħras* 'realgar', *ħamsifa* 'sulfur', *laitondos* 'brass', *paṭeta* 'calomine', *baita* 'barrel', *cora* 'riverboat', *tindigeda* 'anchor', *ieiba* 'bow', *pinda* 'stern', *siobostos* 'brine', *burasos* 'sponge', *dauris* 'seagull', *akulua* 'shark', *raiħ* 'crab', *moreia* 'tuna', *notonis* 'salmon', *busmitrio* 'pearl', *citro* 'lemon', *bidno* 'grapevine', *vinos* 'wine', *moruł* 'carrot', *palaznos* 'gorse', *seła* 'silk', *viôora* 'type of flower', *mapola* 'poppy', *suber* 'cork', *peida* 'type of vine', *kariu* 'happiness', and dozens of toponyms.

Metaiun borrowings **from Caðinor** include *adnedu* 'add', *demedu* 'subtract', *bina* 'list', *leraħ* 'understanding', *aken* 'clear', *ħiitiru* 'sash', *aladaħ* 'grammar', *preħtura* 'history', *kaadau* 'magic', *ygunit* 'knights-and-kings', *kraze* 'rose', *kridu* 'write', *ledu* 'compete', *lureħ* 'beautiful', *lyħ* 'glass', *ciħta* 'box'.

Kebreni borrowings **into Verdurian** include

- financial and accounting terms like *andedau* 'profit', *demedau* 'loss', *dürí* 'credit', *pória* 'liability', *porui* 'debit', *gëméša* 'mortgage', *gocrea* 'balance sheet'; *lagu* 'income', *žüngu* 'expenditures'; *sutam, cürnu, alat, sülcona* 'types of coins'

- commercial words like *susaré* 'shop', *tuyo* 'pipe';

- nautical terms like *culisa* 'fleet', *culso* 'admiral', *nabro* 'ship captain', *navira* 'ship', *čirnu* 'deck', *sefo* 'boy';

- general words like *bakt* 'terrible', *lür* 'woe', *řulo* 'clown', *zevu* 'pal', *vučemu* 'flounder'.

Kebreni borrowings **from Verdurian** include

- technological terms like *aisel* 'key', *beh* 'essence', *cuelu* 'calcine', *skalea* 'gas', *impuźu* 'print', *uvere* 'fashion', *źuśni* 'lace', *śeveħka* 'leggings', *leidi* 'lens'; *otedit* 'watch', *keïnai* 'factory';

- cultural terms like *bemaś* 'cartoon', *kona* 'money', *lic* 'trial', *meika* 'school', *moitu* 'agent', *raline* 'play', *tuta* 'newspaper';

- religious and philosophical words like *aźcita* 'monastery', *nieron* 'holy', *ripriroda* 'philosophy', *kuraiyr* 'logic', *razum* 'mind';

- grammatical terms, mostly loan-translated; e.g. *maźeu* 'trustee' is used for 'pronoun' based on V. *promevec*

- general words like *pruso* 'inn', *meclu* 'mix', *feśu* 'soirée', *fauśu* 'cram', *śekśe* 'cocoa'.

There are also many CALQUES (loan-translations) from Caðinor or Verdurian, such as *babate namar* for 'galena', from *mira plomei* 'mother of lead'; or *zibiśu* for 'entail', from *imfayir*, both formed from 'in' + 'be necessary'; or *miebeu* for 'disciple', 'one who leaves in support of (his beliefs)', based on *profäsec*; or *mitecau* for 'company', based on *cumbutát* 'those with a common goal'.

> You don't need to document borrowings in this way, though it may help monitor your cultural interchanges. Languages are apt to borrow, often quite heavily, from their neighbors or from prestige or literary languages.

> Think about the history and economy of your peoples. What do they produce? What are they good at? The Kebreni happen to be gifted in shipbuilding, banking, and accounting, so there are a lot of Kebreni terms borrowed into neighboring languages in these areas.

Kebreni	Metaiun	Cat	Gloss
abaźe	apače	n	knife ['cutter']
adnedau		n	addition; profit
adnedu		v	add [Caɗ. *admettan*]
Aĥimba	Agibna	n	an ancient kingdom centered on the lower Serea; V. *Ažimbea*. [the name of the Metaiun sea goddess; with augm. *-na*; cf. Caɗ. calque *Agireis*]
aĥnu	asnu	n	donkey, ass
aisel		n	key [Verd. *ansel*]
aken	akni	a	clear, evident [Caɗ. *iacnis*]
akluva	akluwa	n	shark
aladaĥ		n	grammar [Caɗ. *aluatas*]
aladu		v	spend money
alamatu		v	scrounge up cash, get a little money
alat	alati	n	a silver coin [Caɗ. *alatis*]
amma	amua	n	hand
		#	five
anaĥ	anas	n	duck
angen		a	eastern
angu	angu	n	east
ankuva	ankuva	n	sea snake, eel
ansu	ams-	v	touch or feel (with the hands) ['hand' + -*s*-]
aśeve		pron	why, what for [volitional form of *śava* 'what': thus 'wanting what?']
atana	atana	n	army [collective of 'weapon']
atane	atane	n	weapon ['harmer']

Avelah	Awoilas	n	An ancient kingdom opposite Kebri; also its capital, the modern Avéla ['treaty field']
aviza	avisa(r)	n	university, academy [Cuêzi *avissār*]
avon	awoni	n	agreement, treaty
avunu	awun-	v	agree
aźcita		n	monastery [Ver. *ažcita*]

I've just included the A's here (the full lexicon is on my website).

I always indicate an etymology, including the source of foreign words. (Since Meiaiun gets its own column this information is not repeated for many words.) There should be plenty of changes of meaning recorded... I'm afraid I didn't do so well with these words! But notice that the word for 'addition' has been extended to mean 'profit'.

Word lists

This section contains some word lists to help fill out your lexicon. Some are general, some are specific for particular purposes.

They're resources, not achievements. You don't *have* to have all these words. But they're likely to be useful if you want a general vocabulary.

Review the section on vocabulary creation (p. 50); each root you create should produce several words.

The Swadesh list

Morris Swadesh created this 200-item list for the purposes of GLOTTOCHRONOLOGY— estimating the time languages diverged by checking the rate of replacement of basic vocabulary. Glottochronology is no longer widely accepted, largely because the rate of replacement is not in fact a constant; but the list is still a useful set of basic terms.

Swadesh chose words likely to exist in all human cultures, which means it's weak on technology and even common Eurasian animals. You might, for instance, find that you want a word for 'horse' before 'louse'.

Adjectives

Numbers	one two three four five
Colors	black white red green yellow
Oppositions	good bad
	new old
	warm cold
	dry wet
	sharp dull
	near far
	big small
	long short
	wide narrow
	thick thin
	fat heavy
	left right
	few many

241

	some all
Miscellaneous	dirty right (correct) rotten smooth straight other

Nouns

Substances	earth water ice stone fire ashes smoke dust salt sand
Time	day night year
Weather	rain snow cloud fog wind
The sky	sky sun moon star
Geographical	mountain woods lake river sea road
Body parts	head neck back belly hand leg foot skin
The head	ear eye hair mouth nose tongue tooth
Internal	blood bone guts heart liver meat
Animals	animal bird dog fish louse snake worm tail
Bird-related	egg feather wing
Plants	tree flower fruit grass leaf bark seed stick root
People	person man (male) woman child
Family	father mother wife husband
Miscellaneous	fear name rope

Verbs

Life and death	live die kill sleep
Movement	come walk float fly swim turn
Body position	stand sit lie (down) fall
Eating	eat drink bite blow breathe suck vomit
Perception	see hear smell
Cognition	know think
Speech acts	say sing laugh count
Daily life	play hunt sew throw wash wipe
Conflict	fight hit
Tool usage	cut stab tie dig
Manipulation	hold give push pull rub scratch squeeze

Physical states	burn flow freeze split swell

Grammatical words

Conjunctions	and because if not
Prepositions	at in with
Personal pronouns	I thou he we you (pl.) they
Demonstratives	this that
Locatives	here there
Question words	how what when where who

Sophomore list

The Swadesh list won't get you far; but add these additional 350 words and you'll be able to communicate surprisingly well.

I've placed modern technology in another list, since it may be irrelevant if you're creating a language for a fantasy or alien world.

Adjectives

Numbers	zero half quarter (and of course six and up)
Colors	blue brown dark light
Oppositions	beautiful ugly
	fast slow
	first last
	hard soft
	full empty
	smart stupid
	real fake
	upper lower
	expensive cheap
	sweet sour
	strong weak
	different same
Swadesh forgot...	young hot clean wrong rough crooked
Emotions	glad happy sad tired angry crazy
Character	careful lucky smart wise foolish healthy sick
Value	important interesting boring wonderful strange

Abstractions	funny easy difficult alone free normal special probable secret

Nouns

Natural substances	air glass iron gold silver
Territory	nature world land
Time	week month yesterday today tomorrow morning afternoon
The seasons	spring summer fall winter
Geographical	hill farm field island
Body parts	body lip breast butt muscle brain
Animals	cat cow chicken horse pig mouse monkey lion bug wolf
Plants	grain bread branch
People	girl boy girlfriend boyfriend friend baby
Family	family sister brother son daughter
Hierarchy	king boss leader servant
Religion	god devil temple holy evil soul sin
Settlements	city street tavern
Houses	house room wall window door
Furniture	table chair bed corner
School	school university class lesson teacher test
Dining	food lunch dinner wine milk
Clothing	clothes pants dress shoe hat
Technology	machine tool boat clock key net wagon wheel wire
Containers	box bag bottle cup plate knife
Avocations	music art science vacation picture game
Language	language word book pen paper page
Abstract thought	idea message story symbol example
	part number manner group thing
Analysis	system list event reason fact space time map
Money	money price worth debt shop
Respect	honor shame

Politics	war peace sword government law council tax prison minister

Verbs

Life and death	be seem born
Everyday actions	work wake dream cook use grow
Writing	write read translate create study learn copy
Affection	love hate like care want wish marry
Knowledge	understand believe doubt expect remember forget
Emotions	hope worry regret surprise
Modals	can must should
Aspect	begin finish intend to do habitually do
Abstractions	cause mean measure place
Shapes	square circle line edge side
Perception	touch taste
Speech acts	answer ask thank greet lie joke call offer choose
Movement	leave go follow hide run roll
Bodily actions	dance kiss smile cry point
Conflict	annoy hurt crime destroy trick
Society	allow meet help
Manipulation	put take have build fold add
Acquisition	buy sell need get lose search find trade keep
Containers	open close cover

Grammatical words

Conjunctions	but or though until
Prepositions	toward for without against on about behind across over under
Adverbs	perhaps indeed thus
Time	now then again next
Degree	very too enough

Courtesy

> please
> thank you
> you're welcome
> welcome to —
> hello   goodbye
>
> yes

The Modern World

In addition to the words listed, think about days of the week, months of the year, and the names of countries and cities.

Air transport	airplane airport
Cars	car bus license gas station motor taxi truck gasoline
Other transport	bicycle railroad train station subway spaceship
Computers	computer CD-ROM chip CPU
Accessories	floppy disk hard drive modem keyboard mouse monitor
Programs	program video game word processor compiler
Internet	Internet e-mail bulletin board chatroom web website download browser blog post flame lurker newbie chat
Disciplines	physics chemistry biology electricity magnetism mathematics
Physics	atom molecule energy nuclear particle photon proton neutron
Biology	cell evolution gene
Substances	plastic
Appliances	stove sink dishwasher refrigerator washing machine dryer furnace air conditioner
Film	camera film photo movie animation theater
Recording	CD record tape videotape stereo VCR tape recorder
Weaponry	gun rifle tank infantry cavalry artillery bomb
Office technology	fax copier typewriter

Media	newspaper magazine telephone television radio comic strip
Other technology	elevator laser light bulb watch
Optics	lens telescope microscope glasses
Measures	pound foot mile ounce cup gram kilogram meter kilometer milliliter liter
Lifestyle	lifestyle ATM suburb
Jobs	secretary babysitter bureaucrat manager
Education	college university degree
Economy	economy banknote credit card dollar euro expenses income inflation standard of living unemployed union welfare yen taxes
Avocations	chess rock soccer cigarette drugs
Clothing	bikini bra jeans T-shirt lipstick
Health	AIDS allergy addict antibiotic bacteria vaccine virus vitamin
Food	candy hamburger hot dog pizza sushi taco tofu tomato
Belief systems	communism socialism fascism republic democracy Green human rights liberal conservative
Positions	president prime minister representative parliament council dictator party
Religions	Islam Judaism Christianity Hinduism Buddhism

Geographical terms

These are words useful for creating maps. We start with geographical terms, which are not only useful for labeling your map in your own language (*Zëi Mišicama* instead of 'Mišicama Ocean'), but to name cities and regions ('Great Mountain, Seatown, Yellow River, Clear Lake, Ox Pond, Deer Crossing', etc.). Indeed, some towns are nothing but one of these terms (Detroit = 'Straits'; Le Havre = 'the Port'; Ostrov = 'Island').

One of the most popular names for cities is 'New town', which is the meaning of Newton, Neustadt, Neuveville, Naples, Nyborg, Novgorod, Villanueva, Yenişehir, and Xīnchéng.

Other ideas for naming cities:

- after the founder or patron (Jacksonville, Baltimore, Washington, Stalingrad)

- after the god or saint it's dedicated to (San Francisco, Salvador)

- after the people who once lived there (Paris— after the Parisii; Washington— the British town, after the Washings, the followers of Wasa; Andalucía— after the Vandals)

- expressions of thanksgiving or hope

- evocations of the virtues (Concord, Resolution, La Paz, União)

- after a propitious existing city (Lima, Ohio; Paris, Texas; New Amsterdam; Versailles, Argentina)

- how far you are from somewhere interesting (Half Day Road, Ventimiglia)

Geographical names often preserve a region's linguistic history: Amerindian names in the U.S. and Latin America; Spanish and French names in the American West; Celtic names across Europe; Latin and Greek names in the Mediterranean; Bantu names in South Africa; Maori names in New Zealand.

So the older places in your land should be named by whoever got there first, adapted to the language spoken there now. Since these are likely to be chief features of the land— rivers, lakes, mountain ranges, big cities— this is an argument for working out at least *two* naming languages before you get too far with your map.

Geographical terms

Plains	plain savannah meadow field prairie
Forests	forest woods grove copse
Hills and mountains	hill down mountain range plateau crest peak
Valleys	valley canyon cliff
Harsh terrain	marsh swamp desert wilderness jungle
Rivers	river stream brook channel rapids portage source confluence delta bank waterfall spring
Lakes	lake pond
Seas	sea ocean bay strait
Coastlines	coast beach peninsula cape point
Islands	island archipelago atoll

Local features	rock tree bridge ford dam park oasis
Types of trees	aspen birch cedar elm oak palm pine willow

Human terms

Settlements	city town village colony port market capital
Military	fort castle wall camp
Religion	shrine oracle temple church chapel monastery
Other foci	mine inn stopping-point post lodge mill house
Roads	road highway trail way

Useful adjectives

Age	new old
Shapes	round flat wide narrow high low
Location	central upper lower near far
Direction	north south east west
Respect	great grand glorious noble holy royal
Salesmanship	fertile beautiful lucky pleasant quiet gold silver jewel
Descriptive	windy stinky
Color	white black green yellow blue red orange brown
Water quality	fast slow clear muddy noisy laughing reedy
Popular animals	horse ox lion fox deer panther hawk eagle dragon ram

More to read

Web resources

You can do a lot of research on the Web. But links rot quickly, and anything I list here will be likely to disappear in a few years. Instead, I'll maintain a list of web resources on my own site:

> http://www.zompist.com/resources/

There are quite a few other pages of interest on my site (that would be **zompist.com** if you missed it the first time):

- The original web version of the **Language Construction Kit**, including translations into several other languages:

  http://www.zompist.com/kit.html

- The **Sound Change Applier**, which allows you to apply sound changes to a Unicode lexicon in your browser:

  http://www.zompist.com/sca2.html

- **Gen**, a vocabulary generator, which also runs in your browser:

  http://www.zompist.com/gen.html

- The **Zompist Bulletin Board**, where people talk about conlanging and you can get feedback on your own creations:

  (address on web resources page)

- **Virtual Verduria**, documenting over a dozen of my conlangs:

  http://www.zompist.com/resources.html

- The **numbers page**, containing the numbers from 1 to 10 in thousands of languages, plus ethnomathematical information:

  http://www.zompist.com/numbers.shtml

- **Hau to pranownse Inglish**— an investigation into the real rules of English spelling, and how bad it is or isn't:

  http://www.zompist.com/spell.html

- **If English was written like Chinese**— what English writing would look like if it followed the structure of Chinese:

http://www.zompist.com/yingzi/yingzi.htm

- The **Almeopedia**, an encyclopedia of information on Almea:

  http://www.almeopedia.com/

And plenty more!

By the same author

A constructed world (a conworld) is more than just languages— you can work out its geology and biology, the history of its peoples, their culture and technology and belief systems. The companion volume to this book, *The Planet Construction Kit*, covers all of this.

Once you've mastered this volume, you're ready for the sequel— *Advanced Language Construction*. It covers topics I didn't have room for here— logic, pidgins and creoles, sign languages, the linguistic life cycle— and goes into much more detail on case, gender, valence, modality, morphosyntactic alignment, and polysynthesis.

And for the long task of creating the lexicon, there's *The Conlanger's Lexipedia*. It goes subject by subject, giving thousands of etymologies from around the world, suggests ways words can differ from English, and provides the real-world knowledge you need to know about in each area, from colors to kinship systems to law to warfare.

Five books to read

Real linguists read books, I'm afraid. The more you read, the better your conlangs will be. The following would be excellent follow-ups to this book. If you read only one, make it the first one.

J.C. **Catford**, *A Practical Introduction to Phonetics* (1988)

> An excellent introduction to phonetics, including exercises you can do at home to learn each of the sounds discussed. I keep this book close to my desk.

R.L. **Trask**, *Historical Linguistics* (1986)

> There are several good books on historical linguistics; this is one of the best, and covers topics like internal reconstruction, Nostratic, and Proto-World— areas of current interest, and ones I've skimped on because they're less important for conlanging.

Bernard **Comrie**, ed., *The World's Major Languages* (1987)

Meaty descriptions of almost fifty languages, written by experts— like having a stack of grammars on your shelf.

Geoffrey **Sampson**, *Writing Systems* (1985)

A short, very readable survey of writing systems. Best to read this before creating anything more complicated than an alphabet.

C.S. **Lewis**, *Studies in Words* (1960)

Sometimes you learn more from one very detailed case-study than from a wide-scale overview. This book traces a handful of words from their classical origins into modern English; what it should teach conlangers is how thoroughly inadequate their semantic shifts are.

More books

Here's a sampling of additional resources I've found useful either for this book or for my conlangs. Some of these are a bit technical (especially those marked with ✖), but it's nothing you can't handle if you've read some of the above books, or even read this one a couple times.

I mostly leave out grammars of particular languages— but a few of particular interest are included.

Jean **Aitchison**, *Words in the Mind: An Introduction to the Mental Lexicon* (1987)

Billed as an introduction to the lexicon, but really a very readable exploration of semantics.

W. Sidney **Allen**, *Vox Latina: The Pronunciation of Classical Latin* (1965)

What we know of how Latin was pronounced. Allen has a similar book on Greek, *Vox Graeca*. ✖

Mark **Baker**, *The Polysynthesis Parameter* (1995)

An in-depth analysis of polysynthetic languages, focusing on Mohawk. ✖

Laurie **Bauer** and Peter **Trudgill**, *Language Myths* (1999)

Essays debunking popular misconceptions: "French is a logical language", "English spelling is Kattastroffik", "Children can't properly speak or write anymore", "In the Appalachians they speak like Shakespeare", "Some languages are spoken more quickly than others", and more.

Peter **Boyd-Bowman**, *From Latin to Romance in Sound Charts* (1954)

Sound changes from Latin to Spanish, Portuguese, French, and Italian— a systematic resource on a set of actual sound changes.

Penelope **Brown** and Stephen C. **Levinson**, *Politeness: Some universals in language usage* (1978)

The book version of my brief account of politeness. ✖

Carl Darling **Buck**, *A Dictionary of Selected Synonyms in the Principal Indo-European Languages* (1949)

A great resource for inventing etymologies. Look up 'world', for instance, and you'll find half a dozen ways of deriving a word for the concept. ✖

David **Burke**, *Street French: How to Speak and Understand French Slang* (1988)

All the French they didn't teach you in school... which turns out to be quite a lot. Even for non-French students, good to look at to understand the nature of colloquial speech.

Theodora **Bynon**, *Historical Linguistics* (1977)

The first book in historical linguistics I read— enough to fuel the creation of the entire Eastern family.

Noam **Chomsky**, *Syntactic Structures* (1957)

The book that started generative grammar, and still perhaps the best introduction to Chomsky's way of thinking. The analysis of English auxiliary verbs is particularly neat. ✖

Noam **Chomsky**, *Language and Problems of Knowledge* (1988)

Chomsky's theories are constantly changing and highly technical; this is his own attempt at a popular-level explanation. ✖

Michael D. **Coe**, *Breaking the Maya Code* (1999)

How it was realized that those rather ugly little squoggles were a real live language.

Bernard **Comrie**, *Language Universals and Linguistic Typology* (1981)

An introduction to language universals, especially in the area of syntax. ✖

David **Crystal**, *The Cambridge Encyclopedia of Language* (1987)

> A coffee-table book, an illustrated overview of just about everything in linguistics.

Peter T. **Daniels** and William **Bright**, eds., *The World's Writing Systems* (1996)

> The authoritative book on writing systems— it covers basically *everything*, not just pretty pictures but explanations of the mechanics of the scripts.

John **DeFrancis**, *The Chinese Language: Fact and Fantasy* (1984)

> The Chinese writing system has fascinated Westerners for years— and generated an immense load of bullshit. DeFrancis somewhat crabbily sorts out truth from nonsense.

R.M.W. **Dixon**, *The rise and fall of languages* (1997)

> A short book which challenges the family tree model, which Dixon believes applies very well to traditional agricultural regions such as Europe, but badly to Australia and the Amazon. He also bitingly criticizes recent attempts at long-range comparison. ⚒

Umberto **Eco**, *The Search for the Perfect Language* (1997)

> A historical overview of the idea that there is, or was, or could be, a perfect language, better for expressing thought than ordinary languages— a subject that happens to include much of the early history of conlanging.

Suzette Haden **Elgin**, *The Language Imperative: The Power of Language to Enrich Your Life and Expand Your Mind* (2000)

> A better introduction to Whorf than Whorf. How languages affect the mind and society.

Daniel L. **Everett**, *Don't Sleep, There Are Snakes: Life and Language in the Amazonian Jungle* (2008)

> An informal introduction to Pirahã, one of the world's most unusual languages, as well as an entertaining tale of doing fieldwork in the remotest Amazon.

Dick **Geeraerts**, ed., *Cognitive Linguistics: Basic Readings* (2006)

> A dozen essays introducing various aspects of cognitive linguistics, my favorite set of theories; the emphasis is on language as a

general cognitive skill rather than a language organ divorced from the rest of the brain. ✖

François **Grosjean**, *Life with Two Languages: An Introduction to Bilingualism* (1982)

Good for understanding how bilingualism works and how people learn additional languages (and more importantly, when they don't).

Hans Henrich **Hock**, *Principles of Historical Linguistics* (1991)

What to read *after* your first book in historical linguistics; it covers the same topics but in more detail. ✖

Alexander **Humez** and Nicholas Humez, *Latin for People* (1976)

A Latin grammar for fans of Monty Python. It's got all the basics for this most influential language, and also the best linguistic examples EVAR. *Ursus in tabernam introiit et cerivisiam imperāvit...*

R.A. **Hudson**, *Sociolinguistics* (1980)

An introduction to sociolinguistics, which studies the interface between language and culture.

Adam **Jacot** de Boinod, *The Meaning of Tingo* (2006)

Fun book containing odd words from around the world.

Pierre **Janton**, *Esperanto: Language, Literature, and Community* (1993)

An overview of the most successful conlang as well as its predecessors. Good reading for anyone who wants to make an auxiliary language.

Anne **Karpf**, *The Human Voice: How this extraordinary instrument reveals essential clues about who we are* (2006)

The subtitle pretty much explains it. Lots of facts though little theory about what the voice reveals.... most of which isn't directly addressed by linguistics.

William **Labov**, *Principles of Linguistic Change* (1994)

An analysis of sound change, at the phonological and the social level. Labov is particularly notable for studying **ongoing** sound changes. ✖

George **Lakoff** and Mark **Johnson**, *Metaphors We Live By* (1980)

An analysis of common metaphor systems in English and what they mean for cognition.

George **Lakoff**, *Women, Fire, and Dangerous Things* (1987)

A foundational text of what's become cognitive linguistics. Why simple theories of categories are terribly and misleadingly wrong. ✗

Roger **Lass**, *Phonology: An introduction to basic concepts* (1984)

The principles of phonological analysis, which go far beyond listing phonemes.

Stephen C. **Levinson**, *Pragmatics* (1983)

An overview of pragmatics: deixis, conversational implicature, presupposition, speech acts, conversation analysis.

Anatole V. **Lyovin**, *An Introduction to the Languages of the World* (1997)

Much of this is a list of known language families, with touristic highlights; but it's most worthwhile for the grammatical sketches of nine languages, including several missed by Comrie's book.

Charles N. **Li** and Sandra A. **Thompson**, *Mandarin Chinese: A Functional Reference Grammar* (1981)

Another answer to the question "What do I put in the syntax section?" It takes over 600 pages to answer this for Chinese. A great resource if you're thinking of making an isolating language. ✗

James D. **McCawley**, *Everything that Linguists have Always Wanted to Know about Logic (but were ashamed to ask)* (1981)

For awhile logic and generative grammar seemed to be intersecting, and this book helped bring linguists up to speed on propositional and predicate logic, set theory, modal logic, fuzzy logic, and intensional logic, as well as some aspects of pragmatics.

James D. **McCawley**, *The Syntactic Phenomena of English* (1988)

My standard answer to why syntax needs more than one page in your conlang's grammar. In 800 pages, McCawley covers some of the *highlights* of the study of syntax.

Jerry **Norman**, *Chinese* (1988)

Not a grammar, but an overview of Chinese linguistics: its historical phonology, the development of the script, a sketch of Classical Chinese and of the modern language; an overview of each of the dialects.

The Oxford English Dictionary (2nd ed. 1989)

A monument of scholarship and an essential resource on the history of English, best consulted in electronic form.

Thomas E. **Payne**, *Describing Morphosyntax: A Guide for Field Linguists* (1997)

Aimed at linguists describing the morphology and syntax of languages, this also serves as an overview of these fields, with plentiful non-Western examples.

Steven **Pinker**, *The Language Instinct: How the Mind Creates Language* (1994)

A fun, readable introduction to linguistics. Pinker is a little too fond of Chomsky's language organ for my taste, but this is a meaty book full of things to think about.

Geoffrey **Pullum**, *The Great Eskimo Vocabulary Hoax and other irreverent essays on the study of language* (1991)

Humorous (but highly rigorous) essays on linguistics, if you can believe such a thing. You won't get half the jokes till you've read quite a bit of linguistics, however. ✖

Howard **Rheingold**, *They Have a Word For It* (1988)

A catalog of unusual words from many languages.

Edward **Sapir**, *Language: An introduction to the study of speech* (1921)

Old, but still an excellent general introduction, especially notable for Sapir's understanding of Amerindian languages.

Dan **Sperber** & Deirdre **Wilson**, *Relevance: Communication and Cognition* (2006)

An investigation into how people interpret statements in conversations, starting from Grice's maxims. A useful debunking of the conduit metaphor. ✖

Takao **Suzuki**, *Words in Context: A Japanese Perspective on Language and Culture* (1973)

Reflections on how language reflects culture. Not limited to Japanese, though the sections on Japanese ways of referring to people are particularly interesting.

Deborah **Tannen**, *You Just Don't Understand: Women and Men in Conversation* (1990)

A sociolinguist readably explains differences in male and female speech, based on extensive real-world investigation.

Sarah Grey **Thomason** & Terrence **Kaufman**, *Language Contact, Creolization, and Genetic Linguistics* (1988)

A overview of how languages affect each other; most useful for exploding the numerous myths on this subject. (E.g.: English is not an extreme example of language contact; it's not a creole— not many things are creoles, in fact, except for creoles.) ✕

Michael **Tomasello**, *Constructing a Language* (2003)

No, not what it sounds like; it's a detailed look at how children learn language. A thorough demolition of Chomsky's latest parameters-based models. The evidence is that children pick up constructions one by one, only generalizing between them slowly and late. ✕

Benjamin Lee **Whorf**, *Language, Thought, and Reality* (1956)

Various essays on language, many of them expressing what he called linguistic relativity, the idea that the structure of languages reflects and constrains a culture's ways of thought. ✕

Anna **Wierzbicka**, *Cross-cultural pragmatics: the semantics of human interaction* (1992)

How pragmatics differs between cultures— a challenge to views of politeness and maxims of conversation as universals.

Index

THE INTERNATIONAL PHONETIC ALPHABET (revised to 2005)

CONSONANTS (PULMONIC)

© 2005 IPA

	Bilabial	Labiodental	Dental	Alveolar	Post alveolar	Retroflex	Palatal	Velar	Uvular	Pharyngeal	Glottal
Plosive	p b			t d		ʈ ɖ	c ɟ	k g	q ɢ		ʔ
Nasal	m	ɱ		n		ɳ	ɲ	ŋ	N		
Trill	ʙ			r					R		
Tap or Flap		ⱱ		ɾ		ɽ					
Fricative	ɸ β	f v	θ ð	s z	ʃ ʒ	ʂ ʐ	ç ʝ	x ɣ	χ ʁ	ħ ʕ	h ɦ
Lateral fricative				ɬ ɮ							
Approximant		ʋ		ɹ		ɻ	j	ɰ			
Lateral approximant				l		ɭ	ʎ	L			

Where symbols appear in pairs, the one to the right represents a voiced consonant. Shaded areas denote articulations judged impossible.

CONSONANTS (NON-PULMONIC)

Clicks	Voiced implosives	Ejectives
ʘ Bilabial	ɓ Bilabial	ʼ Examples:
ǀ Dental	ɗ Dental alveolar	pʼ Bilabial
ǃ (Post)alveolar	ʄ Palatal	tʼ Dental/alveolar
ǂ Palatoalveolar	ɠ Velar	kʼ Velar
ǁ Alveolar lateral	ʛ Uvular	sʼ Alveolar fricative

OTHER SYMBOLS

ʍ Voiceless labial-velar fricative

w Voiced labial-velar approximant

ɥ Voiced labial-palatal approximant

ʜ Voiceless epiglottal fricative

ʢ Voiced epiglottal fricative

ʡ Epiglottal plosive

ɕ ʑ Alveolo-palatal fricatives

ɺ Voiced alveeolar lateral flap

ɧ Simultaneous ʃ and x

Affricates and double articulations can be represented by two symbols joined by a tie bar if necessary. k͡p t͡s

VOWELS

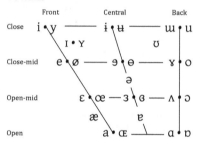

Where symbols appear in pairs, the one to the right represents a rounded vowel.

SUPRASEGMENTALS

ˈ	Primary stress
ˌ	Secondary stress
ː	Long eː
ˑ	Half-long eˑ
˘	Exra-short ĕ
|	Minor(foot) group
‖	Major (intonation) group
.	Syllable break
‿	Linking (absence of a break)

TONES AND WORD ACCENTS

LEVEL			CONTOUR		
e̋ or ˥	Extra high		ě or ˩˥	Rising	
é ˦	High		ê ˥˩	Falling	
ē ˧	Mid		e᷄ ˦˥	High rising	
è ˨	Low		e᷅ ˩˨	Low rising	
ȅ ˩	Extra low		e᷈ ˧˦˧	Rising-falling	
↓	Downstep		↗	Global rise	
↑	Upstep		↘	Global fall	

DIACRITICS Dicacritics may be placed above a symbol with a descender, e.g. ŋ̊

̥ Voiceless	n̥ d̥	̤ Breathy voiced	b̤ a̤	̪ Dental	t̪ d̪
̬ Voiced	s̬ t̬	̰ Creaky voiced	b̰ a̰	̺ Apical	t̺ d̺
ʰ Aspirated	tʰ dʰ	̼ Linguolabial	t̼ d̼	̻ Laminal	t̻ d̻
̹ More rounded	ɔ̹	ʷ Labialized	tʷ dʷ	̃ Nasalized	ẽ
̜ Less rounded	ɔ̜	ʲ Palatalized	tʲ dʲ	ⁿ Nasal release	dⁿ
̟ Advanced	u̟	ˠ Velarized	tˠ dˠ	ˡ Lateral release	dˡ
̠ Retracted	e̠	ˤ Pharyngealized	tˤ dˤ	̚ No audible release	d̚
̈ Centralized	ë	̴ Velarized or pharyngealized	ɫ		
̽ Mid-centralized	e̽	̝ Raised	e̝	ɹ̝ = voicedalveolar fricative
̩ Syllabic	n̩	̞ Lowered	e̞	β̞ = voiced bilabial approximant
̯ Non-syllabic	e̯	̘ Advanced Tongue Root	e̘		
˞ Rhoticity	ɚ	̙ Retracted Tongue Root	e̙		

Printed in the USA
CPSIA information can be obtained
at www.ICGtesting.com
LVHW011802221123
764659LV00003B/133